Using Statistics for Better Business Decisions

Using Statistics for Better Business Decisions

Justin Bateh and Bert G. Wachsmuth

Using Statistics for Better Business Decisions

First published in 2016 by
Business Expert Press, LLC
222 East 46th Street, New York, NY 10017
www.businessexpertpress.com

ISBN-13: 978-1-63157-272-2 (paperback)
ISBN-13: 978-1-63157-273-9 (e-book)

Business Expert Press Quantitative Approaches to Decision Making Collection

Collection ISSN: 2163-9515 (print)
Collection ISSN: 2163-9582 (electronic)

Cover and interior design by Exeter Premedia Services Private Ltd., Chennai, India

First edition: 2016

10 9 8 7 6 5 4 3 2 1

Printed in the United States of America.

Abstract

More and more organizations around the globe are expecting that professionals will make data-driven decisions. Employees, team leaders, managers, and executives who can think quantitatively should be in high demand. This book is for beginners to statistics and covers the role statistics plays in the business world and making data-driven decisions. The goal of this book is to improve your ability to identify a problem, collect data, and organize and analyze data, which will aid in making more effective decisions. You will learn techniques that can help any manager or business person who is responsible for decision making. This book has been created for decision makers whose primary goal is not just to do the calculation and the analysis, but to understand and interpret the results and make recommendations to key stakeholders. You will also learn how using the popular business software, Microsoft Excel, can support this process. This book will provide you with a solid foundation for thinking quantitatively within your company. To help facilitate this objective, this book follows two fictitious companies that encounter a series of business problems, while demonstrating how managers would use the concepts in the book to solve these problems and determine the next course of action. This book is intended for beginners, and the reader does not require prior statistical training. All computations will be completed using Microsoft Excel.

More information, datasets, and supporting materials can be found at http://www.betterbusinessdecisions.org/

Keywords

Analyze data, data-driven decisions, decision making, Microsoft Excel, misuses of data, quantitative thinking, statistical inference, summarize data, visualize data

Contents

CHAPTER 1

Statistics and Statistical Software

Preview: *The study of statistics is vitally important, yet many people have only a vague understanding of it. Statistical analyses play a role in everything from politics and social science to studies of biological diversity, and individuals with a deep understanding of the science are always in high demand. Many people think they understand statistics, but the actual results of a statistical analysis can be counterintuitive. That is why it is so important to move beyond intuition and into the realm of science. It is important to realize that statistics is not an end in itself. Rather, it is a means for the identification and analysis of problems, and it is a useful tool to arrive at better decisions. The statistical method is used to make decisions with ramifications in the real world, and that makes the science a vital part of modern business. Simply put, statistics attempts to make sense of data. Descriptive statistics involves the collection and description of data. Once the data has been collected and described, the researcher is able to understand the context in which the results are presented. Inferential statistics collects data from a subset of the population and uses that information to draw conclusions about the population as a whole. The populations used in a statistical analysis can be anything from a group of water quality measurements in a river system to the heights of soldiers in the U.S. Army. The science behind the analysis is the same no matter where the data are drawn from. No matter what kind of data is being analyzed, the statistical analysis process uses the same steps: problem definition, data collection, data analysis, and reporting the final analysis. This process is designed to be rigorous and scientific, providing an impartial look at the data and an impartial analysis of the results.*

Learning Objectives: At the conclusion of this chapter, you should be able to:

1. Set up Microsoft Excel to run statistical analyses
2. Understand the importance of random sampling
3. Demonstrate how to use Microsoft Excel to identify a random sample
4. Understand basic vocabulary in the statistics field
5. Explain the importance in using statistics for business decision making
6. Identify the sources and types of data used in business.

Introduction

Statistics is one of those strange entities that people describe as *useful* or even *important* without knowing precisely what it is; people seem to intuitively know about statistics (or *think* they know). For example, one of the first questions we ask when teaching a statistics course is (naturally): "What do you think statistics is?" Answers typically range from "statistics consists of compiling lots of numbers [...]" to "statistics deals with collecting and analyzing data"; indeed, most students have something to say. Even prolific writers such as Mark Twain have an opinion about statistics; he is reported to have said: "there are three kinds of lies: lies, damned lies, and statistics" (the exact origin of this phrase is unclear). Contrast that, for example, with what would happen if you ask people what "calculus" is and whether they think it might be useful for them: You most likely earn a majority of blank stares (and not even Mark Twain came up with any quips about calculus).

Thus, statistics as a mathematical topic has an advantage: You do not necessarily have to convince people it is useful; you merely have to ensure they know exactly what it is and how to use it (and how it can be abused). In addition, statistics has a lot to do with data analysis and everybody relies on data in one way or another:

- Corporate presidents decide company policy based on quarterly sales figures.
- Politicians decide on campaign strategy based on polls.
- Teachers decide on grades based on a bell curve.
- You and I decide whether to smoke or not based on the analysis of health records of other people.

As a student studying statistics for decision-making purposes, you should realize that statistics is not the end game. It is a tool, not the ultimate goal of our efforts. We use statistics as a method to identify, analyze, and solve a problem to arrive at a useful decision. That is, the decision is the end game; the statistical methods are just what we are using to help us solve the problem. Thus, in this text we will always opt for mathematical simplicity over detail and we will emphasize how to use statistical analysis to arrive at meaningful decisions as opposed to studying statistics for its own sake. Let us now start for real with a broad definition of statistics.

Definition: Statistics is the study of making sense of data.

In this text we will focus on two basic concepts to make sense of data: *descriptive* statistics (Chapters 1 to 3) and *inferential* statistics (Chapters 5 to 9).

Definition: *Descriptive statistics* involves collecting data, summarizing it, and generally "telling the story" behind the data. This helps describe the data and lets the reader understand the context in which any results should be interpreted. *Inferential statistics*, on the other hand, uses data collected from a subset of the overall study to draw conclusions about the whole.

In real-world problems you frequently have to combine descriptive and inferential statistics.

Example: A tax auditor is responsible for 25,000 accounts. The auditor wants to know how many of these accounts are in error (resulting in a loss of revenue) and how this compares to a (fictional) nationwide error rate of 2.5 percent.

The steps involved in trying to find a suitable answer to this question might be:

- **Identify the objective**: How does the error rate for a particular tax auditor compare to the nationwide average?
- **Collect the data**: The auditor investigates all 25,000 accounts and finds errors with 1,050 of them (say).
- **Analyze the data**: In this case, we simply compute that 1,050/25,000 = 4.2 percent of accounts are in error.

- **Report the analysis**: Based on our data analysis we conclude that 4.2 percent of the accounts are in error. Since the national error rate is 2.5 percent, more accounts than usual are in error.

So far we have conducted descriptive statistics: we computed the exact error rate for one auditor and compared it to the national error rate. Note that the data analysis here, such as it is, was done with the help of a simple calculator. More commonly, special software is used to help with the data analysis, and in fact with all stages of a statistical analysis. In this text we will use Microsoft Excel (any one of the most recent versions should work) to help us perform statistical analysis.

The previous example has the big drawback that it would be very time-consuming to analyze all 25,000 accounts. It would be easier to select only a handful of them, analyze those, and then use the results from that subset to make inferences about *all* accounts. This might not be as precise as checking every account but it might be so much faster and cheaper that the gain in efficiency outweighs the loss of accuracy. Since we are using the analysis of a sample to draw conclusions about all 25,000 accounts, we now engage in inferential statistics.

When we collect data, we have the option of obtaining data from *primary* or from *secondary* sources. Primary sources are sources of data in which the person collecting the data is also using it. Secondary sources are data sets that the person running a study did not collect, but instead were collected from another individual or institution.

Definition: The term *population* stands for the set of *all measurements of interest* while the term *sample* denotes any subset of measurements selected from the population.

A population could be (1) the set of all photographs of Mars, (2) the set of heights of people in the U.S. Army, (3) the set of all measurements for the quality of water taken from the Hudson River, or (4) the set of all problems that can be solved using statistics. On the other hand, samples for these populations could consist of (a) the pictures from a specific region of Mars, (b) the heights of people in a particular division of the U.S. Army, (c) the set of water measurements for the Hudson River taken on July 24, 2013, or (d) the statistical problems we are solving in this class. See Table 1.1.

Table 1.1 Examples of populations and samples

Population	Sample
Set of all photographs of Mars	Pictures from a specific region of Mars
Set of heights of all soldiers in the U.S. Army	Heights of soldiers from the 5th Infantry Division
All water quality measurements from the Hudson River	Water quality measurements taken on July 24, 2015
Set of all problems that can be solved using statistics	Problems that we will solve in this class

We finally need a flexible term to denote what is being measured:

Definition: A *variable* is a characteristic or property of a population where the observations can vary.

Using this terminology, we could refine our four stages of statistical analysis and approach a "generic statistical problem" using these four steps:

- **Problem definition**: What is the population of interest and what are the variables to be investigated?
- **Data collection**: Describe and select a sample from the population.
- **Data analysis**: Make statistical inferences from the analysis of the sample and apply them to the population.
- **Analysis reporting**: Report the inference together with a measure of reliability for the inference.

With this terminology in place we can revisit our previous example of checking accounts.

Example: A tax auditor is responsible for 25,000 accounts. How many of these accounts are in error (resulting in a loss of revenue), and how does this compare to a (fictional) nationwide error rate of 2.5 percent?

The steps involved in trying to find a suitable answer to this question might now be as follows:

- **Defining the problem**: The entire population consists of all 25,000 accounts, and the variable to be investigated is whether an account is in error or not. Thus, we have defined one variable, which has a total of 25,000 values.

- **Data collection and summary**: The auditor decides to select 200 accounts at random, somehow, tests each of them, and finds that 8 of them are in error.
- **Data analysis**: Some statistical theory is applied to allow drawing a conclusion from the sample of 200 accounts and applying it to all 25,000 accounts. In this case, the likely theory involves computing 8/200 = 4 percent.
- **Analysis reporting**: Based on our data analysis we infer that approximately 4 percent of the accounts will be in error. Additional theory (which we will cover in Chapter 5) shows that our guess has an error of ±0.9 percent. Thus, it seems that our accounts contain more errors than the national average of 2.5 percent.

The analysis of the data is usually done by using a calculator, or—more frequently these days—with the help of a software package. In this textbook we will use Microsoft Excel (any recent version of Excel should work) to help us perform statistical analysis.

Samples and "Random Samples"

We have defined the terms population and sample and we were interested in selecting a *random* sample in our last example. The natural question is: What is a random sample, and how do we select one?

Definition: A *random sample of size n* is a sample that is selected by a process such that any other sample of that size *n* has the same chance of being selected.

This definition might seem abstract and perhaps not so useful. We could paraphrase it by saying that a random sample is a sample where the selection has taken place without any bias of any sort. If there was no bias of any kind in making a selection of *n* objects, then any other set of *n* objects would have had the same chance of being selected. Thus, no bias implies a random sample.

There are cases where it is not only more efficient to work with a random sample, but it might even give more accurate answers than trying to work with the population.

Example: Find the average income for people living in New York City (NYC).

This seems straightforward. The most accurate approach apparently would be to ask everyone living in NYC their income, add up all the figures, and divide the sum by the total number of people asked (which will give the precise average). However, that is not only impractical, it would not even work:

- When people are asked their income not everyone will answer (for a variety of reasons).
- People might not answer truthfully (again for a variety of reasons).
- It will be difficult to physically track down everyone living in NYC.
- By the time the last people are asked, others have moved in or out of NYC already.

Therefore, instead of finding the exact—and arguably elusive—average, we should try to *estimate* it. Note that according to the U.S. Constitution, Article 1, Section 2, a census needs to be conducted every 10 years so that the people can have a proper proportion of representation in the U.S. House of Representatives. Instead of attempting to count everyone, as seems required, many statisticians argue that using a carefully selected random sample would in fact give more accurate results. But using such inference might be in violation of the constitution depending on the exact meaning of "census." Discussing constitutional law, however, is way beyond the scope of this text, so, our first problem will simply be to randomly select a small sample, say of size $n = 1,000$, of people living in NYC and find the average income of that sample (which is perfectly within our capabilities). Then we draw conclusions from that sample about the whole population.

Thus, our question now is: How do I select a random sample of size 1,000 from the population of inhabitants of NYC? We might try to use the following procedure:

1. Open the latest NYC phone book.
2. Select one page "at random" (perhaps by throwing the book in the air).
3. Select 1,000 people starting from that page that the book opens up on.

Call those people and ask them for their income. Compute the average of that group and say that this average is representative for the average income of all people in NYC, approximately.

But this is not at all a procedure to obtain a "random sample": all people selected will most likely be from one borough, or all may have a name starting with "Mac" (and are therefore likely to be of Irish ancestry, which introduces bias). Thus, this is *not* a random sample. In fact, it turns out that to select a random sample you need to carefully and deliberately select people from all sociological backgrounds, all races, all cultures, and so on. In other words, contrary to what you might think a random sample must be selected very deliberately in this case.

Random Sample Selection Procedure

While we will generally avoid the problem of random sample selection, we do want to mention at least some way to do this.

Example: Select a random sample of size $n = 5$ from a population of 2,000 measurements.

We proceed as follows:

1. Label all measurements from 1 to 2,000, in any order.
2. Start a computer program that can generate random numbers.
3. Use that computer program to generate five unique random numbers between 1 and 2,000.

4. Select the five measurements from the total population located at those random positions.

This procedure will give a random sample (assuming the computer's random number generator is working correctly). Another approach that works particularly well using Excel is as follows (see Figure 1.1):

1. List all measurements from 1 to 2,000, in any order.
2. Create random numbers between 0.0 and 1.0 and store them with each measurement.
3. Sort all numbers according to their associated random number between 0 and 1.
4. Pick the first five elements from the list of measurements.

For additional details, please see the "Excel Demonstration" section. This works because we are able to list *all* measurements, which is not always possible. For example, if you want to find the average pollution of a certain river, you clearly cannot label all possible measurements (you cannot even take all possible measurements). In the case of NYC, the phone book is indeed a convenient list of people, but it certainly does not contain everyone: some people might opt for unlisted numbers (probably rich, or younger), others might not have a phone at all (presumably poor), and so on.

	A	B
1	Measurement	Random
2	1	0.018211
3	356	0.788832
4	235	0.084765
5	86	0.577049
6	139	0.116619
7	311	0.368515
8	360	0.485389
9	176	0.161761
10	237	0.824249
11	...	...

Values in original order with
associated random number

	A	B
1	Measurement	Random
2	241	0.018211
3	393	0.084765
4	18	0.116619
5	236	0.161761
6	494	0.368515
7	218	0.485389
8	5	0.577049
9	332	0.788832
10	385	0.824249
11	...	...

Values sorted by associated
random number (column B)

Figure 1.1 Selecting a random sample in Excel

From now on, we will take a very simple approach: We will ignore the problem of selecting a random sample and *assume* that a random sample has been selected somehow.

Variables and Distributions

When we are looking at a particular population and selecting samples to make inferences, we need to record our observations or the characteristics of the data we are studying. Recall that a variable is the term used to record a particular characteristic of the population we are studying.

For example, if our population consists of pictures taken from Mars, we might use the following variables to capture various characteristics of our population:

- Quality of a picture
- Title of a picture
- Latitude and longitude of the center of a picture
- Date the picture was taken

It is useful to put variables into different categories, as different statistical procedures apply to different types of variables. Variables can be categorized into two broad categories, numerical and categorical:

Definition: *Categorical variables* are variables that have a limited number of distinct values or categories. They are sometimes called discrete variables. *Numeric variables* refer to characteristics that have a numeric value. They are usually *continuous* variables, that is, all values in an interval are possible.

Categorical variables again split up into two groups, ordinal and nominal variables.

Definition: *Ordinal variables* represent categories with some intrinsic order (e.g., low, medium, high; or strongly agree, agree, disagree, strongly disagree). Ordinal variables could consist of numeric values that represent distinct categories (e.g., 1 = low, 2 = medium, 3 = high). Note that this does not turn them into numeric variables; the numbers are merely codes. To best remember this type of variable, think of "ordinal" containing the word "order."

Nominal variables represent categories with no intrinsic order (e.g., job category, company division, and race). Nominal variables could also consist of numeric values that represent distinct categories (e.g., 1 = male, 2 = female).

It is usually not difficult to decide whether a variable is categorical or numerical.

Example: An experiment is conducted to test whether a particular drug will successfully lower the blood pressure of people. The data collected consists of the sex of each patient, the blood pressure measured, and the date the measurement took place. The blood pressure is measured three times, once before the patient was treated, then one hour after administrating the drug, and again two days after administrating the drug. What variables comprise this experiment?

The characteristics measured in the experiment seem to be the patient's sex, blood pressure, and treatment date, so it looks like we need three variables to capture the outcomes: sex (nominal), blood pressure (numeric), and date (ordinal). But the fact that the blood pressure is measured three times does not quite fit this scheme. In fact, for each patient participating in the study we actually measure *five* characteristics: sex, treatment date, blood pressure prior to treatment, blood pressure right after treatment, and blood pressure two days after treatment. Thus, we really have five variables, not three. In fact, we also have one additional variable, namely, the ID (or name) of the patient. Thus, the data collected for four (fictitious) patients is recorded in six variables as shown in Table 1.2.

Note that many statistical software packages follow this convention to setup variables in columns, one column per variable, and to record the values for each case in rows.

Table 1.2 Recording variables and values in tabular form

Patient ID (nominal)	Sex (nominal)	Date (ordinal)	Pressure (pre) (numeric)	Pressure (post) (numeric)	Pressure (after) (numeric)
1	Male	January 1, 2014	180	135	150
2	Female	January 1, 2014	170	140	145
3	Male	January 3, 2014	200	130	140
4	Male	January 7, 2014	190	160	190

Example: Consider the following survey, given to a random sample of students taking a university course:

Q1: What is your status?

[ ] Freshmen [ ] Sophomore [ ] Junior [ ] Senior [ ] Graduate Student

Q2: What is your major? _____

Q3: What is your age? _____

Q4: How often do you use the following support services?

	Daily	Few times/week	Few times/month	Few times/year	Never
Dining services					
Health services					
Recreation center					
PC support services					
Campus ministry					

Q5. The following student support services are effective:

	1 (Strongly agree)	2	3	4	5 (Strongly disagree)	−1 (No opinion)
Dining services						
Health services						
Recreation center						
PC support services						
Campus ministry						

Note: 1 = Strongly agree, 2 = Agree, 3 = Neutral, 4 = Disagree, 5 = Strongly disagree, −1 = Not applicable.

The survey consists of a total of 13 variables as follows: Q1 (status) is an ordinal variable, Q2 (major) is nominal, and Q3 (age) is numeric. Q4 consists of five variables (one for each row of the table), all being ordinal, and Q5 again consists of five ordinal variables. Note in particular that the five variables in question 5 are *not* numeric. The numbers are simply codes for particular categories. However, ordinal variables share some characteristics of numerical ones, as we will see in Chapter 3. *Following our previous example, we should introduce one additional nominal variable to capture the ID of each subject. This allows us to have a unique identification for each data record.

When the results of a survey or an experiment are recorded, the outcomes usually vary, and the variation of each variable usually occurs with different frequencies. For example, a survey given to a random sample of U.S. citizens might record the sex of the subject. The frequencies of the values for this variable will likely be approximately 52 percent female and 48 percent male. Recognizing patterns in the frequencies of outcomes is in fact one of the goals of statistics.

Definition: The *distribution* of a variable refers to the set of all possible values of a variable and the associated frequencies or probabilities with which these values occur.

Sometimes variables are distributed so that all outcomes are equally, or nearly equally likely. Other variables show results that "cluster" around one (or more) particular value.

Definition: A *heterogeneous distribution* is a distribution of values of a variable where all outcomes are nearly equally likely. A *homogeneous distribution* is a distribution of values of a variable that cluster around one or more values, while other values are occurring with very low frequencies or probabilities.

Example: Suppose you are conducting a survey that tries to determine whether women are typically shorter than men. Thus, your survey, administered to 100 randomly selected people, asks for the respondent's sex and height. Do you anticipate homogeneous or heterogeneous distributions from these variables?

Since approximately half of all people are male and half are female and the survey was given to 1,000 randomly selected participants, there should be approximately the same number of men and women queried. Thus, the variable sex should have a heterogeneous distribution—all possible values are just about equally likely. The second variable, height, however, will likely cluster around one or two most frequent values. Or conversely, few people are really short (4 ft. or less) or really tall (7 ft. or more), so this variable should be homogenously distributed.

Example: Suppose a company issues sales reports for two years, 2014 and 2015, as shown in Figure 1.2. We can consider this report as having two variables (v_2014 and v_2015, say), each one having four values (for North, South, East, and West, separately). Are the distributions of values hetero- or homogeneous?

The values for the 2014 variable (v_2014 if you like) are pretty close to each other. In the chart you can see that all 2014 bars are approximately of equal height. If we looked at the original figures, we would find an (about) equal amount of sales for North, South, East, and West, and no region would stick out, particularly. Thus, each region is equally likely in terms of number of sales—the distribution is heterogeneous (if we checked where an individual, randomly selected, came from, each region would be approximately equally likely).

The values for the 2015 variable (v_2015 in our terminology) differ widely. In Figure 1.2 the 2015 bars are of different heights, with "East" being by far the highest. If we would look at the original figures, we would find that most sales were made in the East. Thus, a sale from the

Sales Report	2014	2015	Totals
North	95	23	118
South	87	47	134
East	105	119	224
West	95	33	128
Total	382	222	604

Figure 1.2 A sample company sales report

East is much more likely than from any other region—the distribution is homogeneous (if we checked where an individual, randomly selected, came from, she would most likely come from the east). This seems somehow counter intuitive:

- If all bars of a distribution are approximately *equally high*, the variable is *heterogeneous*.
- If *some bars* of a distribution *dominate* the others, the variable is *homogeneous*.

Introduction to Microsoft Excel

This text utilizes Microsoft Excel 2013. If you are using Microsoft Excel 2007 or 2010, there will be very minor differences and you should be able to follow along with the examples in this textbook. Understanding the basic workings of Microsoft Excel will be necessary in this course; however, advanced knowledge of the software is not necessary. The guided examples are designed so that anyone with basic knowledge of the software can follow along. If you need additional assistance with the basic functions and working of Excel, such as entering values and formulas, selecting ranges, basic functions, saving and retrieving files, and so on, we recommend spending some time using the resources available on Microsoft's website at https://support.office.com. Search for "Basic Tasks in Excel 2013."

Installing the Analysis ToolPak in Microsoft Excel

Excel contains a variety of "add-ons" that allow you to perform additional calculations beyond the basic features built into Excel from the start. Some of these add-ons might require you to insert the Microsoft Office CD ROM; others can be installed without that disk. In general, the more add-ons you install into Excel, the longer the program takes to start up. Therefore, you only want to install those options that you are really going to use, or uninstall add-ons when you do not need them any longer.

For this text you must install the "Analysis ToolPak," which contains a variety of procedures for conducting statistical analysis. Installing an add-on is simple, but differs slightly depending on your version of Excel. Here is the procedure for the 2013 version of Excel for Windows. (Note that Excel for Mac does *not* include this ToolPak. If you are using a Mac, try and install the free software from www.analystsoft.com/en/products/statplusmacle/ instead.)

- Start Excel as usual with a blank sheet.
- Click on the "File" button in the top left corner.
- Click on "Options" near the bottom of the menu.
- Highlight the "Add-Ins" option on the list on the left.
- Under the "Manage" section, make sure Excel Add-ins is selected and click the "GO" button as shown in Figure 1.3.
- Another dialog box will appear; check the "Analysis ToolPak" and click "OK." (Caution: Be sure *not* to install the Analysis ToolPak—VBA version.)

The functions from the Analysis ToolPak will now be available in the "Data" ribbon as the right-most entry, named "Data" (and not in the "Add-ins" ribbon as you might expect). The specific functions in that add-in are the same for most versions of Excel for Windows. If you select

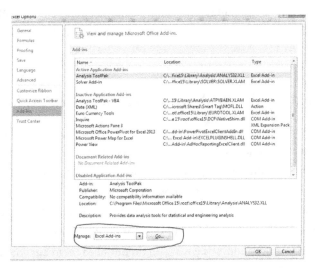

Figure 1.3 Dialog to install the Analysis ToolPak for Excel for Windows

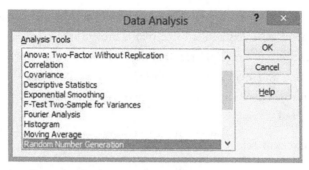

Figure 1.4 Procedures of the Analysis ToolPak

the "Data Analysis ..." option under "Data" you will see the procedures as shown in Figure 1.4 for performing statistical analysis on data in your spreadsheet.

We will explore several of these options in the rest of this course, but you are welcome to click on "Help" now to learn more about the Analysis ToolPak.

Excel Demonstration

In this textbook we will follow two fictitious companies, Company S and Company P. Both of these companies will be faced with common workplace problems as we proceed through the text, and you will be provided with demonstrations on how to arrive at answers for these problems using statistics and Microsoft Excel. Here is a background of the two companies.

Company S is a mid-sized accounting firm with approximately 600 employees. As a service-based organization, Company S provides services such as general accounting, bookkeeping, tax preparation, software consultation, controller services, business accounting, and payroll services. Company S comprises a management team, support staff, and certified public accountants (CPAs). Management is responsible for developing strategies to generate new clients, while the support staff and CPAs fulfill the service requests of their clients.

Company P is a large manufacturer of paper products with approximately 1,000 employees and supplies various paper products to retailers around the United States. These products include industrial supplies, food service supplies, sanitary supplies, and packaging supplies. As a product-based organization, Company P, in addition to management and support staff, has a sales force that is broken into sales teams, with each team given a regional territory. Each sales team is responsible for establishing and managing relationships with retailers and the sale of products to retailers within their territory.

Using Excel to Select a Random Sample

Problem: Company P would like to interview a random sample of 5 of the top 20 clients in the company. Use Excel to select a random sample of size 5 from the population of 20 clients.

The task is to assign a random number to each client and then sort by this number in order to pull a random sample of five clients. First, enter the 20 client names into a new Excel worksheet into column A. Then, next to each client name, enter the Excel function =RAND(). Note that in order to enter an Excel function, you must start with a leading equal sign. If it worked you should see a random number between 0 and 1 in that cell but when you click on it you will see the =RAND() function in the Excel edit bar. You could now type this function into the remaining 19 cells but to speed up the process, "copy and paste" the entry from the first cell value into the following 19 cells in column B. See Figure 1.5.

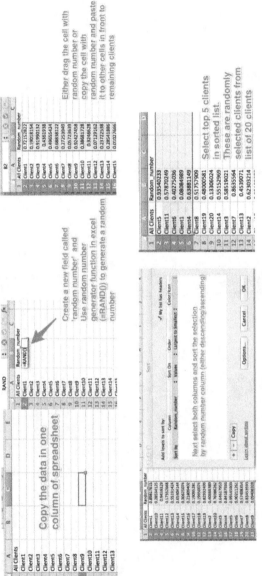

Figure 1.5 Selecting a random sample from a list of client names

CHAPTER 2

Data Visualization

Preview: *Presenting data visually can make it easier to understand and absorb. It is one thing to read a row of figures on the page, but quite another to see those figures presented in a user-friendly chart. The data visualization process aims to make sense of the raw data, presenting it in a manner that is easy to understand even for non experts. Pie charts and bar charts are among the most commonly used data visualization techniques; they can be created easily using common spreadsheet programs like Microsoft Excel. Numerical data can be represented in histograms, while categorical data can be visualized using frequency tables and charts. Cumulative frequencies count the number of data points up to a given value and are used to find the median, quartile, and percentiles in a group of data. Relative frequency, on the other hand, is used to represent how often something happens relative to some total. For example, the relative frequency may be used to show that a given sales team won 10 of its last 13 contracts, while the cumulative frequency will show the median number of contracts won across the entire year. Visualizing data is an important skill, and that ability is important whether you are running a business or teaching a class. You can get a sense of the importance of the data by looking at numbers on a spreadsheet, but a well-chosen visual representation of that data can be much more useful.*

Learning Objectives: At the conclusion of this chapter, you should be able to:

1. Organize data
2. Construct tables and charts for numerical data
3. Construct tables and charts for categorical data
4. Describe the principles of properly presenting graphs
5. Use Microsoft Excel to present data in basic graphs and charts
6. Demonstrate how to create a pivot table and histogram

Introduction

As we have seen in Chapter 1, statistics is the study of making sense of data and consists of four components: defining the problem, collecting and analyzing data, and reporting the results. In this chapter we will concern ourselves with summarizing data and presenting it visually.

Usually when data is collected there are several numbers, results, responses, and so on. In fact, there is often so much data that it needs to be summarized before you can make sense of it; raw data usually does not reveal any patterns or insights. One approach to summarizing data is to summarize it in graphical or tabular form. Since a picture is worth a thousand words, we hope to be able to detect patterns or to draw conclusions once we see data presented graphically.

In this chapter we will discuss a variety of ways to visualize data and how to use Excel to accomplish the visualization. We will also show how charts can be used to emphasize different points of views without modifying or falsifying data.

Pie Charts and Bar Charts

Pie charts are a convenient way to visualize data if the categories that divide the data are not that numerous (eight or less). Pie charts apply to categorical variables (either ordinal or nominal); in most cases pie charts are not appropriate for numerical variables.

Example: Suppose a survey was conducted among 1,000 adults about their job status, with the following results:

No job	One job	More than one job
122	536	342

Use a pie chart to represent this data.

A pie chart divides a circle into segments such that the area of each segment over the total area corresponds to the ratio of each number over the total. A pie chart representing the preceding data is shown in Figure 2.1.

See the following text for the mechanics of creating charts with Excel. Note that Excel has automatically converted the raw data into percentages

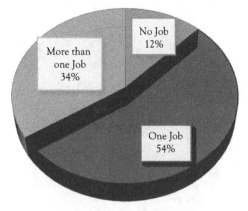

Figure 2.1 Sample pie chart with three segments

of the total and rounded it properly. In other words the figure for "one job" was converted to

536/(122 + 536 + 342) * 100 = 536/1000 * 100 = 53.6 percent, rounded up to 54 percent.

If you move your cursor over the various slices of the pie while inside Microsoft Excel, you will see the total number as well as the number in percentage corresponding to that slice.

Exploding your pie chart: You can also *explode* your pie chart (which sounds a lot more fun than it is). Simply click on one of the pie slices (not any text, though) and drag it outwards a little—your chart will explode! You can either make one slice move out of the pie or all slices. This is useful to highlight one particular slice. In Figure 2.2 we have also colored that slice light gray to further accentuate it.

Bar charts are applicable to categorical variables, just as pie charts, but they can accommodate more categories.

Example: A survey was conducted to find the number of workers employed by major foreign investors. The results are presented in this table.

Great Britain	Germany	Japan	Netherlands	Ireland
6,500	1,450	1,200	200	138

Construct a bar chart representing this data.

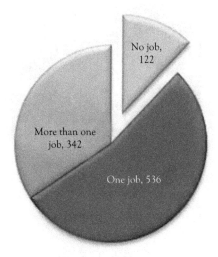

Figure 2.2 A so-called exploding pie chart

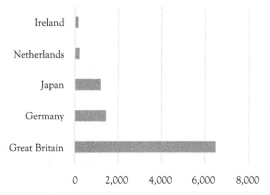

Figure 2.3 A sample bar chart

A bar chart uses vertical or horizontal bars whose length corresponds to the frequency of each category. In our example, the bars represent the number of workers employed by major foreign investors. The first attempt is shown in Figure 2.3.

Nice, but we do not like that the bars go horizontally; it would be nicer if they went vertically. We use some of the options Excel provides to change the bar chart to the one shown in Figure 2.4.

To summarize:

- Pie charts and bar charts can be used to visualize the number of values in each category for a categorical variable. They

Figure 2.4 A bar chart with vertical bars and a title

represent a visual representation of the frequencies of the various categories and are useful to quickly find data that either has a particularly high or low frequency as compared to other data values.

• A pie chart becomes difficult to read if there are more than 6 or 7 categories, while a bar chart can handle up to 20 categories or more.

Frequency Histograms

The previous chart types work well for categorical data since there are usually a limited number of categories. The most important type of graphical data representation for *numerical* data is a *frequency histogram*, or histogram for short. Let us first consider a simple example.

> **Example:** In an anonymous survey of students in a statistics course (like the one you are taking at the moment), students were asked about their sex, male or female. Visualize the responses received: 2, 1, 2, 1, 2, 1, 2, 1, 2, 1, 1, 1, 2, 1, 1, 2, 1, 2, 2, 2, 2, 2, 2, 2, 1, 1, 1, 2, 2, 2, 2, 2, 2, 1, 2, 1, 2, 2, 1, where 1 = male and 2 = female.

First, as a quick review, this is a nominal variable; do not get fooled by the minor detail that the values are all numbers (they are merely codes for the categories).

Second, a usual bar chart (or pie chart) would not work well. We are not really interested in the fact that some responses were 1 and others were 2. Instead we want to know *how many 1's* (men) and *how many 2's* (women) there are, or in the *frequencies* of the various responses. In this case we could (relatively) easily count the values manually to find the following frequencies:

	Frequency
Male (1)	15
Female (2)	24
Totals	39

This frequency table tells us, for example, that more women than men are taking this statistics class. These frequencies directly translate to probabilities: if we meet a person from this class completely at random on the street, there is a "15 in 39" or 38 percent chance it is a man and a "24 in 39" or 62 percent chance it is a woman (we will discuss some probability theory later but this should make common sense). A pie chart could be used to illustrate these figures nicely and shows at a glance that there are more females than males. See Figure 2.5.

In the preceding example we could generate our frequency table manually in an easy manner. But if we have hundreds or thousands of responses, we want to use Excel to generate the frequency table and associated chart automatically. First, however, we will work out a slightly more elaborate frequency histogram manually.

Example: Many communities add fluoride to water to prevent tooth decay. In a 25-day period, these levels of fluoride were measured: 75, 86, 84, 85, 97, 94, 89, 84, 83, 89, 88, 78, 77, 76, 82, 72, 92, 105, 94, 83, 81, 85, 97, 93, 79. Create an appropriate frequency histogram representing this data.

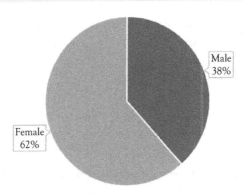

Figure 2.5 Sample pie chart showing counts in each category as percentage

There are too many numbers for a pie or bar chart; in fact we are not interested in the actual numbers as much as we are interested in the frequency with which they occur. Hence, we want to group them into categories, and then graph the frequency counts of these categories instead of the original numbers. We decide, somewhat arbitrarily, to group the data into six categories that we will call *bins*. The smallest data value is 72, the largest is 105, so that the width of each bin should be $(105 - 72)/6 = 5.5$. Thus, our bins are:

$$72.0 \text{ to } 72.0 + 5.5 = 77.5$$
$$77.5 \text{ to } 77.5 + 5.5 = 83.0$$
$$83.0 \text{ to } 83.0 + 5.5 = 88.5$$
$$88.5 \text{ to } 88.5 + 5.5 = 94.0$$
$$94.0 \text{ to } 94.0 + 5.5 = 99.5$$
$$99.5 \text{ to } 99.5 + 5.5 = 105.0.$$

Next we count how many of our data values will fall in each bin. If a number should fall on a boundary between two bins, we will decide to count it in the *lower* bin if possible. The frequencies are shown in Table 2.1.

We can of course construct a bar chart for this frequency table; to distinguish a frequency histogram from a bar chart we set the gap between the columns to zero. See Figure 2.6.

A frequency histogram, in addition to being able to assign probabilities to certain events, also tells you the type of distribution of your variable: homogeneous or heterogeneous. For this example, the variable is heterogeneous.

Table 2.1 Frequencies of fluoride levels in water supplies (in parts per billion [ppb])

Bin	Data	Frequency
less than 77.5	75, 77, 76, 72	4
77.5–83.0	83, 78, 82, 83, 81, 79	6
83.0–88.5	86, 84, 85, 84, 88, 85	6
88.5–94.0	94, 89, 89, 92, 94, 93	6
94.0–99.5	97, 97	2
more than 99.5	105	1

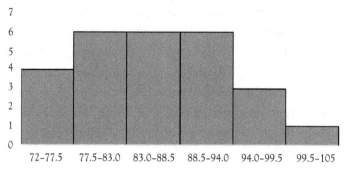

Figure 2.6 A frequency histogram

Example: Open the Excel spreadsheet linked in the following text. It shows the age of respondents to a survey. Generate a frequency histogram and determine if the variable is homogeneous or heterogeneous. Use the default number of categories Excel comes up with.

www.betterbusinessdecisions.org/data/math1101_survey_numeric.xls

The data in that file has the following format:

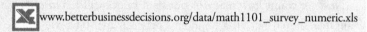

	A	B	C	D	E	F	G	H
1	ID	Age	Weight	Height	NumCDs	TVHours	ExerciseHours	SleepHours
2	55107	18	128	64	70	24	1	7
3	55108	22	240	74	300	4	2	5
4	55110	18	109	62	60	8	2	8
5	55112	18	165	67	100	20	40	5
6	55122	17	140	67	425	3	2	7
7	...	...	...	...	...	...	...	...

We use Excel's histogram tool, which is outlined in detail in the "Using Microsoft Excel" section, to create the chart as shown in Figure 2.7.

According to this histogram, most values are between 20.8 and 24.6. Thus, most values are pretty similar so that this is a homogeneous distribution. Another way to look at this is to say that if we meet a random member of this survey, that person is most likely between 20.8 and 24.6 years old.

Example: The next Excel spreadsheet contains data for salaries of almost 20,000 Major League Baseball (MLB) players from 1988 to 2011. Open the data files and create a histogram for the *salary* variable. Think about whether it is actually a good idea to create this histogram.

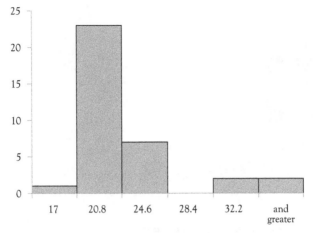

Figure 2.7 Frequency histogram as generated by Excel's histogram tool

www.betterbusinessdecisions.org/data/MLBPlayerSalaries.xlsx

This data set consists of salary information for almost 20,000 MLB players. It has the following format:

	A	B	C	D	E
1	Year	Player	Salary	Position	Team
2	1988	Mike Witt	$ 1,400,000	Pitcher	Los Angeles Angels
3	1988	George Hendrick	$ 989,333	Outfielder	Los Angeles Angels
4	1988	Chili Davis	$ 950,000	Outfielder	Los Angeles Angels
5	1988	Brian Downing	$ 900,000	Designated Hitter	Los Angeles Angels
6	1988	Bob Boone	$ 883,000	Catcher	Los Angeles Angels
7	1988	Johnny Ray	$ 857,000	Second Baseman	Los Angeles Angels
8	...	...	..	...	...

Using Excel's histogram tool with 10 bins, defined manually, gives the histogram shown in Figure 2.8 (you might want to jump to the "Using Microsoft Excel" section to see how to use Excel's histogram tool, and then return here).

This histogram shows again a homogeneous distribution with most players making less than $3.3 million. This diagram is accurate but it does not tell the whole story because it ignores the fact that players' salaries typically increased over the years. A more accurate analysis would perhaps create several histograms, maybe one per decade. That would give a more accurate picture of how salaries changed over time and how they are distributed in each decade.

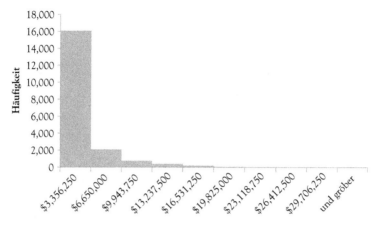

Figure 2.8 Frequencies of MLB salary information

Relative Frequency Histograms

The preceding charts and tables have used the count, or frequency, of each category. In most cases, though, we are not interested in the raw numbers but in *relative* frequencies.

Example: Convert the frequencies in Table 2.1 showing the level of fluoride in drinking water to obtain show relative frequencies. How often did the fluoride level go beyond 94 ppb?

Recall the data from that example (see Table 2.2 on the left). It clearly shows that the fluoride level went beyond 94 ppb on three days. However, that raw count tells us little. To interpret it and to put it in perspective we need to relate it to the total number of days that measurements were

Table 2.2 Frequencies and relative frequencies

Bin	Frequency	Bin	Frequency	Relative frequency %
72.0–77.5	4	72.0–77.5	4	4/25 = 16
77.5–83.0	6	77.5–83.0	6	6/25 = 24
83.0–88.5	6	83.0–88.5	6	6/25 = 24
88.5–94.0	6	88.5–94.0	6	6/25 = 24
94.0–99.5	2	94.0–99.5	2	2/25 = 8
99.5–105	1	99.5–105	1	1/25 = 4
Total	25	Total	25	100

taken. In this case, the level went above 94 ppb on 3 out of 25 days, or 12 percent of the time. In fact, we can convert each frequency into a relative frequency by dividing it by the sample size n, as in Table 2.2 on the right.

Usually we are interested in relative frequencies, since they put the raw count in perspective. However, if the sample size is particularly small, relative frequencies can be misleading.

Example: A sample of size 3 was selected from a survey of teacher evaluations. Two respondents were male and one was female. Discuss the merits of relative versus raw frequencies.

The relative frequencies of the sample are clear: 33 percent of the samples were female and 67 percent were male. This seems to suggest that about 33 percent of *all* evaluations were submitted by females, 67 percent by males. However, since the sample size is so small, these figures are likely to be incorrect. Thus, if the sample size is small, relative frequencies might convey a false sense of certainty.

Perhaps a reasonable solution is to state the relative frequency as a ratio, not in percentage. In other words, one out of three evaluations was female and two out of three were male.

Example: Consider the same data set of MLB salaries and create a relative frequency table and corresponding histogram for the salaries in 2011 only. How many players, approximately, made less than $13 million in 2011?

To create a relative frequency table, we first create a standard frequency table; as before, then we convert each frequency into a relative frequency by dividing it by the sample size. Figure 2.9 shows the resulting table, using 10 categories, of MLB salaries in 2011. We added a column containing the relative frequencies by dividing each frequency by the sample size $n = 843$. Now it is easy to see that approximately $6.5 + 64.8 + 12.9 + 5.8 = 90\%$ of MLB players made less than $13 million in 2011.

Note that a frequency histogram and a relative frequency histogram will have the exact same shape. The only difference between the two would be the scale on the (vertical) y-axis.

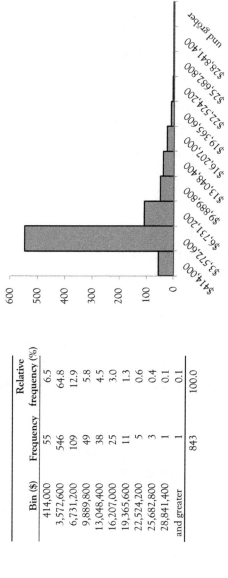

Bin ($)	Frequency	Relative frequency (%)
414,000	55	6.5
3,572,600	546	64.8
6,731,200	109	12.9
9,889,800	49	5.8
13,048,400	38	4.5
16,207,000	25	3.0
19,365,600	11	1.3
22,524,200	5	0.6
25,682,800	3	0.4
28,841,400	1	0.1
and greater	1	0.1
	843	100.0

Figure 2.9 Relative frequencies of MLB salaries in 2011

Table 2.3 *Relative and cumulative frequency table for MLB salaries in 2011*

Bin ($)	Frequency	Relative frequency (%)	Cumulative frequency (%)
414,000	55	6.5	6.5
3,572,600	546	64.8	6.5 + 64.8 = 71.3
6,731,200	109	12.9	71.3 + 12.9 = 84.2
9,889,800	49	5.8	84.2 + 5.8 = 90.0
13,048,400	38	4.5	90.0 + 4.5 = 94.5
16,207,000	25	3.0	94.5 + 3.0 = 97.5
19,365,600	11	1.3	97.5 + 1.3 = 98.8
22,524,200	5	0.6	98.8 + 0.6 = 99.4
25,682,800	3	0.4	99.4 + 0.4 = 99.8
28,841,400	1	0.1	99.8 + 0.1 = 99.9
and greater	1	0.1	99.9 + 0.1 = 100
	843	100.0	

Cumulative Frequency Histograms

Another frequency that is often used is the *cumulative frequency*. It is defined as the sum of the relative frequencies up to the given bin.

Example: Consider the salaries of MLB players in 2011 and add cumulative frequencies to the table.

To compute the cumulative frequency for a row, we add the relative frequencies up to and including that row, or equivalently we add the current *relative* frequency to the prior *cumulative* frequency (see Table 2.3).

We already saw that relative frequencies translate to probabilities. Cumulative frequencies, on the other hand, will be useful to find median, quartiles, and percentiles (see Chapter 3).

Excel provides a number of additional charts as well as variations on existing types. It is easy to experiment so feel free to check out other types of charts.

Bending the Rules: Lying or Exaggeration

Using graphical data representation provides a great opportunity to visualize data so that it conveys a particular point of view. This is not cheating; it is simply using some visual aids to make your data appear to support one particular point of view over another without actually changing the data. Table 2.4 shows, for example, some data of how much different states spent per student in dollars in 2013.

It is easy to see that of the states listed, New Jersey (NJ) spends the most per student, about twice as much as states like Arkansas (AR) or Mississippi (MS). The difference between NJ and AR is pretty clear (see Figure 2.10).

Now suppose we want to give a presentation in which the state of AR is supposed to look reasonably good as compared to the state of NJ. We could create a bar chart that minimizes the visual differences in state spending by using a particularly "large" scale on the y-axis. See Figure 2.11.

We are also de-emphasizing the empty space that results in choosing a large y-scale by placing the chart title into that area. In this chart it is still clear that NJ spends the most per student—after all, we cannot change the actual data—but the difference does not look quite so stark any more. As another option, we could remove the horizontal gridlines to make it harder to see exactly how much money the different states actually spend.

Table 2.4 Money spent per student in select states in 2013

State	$ per student	State	$ per student
Arkansas	9,394	Idaho	6,791
Mississippi	8,130	New Jersey	17,572
North Dakota	11,980	Washington	9,672

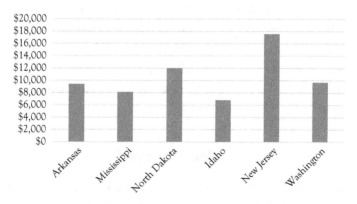

Figure 2.10 Standard bar chart representing money spent per student in 2013

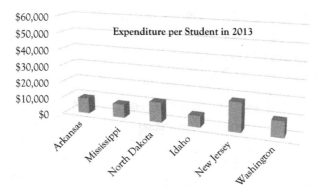

Figure 2.11 Spending per student, de-emphasizing differences between states

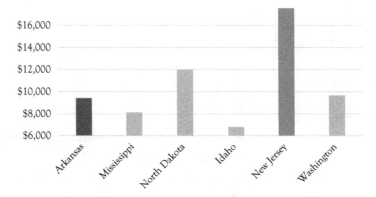

Figure 2.12 Spending per student, emphasizing the difference between AR and NJ

Now let us try the opposite: we want to give a presentation in which the state of AR looks bad as compared to the state of NJ. Thus, we pick a scale on the y-axis that makes sure that the difference between AR and NJ appears as large as possible. In particular, we choose a y-scale that starts at 6,000 and ends at 17,600 instead of the standard values. See Figure 2.12.

We can also pick an "aggressive" color (such as red) for the AR figure and a "calm" color (such as green) for NJ, emphasizing the fact that we want to represent AR as "bad" and NJ as "good." In this chart AR indeed looks pretty bad compared to NJ—in fact, it seems as if NJ spends many times more money per student than AR—but we have not changed the actual data values.

All three charts represent the same data and are perfectly valid. Yet visually they tell different stories. There are many other tricks that can be used to represent data in such a way as to support one particular point of view without outright changing the data.

Exercise: Suppose you have some data showing the cases of H1N1 influenza infections per region as follows:

- Region 01—Boston: 215
- Region 02—New York: 229
- Region 03—Philadelphia: 193
- Region 04—Atlanta: 301
- Region 05—Chicago: 1,788
- Region 06—Dallas: 734
- Region 07—Kansas City: 164
- Region 08—Denver: 175
- Region 09—San Francisco: 1,080
- Region 10—Seattle: 420

If you were a health official in Dallas, you might want to use this data to try to get people in your region to vaccinate against the H1N1 flu or to encourage a government agency to fund prevention and treatment programs in Dallas. Thus, you are trying to create a chart that emphasizes the number of cases in Dallas versus the other regions so that your citizens are motivated to get vaccinated or that funding is approved. Figure 2.13 shows a few suggestions.

Try this: check your local newspaper or online news source to find some charts. See if these charts try to promote any particular point of view or if they are relatively neutral.

Using Microsoft Excel

Usually we use Excel for help with some calculations only. This is relatively easy and needs no further explanation. However, Excel also includes some more complex procedures useful for statistics; we will explore some of them in this section.

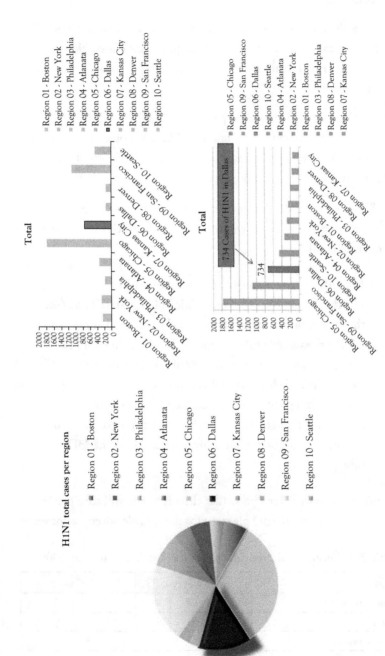

Figure 2.13 Tricks to highlight a particular data point without changing the data

Creating Charts

We have already seen bar charts and pie charts to summarize our data. Such charts can be created in Excel with just a few clicks. Note that the following instructions are for Excel 2013 but other versions of Excel offer similar capabilities.

Example: Table 2.5 shows the percentage of the population living in poverty and the violent crime rate per 100,000 people in 2009 (from census.gov) in the six New England states. Decide if a bar chart or pie chart is better to represent the data.

We have only six categories for our data, so neither a bar chart nor a pie chart can be excluded. We will create both to see which one seems more meaningful.

- Enter the data into an empty spreadsheet in Excel.
- Use the mouse (or cursor keys while holding SHIFT) to select the cells in the first two columns, including the first row containing the variable names; ignore the third column for now.
- Select the "Insert" ribbon. You should see an icon for "recommended chart" as well as icons for specific chart types. It is usually a good idea to check the recommended chart. In our case, though, we know which chart type we want, so we directly click on the pie chart icon and select the "3D" subtype.

While you hover over a particular chart type you will see a preview of the chart. In our case the 3D pie chart for the variable poverty is shown in

Table 2.5 Poverty and crime data for New England states in 2009

State	Poverty	Crime
Connecticut	9.4	306.7
Maine	12.3	119.4
Massachusetts	10.3	466.2
New Hampshire	8.5	166
Rhode Island	11.5	252.8
Vermont	11.4	140.8

Figure 2.14 on the left. We repeat the procedure to produce a 3D column bar chart, shown on the right in Figure 2.14.

The pie chart is not very helpful. It is difficult to grasp which slice represents what state and it is difficult to see the actual poverty rate for each slice. In addition, Excel recommends pie charts if the various category values add to 100 percent. This is not the case, so this chart type is out. The bar chart in Figure 2.14 on the right side has more potential but at the moment it is not looking its best.

- Click on the chart title "Poverty" and press Delete. The title will disappear and the chart will grow slightly.
- Excel offers some "styles" on the "Insert" ribbon that can further improve the look of a chart. We pick, for example, the third option called "style 3" to get a nicely formatted, readable chart as shown in Figure 2.15.

To create a chart for the "crime" variable we first switch the second and third columns with each other via cut and paste—for simple charts it is easiest to make sure that the data and the labels are next to each other. If you select all three columns, Excel will recommend a "stacked" chart, which is not appropriate for this data. Alternatively, you could use the cursor keys together with CTRL to select the non-adjacent columns "State" and "Crime." We leave the details to you.

For additional help and information, see "How to use the Chart Wizard," available at https://support.microsoft.com/en-us/kb/304421

Excel's Histogram Tool

The Analysis ToolPak provides a convenient tool to create histograms for numerical variables.

Example: Many communities add fluoride to water to prevent tooth decay. In a 25-day period, these levels of fluoride were measured: 75, 86, 84, 85, 97, 94, 89, 84, 83, 89, 88, 78, 77, 76, 82, 72, 92, 105, 94, 83, 81, 85, 97, 93, 79. Create an appropriate frequency histogram representing this data, using the appropriate Analysis ToolPak tool.

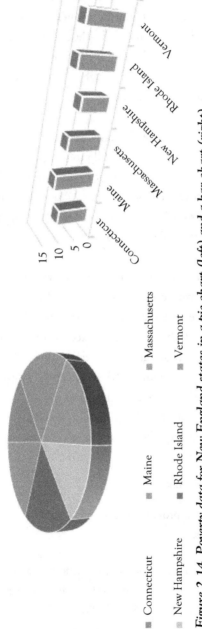

- Connecticut
- New Hampshire
- Maine
- Rhode Island
- Massachusetts
- Vermont

Figure 2.14 Poverty data for New England states in a pie chart (left) and a bar chart (right)

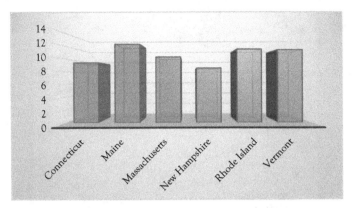

Figure 2.15 Nicely formatted bar chart for poverty data

Here is a quick walk-through of this procedure:

- Start Excel and enter the preceding numbers, all in one column. You do not need to enter a title or anything else, just the numbers in one column, one number in each row.
- Bring up the "Data Analysis ..." dialog (remember, it is available on the "Data" ribbon). If you do not see this item, you must first install the "Analysis ToolPak" as described in Chapter 1. You will see a dialog box listing all procedures available in this Analysis ToolPak. Highlight the entry "Histogram"; then click "OK."
- Next, enter the options for a (frequency) histogram, including the location of the data to use and, optionally, the categories (bin ranges) that you want to define. See Figure 2.16 for details.

To define the input range, you can use the "cell selector" icon ▦ next to the "Input Range" field. Click it and use the mouse or cursor keys to select the appropriate cells by highlighting them. Click the "Return" icon to return to the original "Histogram" dialog box. Leave the "Bin Range" empty for now so that the tool will automatically pick the bins for the data. Make sure to check "New Worksheet Ply" as your output options, check the "Chart Output," and click OK. Note that if your first cell contained a variable label instead of the first value, you would need

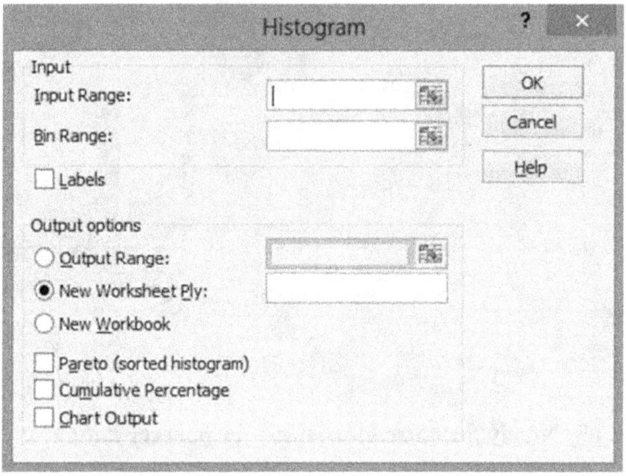

Figure 2.16 Options for the histogram procedure in Analysis ToolPak

to check the "Labels" option as well. The resulting histogram is shown in Figure 2.17.

As usual, we can now customize our chart by double-clicking on its components to replace the various titles by more meaningful names, and removing the "Frequency" label. In this example Excel determined the categories for our numerical variable (the "bins") automatically.

- Category 1 includes all numbers less than 72 and includes one measurement.
- Category 2 goes from 72 to 78.6 and includes four measurements.
- Category 3 goes from 78.6 to 85.2 and includes nine measurements.
- Category 4 goes from 85.2 to 91.8 and includes four measurements.
- Category 5 goes from 91.8 to 98.4 and includes six measurements.
- Category 6 includes everything above 98.4 and includes one measurement.

If we want to define the bin boundaries manually, we would add the numbers representing the bin boundaries in increasing order somewhere

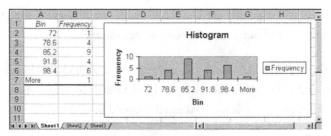

Figure 2.17 A histogram with automatically generated bins

in a column and select them by clicking the cell selector icon in the "Bin Range" field.

Example: Use Excel to create another histogram for the fluoride data that has four bins.

We need to determine the boundaries of the bins so that we end up with exactly four bins. We can use Excel's =min(RANGE) and =max(RANGE) functions to determine the smallest and largest data point. Then, if we use bins with width of (max − min)/(number of bins), we will end up with the right number of equally spaced bins:

min = 72, max = 105, bin width = (105 − 72)/4 = 8.25.

Now we add a column to the Excel table where we define the bin boundaries:

min + width = 80.25
min + 2 * width = 88.5
min + 3 * width = 96.75.

Note that we need three bin boundaries to define four bins:

less than 80.25
between 80.25 and 88.5
between 88.5 and 96.75
bigger than 96.75.

Finally, start the histogram procedure from our Analysis ToolPak. Define the data range as usual, but also define as bin range the three bin boundaries we just computed. The resulting histogram will now have four bars, as desired.

Students frequently have trouble using the histogram tool with a given number of bins, so here is one more example.

Example: Consider the Excel spreadsheet containing salary data of almost 20,000 MLB players from 1988 to 2011. Create a histogram for the salary variable with 10 equally spaced bins.

 www.betterbusinessdecisions.org/data/MLBPlayerSalaries.xlsx

We first compute the minimum and maximum data values and then use them to define the bin widths for our bins. Finally we create 9 bin boundaries to define our 10 bins, letting Excel do the actual computations (see Figure 2.18).

With these boundaries in place, start the histogram tool as usual. Enter the range for the salary data C2:C19544 and use the boundaries we just computed as bin range (H6:H14). Make sure the option for "Chart Output" is checked to generate this histogram chart in addition to the table. The resulting histogram should look like the one in Figure 2.8.

Excel's Pivot Tool: Charts for Categorical Data

Often one would like to know the frequency of occurrence of values for a variable in percentage. This is similar to a frequency histogram we studied

⊿	G	H	I
1	min	$ 62,500	=MIN(C2:C19544)
2	max	$ 33,000,000	=MAX(C2:C19544)
3	num bins	10	
4	bin width	3293750	=(H2-H1)/10
5			
6	boundaries	$ 3,356,250	=H1+H4
7		$ 6,650,000	=H1+2*H4
8		$ 9,943,750	=H1+3*H4
9		$ 13,237,500	=H1+4*H4
10		$ 16,531,250	=H1+5*H4
11		$ 19,825,000	=H1+6*H4
12		$ 23,118,750	=H1+7*H4
13		$ 26,412,500	=H1+8*H4
14		$ 29,706,250	=H1+9*H4

Figure 2.18 Computing bin boundaries for MLB data

earlier, but a *histogram* only applies to numerical variables, while the procedure outlined in this section applies to *categorical* variables.

Example: A survey was conducted in the summer of 2014, asking several students in a statistics course a number of questions about their background and musical taste. The data can be found by clicking on the following link. Display a bar chart for the race of the students. In other words, compute how many of the students are White, Black, Hispanic, and so on and display those figures in a bar chart.

 www.betterbusinessdecisions.org/data/student-survey.xls

Loading this data into Excel, we see in Figure 2.19 that the column of interest is column E titled "Race." However, that column represents a categorical variable (ordinal or nominal?), so we cannot compute a frequency histogram.

Before we figure out how Excel can generate the desired data automatically let us do it by hand. Inspecting the data we see that there are five categories: White, Black, Hispanic, Pacific Islander, and Other. We can manually count how many people are contained in each category (see Figure 2.20).

Our manual procedure worked because we did not have that much data. For large data sets we need to figure out an automatic procedure to generate the appropriate table. Fortunately, Excel has just such a procedure, called a *Pivot Table*. The pivot tool is found as the first button of the "Insert" ribbon. It looks slightly different depending on your version of Excel but the differences are pretty minor. To use the pivot tool:

	A7	▼	f_x	20046		
	A	B	C	D	E	F
3	20080	Female	155	66	White	0
4	20041	Female	115	60	Other	1
5	20044	Male	220	72	White	2
6	20096	Female	125	64	Hispanice	5
7	20046	Female	115	63	White	5
8	20050	Female	103	62	Black	2
9	20065	Male	130	67	Pacific Isl	3

Survey, Text Values

Figure 2.19 Excerpt of data from a student survey

28	White	15
29	Black	3
30	Hispanic	2
31	Pacific Isl	1
32	Other	2

Figure 2.20 A frequency table generated manually

- Load the preceding spreadsheet into Excel and click anywhere *outside* the data area, for example, below the last row of data (otherwise the pivot tool may be disabled).
- Select "Insert | Pivot Table" and choose the entire data table for the Input Range field, using the by now familiar range selector. Make sure to pick the entire data table, including the first row containing labels. Excel should by default have selected the entire table already for your convenience.
- Choose to put the resulting pivot table into a new spreadsheet and click "Okay" to generate the pivot table, which will initially be empty.

You will see a "potential frequency table" containing labels such as "Drop Row Field Here," "Drop Column Fields Here," and so on, but no data values are yet contained in the table (see Figure 2.21). There will also be a list containing the available variables from your data, in our case "id," "Sex," "Weight," "Height," "Race," and so on. You can "drag and drop" these variables onto the various slots in the table to create a variety of useful tables for data analysis.

- Drag the variable "Race" from the field list into the "Drop Row Fields" area of the table. Your table will adjust, showing you all available "Race" categories but as for now no frequencies (counts).
- Next, again drag the variable "Race" from the field list, but this time drag it to the "Drop Value Fields" area in the middle.

Figure 2.21 An empty pivot table with a list of named fields

	A	B
1		
2		
3	Count of Race	
4	Race	Total
5	Black	3
6	Hispanice	2
7	Other	2
8	Pacific Islander	1
9	White	15
10	(blank)	
11	Grand Total	23
12		

Figure 2.22 A pivot table showing the counts in the race categories

You will now see the counts of how many occurrences fell inside each race category, which of course will turn out similar to the one we created manually before in Figure 2.17, except this time it includes the "blank" category (and the order may be different). See Figure 2.22 for the finished pivot table.

See if you can eliminate the "blank" response row. (Hint: Maybe you can find a drop-down menu somewhere where you can "uncheck" unwanted categories.) Also, when you double-click the "Count of Race" label in the table you can specify exactly what type of counts should be shown and in which way it should be formatted. Try, for example, to get your counts to appear as percentage of the overall total.

You can now create a bar chart as usual, including or excluding the blank response as you see fit. We will later revisit the pivot table tool and investigate additional options and possibilities.

CHAPTER 3

Numerical Data Summary

Preview: *Charts and graphs are useful for representing data in a user-friendly format, but there are times when it is more important to summarize data numerically. A quality numerical data summary has meaning even to individuals who have no previous experience with the data being presented. You do not have to be a scientist or a doctor to understand that the average cholesterol for a given male population is 220, while the cholesterol level for women in the same population is 190. In order to understand the power of numerical data summary, it is important to understand the difference between the median and the mean: the mean is the average of all observations, while the median is the point at which half the numbers are larger and half are smaller. The mode is another important numerical data representation: it is the observation that occurs most frequently. The mean, median, and mode are important, but so is the variance. The term variance is used to measure how widely, or narrowly, spread out a group of numbers is. For instance, a set of numbers in which all values are 7 has zero variance. These terms are used to summarize a set of numbers and help the observer make sense of the results. Whether the data being represented is a list of baseball statistics, salary data for a Fortune 500 company, or the cholesterol levels of heart patients, the summarization techniques are the same.*

Learning Objectives: At the conclusion of this chapter, you should be able to:

1. Describe the properties of central tendency, variation, and shape in numerical data
2. Compute descriptive summary measures for a population
3. Construct and interpret a box plot

Introduction

As we have seen in Chapter 1, statistics is the study of making sense of data and consists of four components: collecting, summarizing, analyzing, and presenting data. In Chapter 2 we focused on summarizing data graphically; in this chapter we will concern ourselves with summarizing data numerically.

While charts are certainly very nice and often convincing, they do have at least one major drawback: they are not very "portable." In other words, if you conduct an experiment measuring cholesterol levels of male and female patients, it is certainly suited to create appropriate histograms and colorful charts to illustrate the outcome of your experiment. However, if you are asked to summarize your results, for example, for a radio show or just during a conversation, charts will not help much.

Instead you need a simple, short, and easy-to-memorize summary of your data that—despite being short and simple—is meaningful to others with whom you might share your results.

For example, in our study of levels of cholesterol we could condense the results by stating that the "average" level of cholesterol for men is X, while the average for women is Y, and most people would understand. Of course, when we condense data in this way, some level of detail is lost, but we gain the ease of summarizing the data quickly.

This chapter will discuss some numbers (or "statistics" as they will be called) that can be used to summarize data numerically while still trying to capture much of the structure hidden in the data. Among the descriptive statistics we will study are the mean, mode, and median; the range, variance, and standard deviation; and more detailed descriptors such as percentiles, quartiles, and skewness. Toward the end of this chapter we will learn about the "box plot" that combines many of the numerical descriptors in one structure.

Measures of Central Tendency

While charts are commonly very useful to visually represent data, they are inconvenient for the simple reason that they are difficult to display and reproduce. It is frequently useful to reduce data to a couple of numbers that are easy to remember and easy to communicate, yet capture the essence of the data they represent. The mean, median, and mode are our first examples of such computed representations of data.

Mean, Median, and Mode

Definition: The *mean* represents the average of all observations. It describes the "quintessential" number of your data by averaging all numbers collected. The formula for computing the mean is:

mean = (sum of all measurements)/(number of measurements).

In statistics, *two* separate letters are used for the mean:

- The Greek letter μ (mu) is used to denote the mean of the entire population, or *population mean.*
- The symbol $\bar{x}$ (read as "x bar") is used to denote the mean of a sample, or *sample mean.*

Another way to show how the mean is computed is:

$$mean = \frac{1}{n}\sum_{i=1}^{n} x_i = \frac{1}{n}\left(x_1 + x_2 + \cdots + x_n\right).$$

Here n stands for the number of measurements, x_i stands for the individual i-th measurement, and the Greek symbol sigma Σ stands for "sum of." This formula is valid for computing either the population mean μ or the sample mean $\bar{x}$.

Of course, the idea—ultimately—is to use the sample mean (which is usually easy to compute) as an estimate for the population mean (which is usually unknown). For now, we will just show examples of computing a mean, but later we will discuss in detail how exactly the sample mean can be used to estimate the population mean.

Example: A sample of seven scores from people taking an achievement test was taken. Find the mean if the numbers are:
95, 86, 78, 90, 62, 73, 89.

The mean of that sample is:
$\bar{x}$ = (95 + 86 + 78 + 90 + 62 + 73 + 89)/7 = 573/7 = 81.9.

The mean applies to numerical variables, and in some situations to ordinal variables. It does not apply to nominal variables.

Another, and in some sense better, measure of central tendency is the median, or middle number.

Definition: The *median* is that number from a population or sample chosen so that half of all numbers are larger and half of the numbers are smaller than that number. The computation is different for an even or odd number of observations.

Important: Before you try to determine the median you must first *sort your data* in ascending order.

Example: Compute the median of the numbers 1, 2, 3, 4, and 5.

The numbers are already sorted, so that it is easy to see that the median is 3 (two numbers are less than 3 and two are bigger).

Example: Compute the median of the numbers 1, 2, 3, 4, 5, and 6.

The numbers are again sorted, but neither 3 nor 4 (nor any other of the numbers) can be the median. In fact, the median should be somewhere between 3 and 4. In that case (when there is an even number of numbers) the median is computed by taking the "middle between the two middle numbers." In our case the median, therefore, would be 3.5 since that is the middle between 3 and 4, computed as $(3 + 4)/2$. Note that indeed three numbers are less than 3.5, and three are bigger, as the definition of the median requires. For larger data sets, the median can be selected as follows:

Sort all observations in ascending order.

- *If n is odd*, pick the number in the $\dfrac{n+1}{2}$ position of your data.

- *If n is even*, pick the numbers at positions $\dfrac{n}{2}$ and $\dfrac{n}{2}+1$ and find the middle of those two numbers.

This does not imply that the median is $\dfrac{n+1}{2}$ (if n is odd) but rather that the median is *that* number which can be *found at position* $(n + 1)/2$.

The median is usually easy to compute when the data is sorted and there are not too many numbers. For unsorted numbers, in particular several numbers, the median becomes quite tedious, mainly because you have to sort the data first. The median applies to numerical variables, and in some situations to ordinal variables. It does *not* apply to nominal variables.

The final measure of central tendency is the mode. It is the easiest, most applicable, but least useful of the measures of central tendency.

Definition: The mode is that observation that occurs most often.

The mode is frequently not unique and is therefore not that often used, but it has the advantage that it applies to numerical as well as categorical variables. As with the median, the mode is easy to find if the data is small and sorted.

Example: Scores from a test were: 1, 2, 2, 4, 7, 7, 7, 8, 9. What is the mode?

The mode is 7, because that number occurs more often than any other number.

Example: Scores from a test were: 1, 2, 2, 2, 3, 7, 7, 7, 8, 9. What is the mode?

This time the mode is 2 and 7, because both numbers occur thrice, more than the other numbers. Sometimes variables that are distributed this way are called bimodal variables.

Pros and Cons

Since there are three measures of central tendency (mean, median, and mode), it is natural to ask which of them is most useful (and as usual the answer will be ... "it depends").

The usefulness of the *mode* is that it applies to any variable. For example, if your experiment contains nominal variables then the mode is the only meaningful measure of central tendency. The problem with the mode, however, is that it is not necessarily unique, and mathematicians do not like it when there are more than one correct answers.

Mean and *median* usually apply in the same situations, so it is more difficult to determine which one is more useful. To understand the difference between median and mean, consider the following example.

Example: Suppose we want to know the average income of parents of students in this class. To simplify the calculations and to obtain the answer quickly, we randomly select three students to form a random sample. Let us consider two possible scenarios:

- Case 1: The three incomes were, say, $25,000, $30,000, and $35,000.
- Case 2: The three incomes were, say, $25,000, $30,000, and $1,000,000.

Compute mean and median in each case and discuss which one is more appropriate.

The actual computations are pretty simple:

- In Case 1 the mean is $30,000 and the median is also $30,000.
- In Case 2 the mean is $351,666 whereas the median is still $30,000.

Clearly we were unlucky in Case 2: one set of parents in this sample is very wealthy, but that is—probably—not representative for the students of the class. However, we selected a random sample, so scenario 1 is equally likely as scenario 2. Therefore, it seems that the median is actually a better measure of central tendency than the mean, especially for small numbers of observations. In other words:

- The mean is influenced by extreme values, more so than the median.
- The median is more stable and is therefore the better measure of central tendency.

However, for large sample sizes the mean and the median tend to be close to each other anyway, and the mean does have two other advantages:

- The mean is easier to compute than the median since it does not require sorted observations (this is true even if you use Excel: sorting numbers is time-consuming even for a computer, but in most cases the sample size is so small that we do not notice this).
- The mean has nice theoretical properties that make it more useful than the median.

We will use both mean and median in the remainder of this course, while the mode will be less useful for us and will usually be ignored.

Mean, Median, and Mode for Ordinal Variables

As mentioned, the mean and median work best for numerical values, but you can compute them for ordinal variables as well if you properly interpret the results.

Example: Suppose you want to find out how students like a particular statistics lecture, so you ask them to fill out a survey, rating the lecture "great," "average," or "poor." The 14 students in the class rank the lecture as:

great, great, average, poor, great, great, average, great, great, great, average, poor, great, average.

Compute the mean, the mode, and the median.

Obviously the mode is "great," since that is the most frequent response. For the other measures of central tendency we have to introduce numerical codes for the responses. We could define, for example:

"great" = 1, "average" = 2, and "poor" = 3.

Then the preceding ordinal data is equivalent to

1, 1, 2, 3, 1, 1, 2, 1, 1, 1, 2, 3, 1, 2.

Now it is easy to see that the average is $22/14 = 1.57$ and the median is 1. Of course the actual values for these central tendencies depend on the numerical code we are using for the original variables. We would need to justify or at least mention the codes we are using in a report so that the answers can be put in proper context. In other words, instead of

	Strongly agree	Agree	Undecided	Disagree	Strongly disagree
1. The software I wanted was easy to find	1	2	3	4	5
2. The checkout process was easy	1	2	3	4	5

Figure 3.1 A survey with a Likert scale

reporting mean and median as 1.57 and 1, respectively, it would be more appropriate to report that the median category was "great" (1), and the average category was between "great" (1) and "average" (2). In a proper survey we would in fact list the code values together with the responses.

One particular type of response that is frequently used in surveys is a Likert scale.

Definition: A *Likert scale* is a sequence of items (responses) that are usually displayed with a visual aid, such as a horizontal bar, representing a simple scale (see Figure 3.1).

For a Likert scale like this, it should be clear that we could compute mean and median in addition to mode, even though the two variables are ordinal.

Mean, Median, and Mode for Frequency Distributions

We have seen how to compute mean, mode, and median for numerical data, and how to create frequency tables for categorical variables and histograms for numerical ones. As it turns out, it is possible to compute these measures of central tendency even if only the aggregate data in terms of a frequency table or histogram is available.

Example: Suppose the sizes of widgets produced in a certain factory are:

3, 2, 5, 1, 4, 11, 3, 8, 23, 2, 6, 17, 5, 12, 35, 3, 8, 23, 6, 14, 41, 7, 16, 47, 8, 18, 53, 10, 22, 65, 9, 20, 59.

Suppose we previously constructed a frequency table as seen in Table 3.1 from this data.

Table 3.1 Frequency table

Category	Count
13.8 and less	19
Between 13.8 and 26.6	8
Between 26.6 and 39.4	1
Between 39.4 and 52.2	2
Bigger than 52.2	3
Total	33

Based solely on this table (and not on the actual data values), estimate the mean and compare it with the true mean of the full data.

If all we knew was this table, we would argue as follows:

- Nineteen data points are between 1 and 13.8, that is, 19 data points are averaging $(1 + 13.8)/2 = 7.4$.
- Eight data points are between 13.8 and 26.6, that is, eight data points are averaging $(26.6 + 13.8)/2 = 20.2$.
- One data point is between 26.6 and 39.4, or one data point averages $(26.6 + 39.4)/2 = 33.0$.
- Two data points average $(39.4 + 52.2)/2 = 45.8$.
- Three data points are above 52.2, or between 52.2 and 65.0, so that three data points average $(52.2 + 65)/2 = 58.6$.

Thus, we could estimate the total sum as:

$$19 * 7.4 + 8 * 20.2 + 1 * 33 + 2 * 45.8 + 3 * 58.6 = 602.6$$

and therefore the average should be approximately $602.6/33 = 18.26$.

The true average of the original data is 17.15. Thus, our estimated average is pretty close to the true average.

Of course if you had the original data, you would not need to do this estimation—you would use that data to compute the mean. But there are

Example: Table 3.2 shows the salaries of graduates from a university. Assume we do not have access to the original raw data and estimate the mean based only on the summary data.

cases where you only have the aggregate data in table form, in which case you could use this technique to find at least an approximate value for the mean.

We will use Table 3.3 (hopefully together with Excel) to get organized.

To estimate the average, we compute the *range midpoints* and *product* entries in Table 3.3. Then we divide the sum of the products by the sum of the counts to get as average $29,047,920/1,100 = $26,407.20.

There is no way to determine the actual average from this table, since we do not know how the numbers fit into the various intervals. We would need access to the original raw data to find the true mean. In a similar way you can compute the mean of an ordinal variable as long as you can assign some numerical value to the categories.

That settles finding the mean, but how do we find the median or the mode? Well, that is actually much easier than the mean:

- Compute the percentages for the frequency table:
    - *The mode is the category with the largest percentage.*
- Add a column named "cumulative percentage" to the frequency table by computing the sum of all percentages of all categories below the current one:
    - *The median is the first category where the cumulative percentage is above 50 percent.*

Table 3.2 Frequency table for salary data

Salary range ($)	Count
7,200–18,860	130
18,860–30,520	698
30,520–42,180	254
42,180–53,840	16
53,840–65,500	2

Table 3.3 Augmented frequency table to compute average

Salary range ($)	Range midpoint	Count	Product
7,200–18,860	13,030	130	1,693,900
18,860–30,520	24,690	698	17,233,620
30,520–42,180	36,350	254	9,232,900
42,180–53,840	48,010	16	768,160
53,840–65,500	59,670	2	119,340
Total		1,100	29,047,920

Table 3.4 Frequency table with cumulative percent

Salary range ($)	Count	Percentage	Cumulative percentage
7,200–18,860	130	130/1100 = 11.8	11.8
18,860–30,520	698	698/1100 = 63.5	63.5 + 11.8 = 75.3
30,520–42,180	254	254/1100 = 23.1	75.3 + 23.1 = 98.4
42,180–53,840	16	16/1100 = 1.4	98.4 + 1.4 = 99.8
53,840–65,500	2	2/1100 = 0.2	99.8 + 0.2 = 100
Total	1100	100	

Example: Find the median and the mode for the salary (Table 3.2).

We add two columns to the table: one containing the frequency as percentage and the second containing the cumulative percentage (see Table 3.4).

We can see that the mode is the second category $18,860–$30,520 since it occurs most often with a relative frequency of 63.5 percent. The median is also the second category, since it is the first where the cumulative percentage is above 50 percent.

Note that finding the median depends on the fact that the categories are ordered, of course, which means that the variable must be ordinal (or numerical in the case of a histogram).

While an average often helps in understanding the essence of data, it is not always helpful. For example, if a quarterback throws the ball one foot too far half the time and one foot short the other half, then on average he has a perfect game yet he does not make a single completion. As another example, suppose that school attendance in a particular school has risen from 80 to 95 percent over the past five years. To evaluate next year's attendance, we compare it to the average over the past five years, which is 87 percent. Suppose attendance comes in at 90 percent. We think we had an improvement in attendance as compared to the five-year average, yet in reality attendance dropped from the previous year.

Measures of Dispersion:
Range, Variance, and Standard Deviation

While mean and median tell you about the center of your observations, it says nothing about the spread of the numbers.

Example: Suppose two machines produce nails that are on average 10 in. long. A sample of 11 nails is selected from each machine and each length is recorded, as denoted in the following text. Which machine is "better" (justify your choice)?

Machine A: 6, 8, 8, 10, 10, 10, 10, 10, 12, 12, 14.

Machine B: 6, 6, 6, 8, 8, 10, 12, 12, 14, 14, 14.

First we verify that the average length of the sample is 10:

Mean for machine A: $\bar{x} = \dfrac{110}{11} = 10$.

Mean for machine B: $\bar{x} = \dfrac{110}{11} = 10$.

In both cases, the mean is 10, indeed. However, the first machine seems to be the better one, since most nails are close to 10 in. Therefore, we must find additional numbers indicating the spread of the data.

Range, Variance, and Standard Deviation

The easiest measure of the data spread is the range.

Definition: The *range* is the difference between the highest and the lowest data value.

In the preceding example, the range is the same for both machines, namely, $14 - 6 = 8$. The range is, while useful, too crude a measure of dispersion. As a case in point, both machines in the preceding example have the same range, so that figure cannot be used to differentiate between the two machines.

We now want to find out how much the data points are spread around the mean. To do that, we could find the difference between each data point and the mean, and average these differences. However, we want to measure these differences regardless of the sign (positive and negative differences should not cancel out). Therefore, we could find the absolute value of the difference between each data point and the mean, average these differences. But for theoretical reasons an absolute value function is not easy to deal with, so that one chooses a square function instead, which also neutralizes signs. Finally, for yet other theoretical reasons we shall use not the sample size n to compute an average but instead $n - 1$. Hence, we will use the following formulas to compute the data spread, or variance.

Definition: The *variance* measures the spread of the data around the mean. Its definition depends on whether you want to find the population or sample variance. There are two symbols for the variance, just as for the mean:

$$\sigma^2 = \frac{1}{N} \sum_{i=1}^{N} \left(x_i - \mu \right)^2 \text{ is the variance for a population.}$$

$$s^2 = \frac{1}{n-1} \sum_{i=1}^{n} \left(x_i - \overline{x} \right)^2 \text{ is the variance for a sample.}$$

In virtually all applications we will use the second formula (the sample variance). This is true in particular when we do not specify which of the two formulas to use: the default formula is the one for sample variance.

Note that the two formulas are very similar: The *population* variance involves the population mean μ, the population size N, and divides the sum by N, whereas the *sample* variance uses the sample mean $\overline{x}$, the sample size n, and divides the sum by $n - 1$. As mentioned in the definition, we will use the formula for the sample variance exclusively. For some information about sample versus population variance, see https://en.wikipedia.org/wiki/Variance.

It is useful to compute the variance at least once "manually" before we show how to use some shortcuts (and more Excel to accomplish the same feat quickly and easily).

How to Find the (Sample) Variance Manually

- Make a table of all x values.
- Find the mean of the data.

- Add a column with the difference of each data point to the mean.
- Add a column with the square of that difference.
- Sum up the last column and divide the sum by $(n - 1)$.

Table 3.5 shows the results of this procedure for the preceding sample of nails from machines A and B. Note that the mean is the sum of column 1 divided by $N = 11$, which we need to compute first before we can determine column 2 or 3.

Thus we have the following:

- The variance of machine A is $\dfrac{1}{n-1}\sum(x - \mu)^2 = \dfrac{1}{10} \cdot 48 = 4.8$.
- The variance of machine B is

$$\frac{1}{n-1}\sum(x - \mu)^2 = \frac{1}{10} \cdot 112 = 11.2.$$

Thus, the spread around the mean for machine A is 4.8 and that for machine B is 11.2. This means that machine A, as a rule, produces nails that stick pretty close to the average nail length. Machine B, on the other hand, produces nails with more variability than machine A. Therefore, machine A would be preferred over machine B.

Table 3.5 Computing variances

X	$x - \mu$	$(x - \mu)^2$	X	$x - \mu$	$(x - \mu)^2$
6	4	16	6	4	16
8	2	4	6	4	16
8	2	4	6	4	16
10	0	0	8	2	4
10	0	0	8	2	4
10	0	0	10	0	0
10	0	0	12	-2	4
10	0	0	12	-2	4
12	-2	4	14	-4	16
12	-2	4	14	-4	16
14	4	16	14	-4	16
110	0	48	110	0	112

| *Machine A* | *Machine B* |

Note: The unit of the variance is the *square* of the original unit, which is unfortunate; we would prefer the same unit as the original data. Therefore, one introduces an additional statistic, called the standard deviation, to fix this unit problem.

Definition: The *standard deviation* measures the spread of the data around the mean, using the same unit as the data. It is defined as the square root of the variance. As with the mean, there are two letters for variance and standard deviation:

$\sigma = \sqrt{\sigma^2}$ is the population standard deviation.

$s = \sqrt{s^2}$ is the sample standard deviation.

Example: Consider the sample data 6, 7, 5, 3, 4. Compute the standard deviation for that data.

To compute the standard deviation, we must first compute the mean, then the variance, and finally we can take the square root to obtain the standard deviation. In this case we do not need to create a table since there are very few numbers:

- The mean: $\dfrac{1}{5}(6+7+5+3+4)=\dfrac{25}{5}=5$
- The variance:

$$\frac{1}{4}\left((6-5)^2+(7-5)^2+(5-5)^2+(3-5)^2+(4-5)^2\right)=\frac{10}{4}=2.5$$

- Standard deviation: $\sqrt{2.5}=1.58$

Shortcut for Variance

It is somewhat inconvenient that we first have to compute the mean before getting to the standard deviation. In particular, if we compute the standard deviation of n data points and then for some reason add one more data point, we have to redo the entire calculation. Fortunately there is a nice shortcut to compute the variance (and thus the standard deviation) that can be proved as an exercise:

$$s^2 = \frac{1}{n-1}\sum\left(x-\mu\right)^2 = \frac{1}{n-1}\left(\sum x^2 - \frac{\left(\sum x\right)^2}{n}\right).$$

Table 3.6 Applying shortcut to compute variance

x	x^2
6	36
6	36
6	36
8	64
8	64
10	100
12	144
12	144
14	196
14	196
14	196
110	1212

At first this second formula looks much more complicated, but it is actually easier since it does not involve computing the mean first. In other words, using the second formula we can compute the variance (and therefore the standard deviation) without first having to compute the mean.

In our preceding example of machine B we would compute the variance using this shortcut as shown in Table 3.6.

Thus $\sum x = 110$ and $\sum x^2 = 1212$ so that the variance is

$$\frac{1}{n-1}\left(\sum x^2 - \frac{\left(\sum x\right)^2}{n}\right) = \frac{1}{10}\left(1212 - \frac{110^2}{11}\right) = \frac{1}{10}\left(1212 - 1100\right) = 11.2,$$

which of course is the same number as before, but a little easier to arrive at. If you need to compute the variance manually, you should always use this shortcut formula. For practice, compute the variance of machine A using this shortcut method.

Variance and Standard Deviation for Frequency Tables

Just as we were able to approximate the mean and median of a variable from its distribution (frequency table or histogram) we can do something similar for the variance (and hence the standard deviation).

Example: Table 3.2 shows a frequency table of study of salaries of graduates from a university. Assuming the original data is unavailable, estimate the standard deviation.

Create Table 3.7 to get organized.

To estimate the variance we use the shortcut formula:

$$\frac{1}{n-1}\left(\sum x^2 - \frac{\left(\sum x\right)^2}{n}\right) = \frac{1}{1099}\left(827,185,889,200 - \frac{29,047,920^2}{1100}\right) = 54,696,684.42 .$$

Thus, the variance is approximately 54,696,684.42 and therefore the standard deviation, which has the unit of "dollars," is the square root of that number, or $7,395.72.

The numbers in this example turned out to be huge, which made the process somewhat confusing. For smaller numbers, everything seems slightly easier, hopefully.

Example: The evaluation of a statistics lecture resulted in the frequency distribution shown in Table 3.8. Find the mean, median, variance, and standard deviation.

Of course this is an ordinal variable so that we need to come up with (more or less arbitrary) numerical code values. With those codes chosen, we will expand the table as shown in the previous example (see Table 3.9).

Therefore, the mean is 2.04 and the standard deviation is 1.21 as you can confirm with a calculator. In other words, the average category is "good" and the spread is relatively small, about one category.

Table 3.7 Augmented frequency table to compute the variance

Salary range ($)	Count	Mid	Count * mid	Mid²	Count * mid²
7,200–18,860	130	13,030	1,693,900	169,780,900	22,071,517,000
18,860–30,520	698	24,690	17,233,620s	609,596,100	425,498,077,800
30,520–42,180	254	36,350	9,232,900	1,321,322,500	335,615,915,000
42,180–53,840	16	48,010	768,160	2,304,960,100	3,687,841,600
53,840–65,500	2	59,670	119,340	3,560,508,900	7,121,017,800
Total	1,100		29,047,920		827,185,889,200

Table 3.8 *Frequency table for course evaluation*

Category	Count
Very good	10
Good	5
Neutral	4
Poor	2
Very poor	1

Table 3.9 *Augmented frequency table to compute variance*

Category	Code	Count	Count * code	Code^2	Count * code^2
Very good	1	10	10	1	10
Good	2	5	10	4	20
Neutral	3	4	12	9	36
Poor	4	2	8	16	32
Very poor	5	1	5	25	25
Total		22	45		123

Quartiles and Percentiles

At this point we can describe the results of an experiment using two numbers (or parameters): a measure of central tendency (mean or median) and a measure of dispersion (the standard deviation, computed from the variance). That will tell us the "center" of the distribution of values (mean) and the "spread" around that center (standard deviation). For example, if we measure the height of U.S. army soldiers, we might find that the average height of U.S. soldiers is 1.73 m, with a standard deviation of 0.15 m (the numbers are made up). This gives you a reasonable idea about how a generic soldier looks (he/she is about 1.73 m tall) and how much variation from that generic look there is. To describe the distribution in more detail we need additional descriptive measures, starting with the lower and upper quartiles.

Definition: The *lower quartile* Q_1 is that number such that 25 percent of observations are less than it and 75 percent are larger, or to be more precise, at least 25 percent of the sorted values are less than or equal to Q_1 and at least 75 percent of the values are greater than or equal to Q_1. The *upper quartile* Q_3 is that number such that 75 percent of observations are less than it and 25 percent are larger, or to be more precise, at least 75 percent of the sorted values are less than or equal to Q_3, and at least 25 percent of the values are greater than or equal to Q_3.

Following this notation, the median should actually be called the "middle quartile" Q_2, since it is that number such that 50 percent are less than it and 50 percent are larger; traditionally, however, the term median is used.

Important: To find the quartiles, you must first sort your data (similar to finding the median).

Example: Compute the upper and lower quartiles of the numbers 2, 4, 6, 8, 10, 12, 14.

The numbers are already sorted, so that it is easy to see that the median is 8 (three numbers are less than 8 and three are bigger). In other words, 8 splits our numbers up into the set of smaller numbers {2, 4, 6} and the set of larger ones {10, 12, 14}. The quartiles, in turn, split up these sets in the middle again, so that $Q_1 = 4$ and $Q_3 = 12$.

Note that the numbers 2 and 4 are less than or equal to the lower quartile, while 4, 6, 8, 10, 12, 14 are larger than or equal to Q_1. Therefore, 2 out of 7 or 28 percent of values are less than or equal to Q_1 and 6 out of 7 = 86 percent are larger than Q_1.

Example: Compute the upper and lower quartiles of the numbers 1, 2, 3, 4, 5.

Now the median is 3, leaving two sets {1, 2} and {4, 5}. To split these numbers in the middle does not work, so it is not immediately clear what the quartiles are.

- If $Q_1 = 1$, then one value out of five is less than or equal to Q_1, or 20 percent. According to our definition that is not enough, so Q_1 must be bigger than 1.
- If $Q_1 = 2$, then two values out of five are less than or equal to Q_1, or 40 percent. Similarly, four values out of five, or

80 percent, are larger than or equal to Q_1 so that the lower quartile is indeed 2.
- Similarly, the upper quartile can be shown to be 4.

Note that the preceding definition of quartiles does not necessarily produce a unique answer. For example, for the data set {2, 4, 6, 8} *any* number between 2 (included) and 4 (excluded) would be a valid lower quartile, because for any such number one out of four data values are smaller, while three out of four values are larger. Thus, we select a slightly different and constructive algorithm to define quartiles (uniquely).

Definition: We compute upper and lower quartiles as follows. For the lower quartile:

- Sort all observations in ascending order.
- Compute the position $L_1 = 0.25 * N$, where N is the total number of observations.
- If L_1 is a whole number, the lower quartile is midway between the L_1-th value and the next one.
- If L_1 is not a whole number, change it by rounding up to the nearest integer. The value at that position is the lower quartile.

For the upper quartile:

- Sort all observations in ascending order.
- Compute the position $L_3 = 0.75 * N$, where N is the total number of observations.
- If L_3 is a whole number, the lower quartile is midway between the L_3-th value and the next one.
- If L_3 is not a whole number, change it by rounding up to the nearest integer. The value at that position is the lower quartile.

Examples: Find the quartiles for the values 2, 4, 6, 8, 10, 12, 14 and also for the values 2, 4, 6, 8 using this new method.

First we observe that the data set(s) are already sorted. For the set 2, 4, 6, 8, 10, 12, 14 we have $N = 7$. Thus:

- $L_1 = 0.25 * 7 = 1.75$, which gets rounded up to 2. Thus, take the number in the second position to be the lower quartile so that $Q_1 = 4$.
- $L_3 = 0.75 * 7 = 5.25$, which gets rounded up to 6. Thus, take the sixth number to be the upper quartile so that $Q_3 = 12$.

For the set 2, 4, 6, 8 we have $N = 4$. Thus:

- $L_1 = 0.25 * 4 = 1$, a whole number. Thus, we again take the number between the first and second positions to be the lower quartile, that is, $Q_1 = 3$.
- $L_3 = 0.75 * 4 = 3$. Thus, we take the number between the third and fourth values, that is, $Q_3 = 7$.

Note that there are at least a dozen different ways to compute quartiles. The preceding procedures are the preferred way in this text but depending on the software package used (such as SAS, JMP, MINITAB, or Excel), other numbers are possible. We will revisit the quartiles to figure out what these numbers can tell us about the distribution of our data. Before we do that, though, we will expand the idea of quartiles to "percentiles."

Quartiles are useful and they help to describe the distribution of values as we will see later. However, we often want to know how one particular data value compares to the rest of the data. For example, when taking standardized test scores such as SAT scores, I want to know not only my own score, but also how my score ranks in relation to all scores. Percentiles are perfect for this situation.

Definition: The *k-th percentile* is that number such that k percent of all data values are less and $(100 - k)$ percent are larger than it. More precisely, at least k percent of the sorted values are less than or equal to it and at least $(100 - k)$ percent of the values are greater than or equal to it.

Note: The lower quartile is the same as the 25th percentile, the median is the same as the 50th percentile, and the upper quartile is the same as the 75th percentile.

Example: A student took the SAT test. Her score in the math portion of the test puts her in the 95th percentile. Did she do well or poorly on the test?

If a score is ranked as the 95th percentile, then by definition 95 percent of all scores are less than the given score, while only 5 percent of students scored higher. That would be a pretty good result with only 5 percent of students who scored higher than that student. In other words, our student would be in the top 5 percent.

To find the k-th percentile:

- Sort all observations in ascending order.
- Compute the position $L = (k/100) * N$, where N is the total number of observations.
- If L is a whole number, the k-th percentile is the value midway between the L-th value and the next one.
- If L is not a whole number, change it by rounding up to the nearest integer. The value at that position is the k-th percentile.

Example: Consider the following cotinine levels of 40 smokers:

0	87	173	253	1	103	173	265	1	112
198	266	3	121	208	277	17	123	210	284
32	130	222	289	35	131	227	290	44	149
234	313	48	164	245	477	86	167	250	491

Find the quartiles and the 40th percentile.

First note that before we start our computations we must sort the data—computing percentiles for non sorted data is the most common mistake. Here is the same data again, this time sorted:

0	1	1	3	17	32	35	44	48	86
87	103	112	121	123	130	131	149	164	167
173	173	198	208	210	222	227	234	245	250
253	265	266	277	284	289	290	313	477	491

Now we can do our calculations, with $N = 40$ (number of values in our data set):

- Lower quartile: $0.25 * 40 = 10$, so we need to take the value midway between the 10th value, which is 86, and the 11th value, which is 87. Hence, the lower quartile is 86.5.
- Upper quartile: $0.75 * 40 = 30$, so we need to take the value midway between the 30th value, which is 250, and the 31st value, which is 253. Hence, the upper quartile is (250 + 253)/2 = 251.5.
- 40th percentile: $0.4 * 40 = 16$, so the 40th percentile is $(130 + 131)/2 = 130.5$.

However, for percentiles another question is usually asked: given a particular value, find that percentile that corresponds to this value. In other words, determine how many values are lesser and how many values are larger than the particular value.

Definition: The *percentile value* of a number x is:
Percentile value of x = (number of values less than x)/(total number of values) * 100.

Example: Suppose you took part in the preceding study of cotinine levels and your personal cotinine level was 245. What is the percentile value of 245, and how many people in the study had a higher cotinine level than you?

First note that in our sorted data the value 245 is in the 29th position. Therefore, according to our formula:

Percentile value of $245 = 29/40 * 100 = 72.5$.

Thus, by definition of percentiles, 72.5 percent of values are less than 245 while (100 − 72.5) = 27.5 percent are larger than 245.

Box Plot and Distributions

By now we have a multitude of numerical descriptive statistics that describe some feature of a data set of values: mean, median, range, variance, quartiles, percentiles, ranks, and so on. There are, in fact, so many different descriptors that it is going to be convenient to combine many of them into a suitable graph called the box plot.

Definition: The *box plot*, sometimes also called "box and whiskers plot," combines the *minimum* and *maximum* values (and therefore the range) with the *quartiles* and the *median* into one useful graph. It consists of a horizontal line, drawn according to scale from the minimum to the maximum data value, and a box drawn from the lower to upper quartile with a vertical line marking the median.

Example: In an earlier example we considered the following cotinine levels of 40 smokers. Draw a box plot for that data.

0	87	173	253	1	103	173	265	1	112
198	266	3	121	208	277	17	123	210	284
32	130	222	289	35	131	227	290	44	149
234	313	48	164	245	477	86	167	250	491

We already computed the lower and upper quartiles to be $Q_1 = 86.5$ and $Q_3 = 251.5$, respectively. It is easy to see that the minimum is 0 and the maximum is 491. A quick computation shows that the median is 170. The corresponding box plot is shown in Figure 3.2.

You can see that the horizontal line (sometimes called the "whiskers") goes from 0 to 491 (minimum to maximum), while the inside box

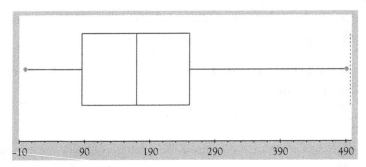

Figure 3.2 Box plot

extends from 86.5 (= Q_1) to 251.5 (= Q_3) with a middle vertical line at 170 (the median).

For some data sets you will see some points beyond the line indicating the whisker. Those points are *outliers*; they are exceptionally small or large compared to the rest of the data. Technically these outliers are part of your data but for certain purposes it will be advantageous to dismiss them. The exact definition of an outlier is provided in the following text.

Definition: The *inter quartile range (IQR)* is defined as the difference between the upper and lower quartiles. It is used, among other things, to define outliers.

Example: Find the IQR for the life expectancy data in 2014:

 www.betterbusinessdecisions.org/data/life.xlsx

The life expectancy data lists average life expectancy and literacy rates in 223 countries of the world in 2014. We sort the data from the smallest to the largest and compute the quartiles and the medium:

Q_1: position = 223 * 0.25 = 55.75, Q_1 = 66.85 (for Papua New Guinea)

Q_3: position = 223 * 0.75 = 167.25, Q_3 = 78.3 (for Panama)

Median: position = 223 * 0.5 = 111.5, median = 74.33 (for Bulgaria)

Thus, the "lower hinge" of the box is Q_1 = 66.85 and the upper hinge is Q_3 = 78.3. By definition, that makes the IQR = 78.3 − 66.85 = 11.45.

In addition to giving you a quick view of the range, the quartiles, the median, and the IQR, the box plot also indicates the shape of the histogram for this data, that is, its distribution:

- The histogram would look slightly skewed to the *left* if the box in the box plot is shifted somewhat toward the *right*.
- The histogram would look slightly skewed to the *right* if the box in the box plot is shifted toward the *left*.

In fact, even though the box plot does not directly contain the mean (it only shows the median) it is possible to estimate whether the mean is less than or greater than the median by looking whether the box plot is skewed to the left or to the right. First, let us look again at histograms and define what we mean by "skewed" histograms (and distributions).

Definition: A histogram (distribution) is called *bell-shaped* or *normal* if it looks similar to a symmetric "bell curve." Most data points fall in the middle; there are few exceptionally small and few exceptionally large values. Compare with Figure 3.3.

A histogram (distribution) is called *skewed to the right* if it looks *like* a bell curve with a longer tail on the right and the mount pushed somewhat to the left. Most data points fall to the left of the middle; there are more smaller than larger values, but there are a few extreme values on the right. Compare with Figure 3.4.

A histogram (distribution) is called *skewed to the left* if it looks like a bell curve with a longer tail on the left and the mount pushed somewhat to the right. Most data points fall to the right of the middle; there are more larger than smaller values, but there are a few extreme values on the left. See Figure 3.5.

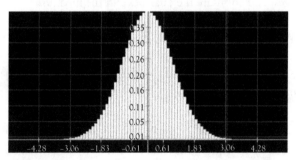

Figure 3.3 A normal distribution

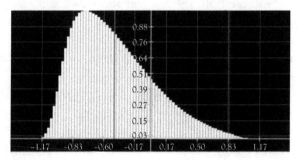

Figure 3.4 A distribution skewed to the right

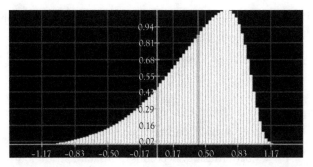

Figure 3.5 A distribution skewed to the left

You can tell the shape of the histogram (distribution)—in many cases at least—just by looking at the box plot, and you can also estimate whether the mean is less than or greater than the median. Recall that the mean is impacted by especially large or small values, even if there are just a few of them, while the median is more stable with respect to exceptional values. Therefore:

- If the distribution is *normal*, there are few exceptionally large or small values. The *mean will be about the same as the median* and the box plot will look symmetric.
- If the *distribution is skewed to the right* most values are "small," but there are a few exceptionally large ones. Those large exceptional values will impact the mean and pull it to the right, so that the *mean will be greater than the median.* The box plot will look as if the box was shifted to the left so that the right tail will be longer, and the median will be closer to the left line of the box in the box plot.
- If the distribution is *skewed to the left*, most values are "large," but there are a few exceptionally small ones. Those exceptional values will impact the mean and pull it to the left, so that the *mean will be less than the median.* The box plot will look as if the box was shifted to the right so that the left tail will be longer, and the median will be closer to the right line of the box in the box plot.

As a quick way to remember skewedness and its implications:

- Longer tail on the left ⇒ skewed to the left ⇒ mean on the left of median (smaller)

- Longer tail on the right $\Rightarrow$ skewed to the right $\Rightarrow$ mean on the right of median (larger)
- Tails equally long $\Rightarrow$ normal $\Rightarrow$ mean about equal to median

Example: Consider the (fictitious) data in an Excel sheet for three variables named *varA*, *varB*, and *varC*:

 www.betterbusinessdecisions.org/data/distribution-data.xls

Create a box plot for the data from each variable and decide, based on that box plot, whether the distribution of values is normal, skewed to the left, or skewed to the right, and estimate the value of the mean in relation to the median. Then compute the values and compare them with your conjecture.

Note that Excel does not include a facility to produce a box plot automatically, but we will introduce a convenient alternative later. For your convenience, we have created the corresponding box plots in Figures 3.6 to 3.8.

One of the data columns results in the box plot shown in Figure 3.6 (note that there is one outlier on the left). The distribution is shifted to the left, and the mean should be less than the median (the exact numbers are: mean = 0.3319, median = 0.4124).

The other data column has the box plot shown in Figure 3.7 (it has two outliers on the right). The distribution is shifted to the right, and the

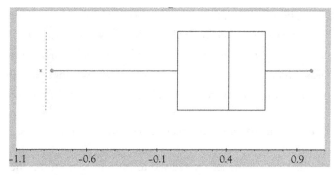

Figure 3.6 Box plot skewed to the left

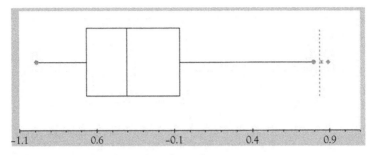

Figure 3.7 Box plot skewed to the right

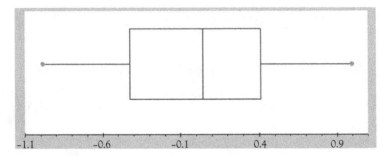

Figure 3.8 Box plot for normal distribution

mean should be greater than the median (the exact numbers are: mean = −0.3192, median = −0.4061).

The final data column has the box plot shown in Figure 3.8. The distribution is (approximately) normal, and the mean and median should be similar (the exact numbers are: mean = 0.013 median = 0.041).

Unfortunately, we forgot to write down which of these cases correspond to *varA*, *varB*, and *varC*—can you figure it out?

Outliers and the Standard Deviation

We have seen that even though the box plot does not explicitly include the mean, it is possible to get an approximate idea about it by comparing it against the median and the skewness of the box plot:

- If the distribution is *skewed* to the *left*, the mean is *less* than the median.
- If the distribution is *skewed* to the *right*, the mean is *bigger* than the median.

In a somewhat similar fashion you can estimate the standard deviation based on the box plot.

Definition: The relation between *range*, *IQR*, and *standard deviation* is:

- The standard deviation is approximately equal to range/4.
- The standard deviation is approximately equal to 3/4 * IQR.

Both estimates work best for normal distribution, that is, distributions that are not skewed, and the first approximation works best if there are no outliers.

Another useful application for the IQR is to define outliers.

Definition: *Outliers* are data points that fall *below* $Q_1 - 1.5 * IQR$ or *above* $Q_3 + 1.5 * IQR$.

Example: Consider the preceding data on cotinine levels of 40 smokers. Find the IQR and use it to estimate the standard deviation. Also identify any outliers.

The data ranges from 0 to 491 (from minimum to maximum), while $Q_1 = 86.5$ and $Q_3 = 251$. Thus, we have two estimates for the standard deviation:

- s is approximately equal to range/4 = 491/4 = 122.75.
- s is approximately equal to 3/4 * IQR = 0.75 * (251 − 86.5) = 123.375.

The estimates are pretty close to each other and since the true standard deviation is 119.5, they are both pretty close to the actual value. The best part of these estimates is, however, that they are very simple to compute and thus they give you a quick ballpark estimate for the standard deviation. As for any outliers, they would be data values:

- Above $Q_3 + 1.5 * IQR = 251 + 1.5 * 164.5 = 497.75$: none
- Below $Q_1 − 1.5 * IQR = 86.5 − 1.5 * 164.5 = −160.1$: none

So there are no outliers in this case (which is one reason why the estimate of range/4 works so well).

Example: Find all outliers for the life expectancy data we looked at before:

 www.betterbusinessdecisions.org/data/life.xlsx

For that data set we found that IQR = 78.3 − 66.85 = 11.45 and therefore the outliers would be data values:

- Above Q_3 + 1.5 * IQR = 78.3 + 1.5 * 11.45 = 95.475
- Below Q_1 − 1.5 * IQR = 66.85 − 1.5 * 11.45 = 49.675

Thus, two data points for South Africa (49.56) and Chad (49.44) are outliers below, while there are no outliers above. Note that since there are outliers, the *range*/4 estimate for the standard deviation should not work as well as the estimate based on the IQR. Confirm that!

Descriptive Statistics Using Excel

Excel of course provides simple functions for computing measures of central tendency:

= average(RANGE)	Computes the average (mean) of the numbers contained in the RANGE. Ignores cells containing no numerical data, that is, cells that contain text or no data do not contribute anything to the computation of the mean.
= count(RANGE)	Computes the amount of numbers contained in the RANGE.
= mode(RANGE)	Computes the mode of the numbers contained in the RANGE. If the cell range consists of several numbers with the same frequency, the function returns only the first (smallest) number as the mode. If all values occur exactly once, the Excel mode function returns N/A for "not applicable."
= median(RANGE)	Computes the median of the numbers contained in the RANGE. Ignores cells containing no numerical data.
= sum(RANGE)	Computes the sum of the numbers contained in the RANGE.
= skew(RANGE)	Returns the skewness: if negative, data is left skewed. If positive, data is right skewed.

Let us use our new formulas on an interesting data set: the salaries of Major League Baseball (MLB) players from 1988 to 2011.

Exercise: Find the mean, mode, and median of the salary of MLB players. Why are they so different? Which one best represents the measure of central tendency? Did we compute the population mean (or median) or the sample mean (or median)?

 www.betterbusinessdecisions.org/data/MLBPlayerSalaries.xlsx

Figure 3.9 shows the formulas that were used together with the resulting values. The mean is $1,916,817, which is indeed very different from the median of $565,000. To explain the difference, we also computed the skewness factor, which is 3.0. That means that the distribution is (heavily) skewed to the right, that is, there are a few exceptionally large values that will pull the mean up above the median. Indeed, there are a few superstar baseball players who impact the mean but not the median. Leading the pack is Alex Rodriguez from the New York Yankees with $33,000,000 per year in 2009 and 2010 and a combined salary of over $284,000,000 between 2001 and 2011. Most players do not come close to this figure; in fact, 50 percent of players make less than the relatively modest $565,000, since that is the median.

For the fun of it, we used the pivot tool to compute the average salary per ball club for the combined years (see Figure 3.10). As most of you probably suspected, the team with the highest average salary (by far) is the New York Yankees, followed by the Boston Red Sox and the New York Mets. Bringing up the rear are the Washington Nationals and the Pittsburgh Pirates.

	A	B	C	D	E	F	G
1	Year	Player	Salary	Position	Team		
2	1988	Mike Witt	$ 1,400,000	Pitcher	Los Angeles Angels	=AVERAGE(C2:C19544)	$1,916,817
3	1988	George Hendrick	$ 989,333	Outfielder	Los Angeles Angels	=MEDIAN(C2:C19544)	$ 565,000
4	1988	Chili Davis	$ 950,000	Outfielder	Los Angeles Angels	=MODE(C2:C19544)	$ 200,000
5	1988	Brian Downing	$ 900,000	Designated Hitter	Los Angeles Angels	=SKEW(C2:C19544)	$ 3
6	1988	Bob Boone	$ 883,000	Catcher	Los Angeles Angels		
7	1988	Johnny Ray	$ 857,000	Second Baseman	Los Angeles Angels		
8	1988	Dan Petry	$ 785,000	Pitcher	Los Angeles Angels		
9	1988	Butch Wynegar	$ 733,333	Catcher	Los Angeles Angels		
10	1988	Dick Schofield	$ 552,222	Shortstop	Los Angeles Angels		

Figure 3.9 Mean, mode, and median for MLB data

New York Yankees	$3,795,448	Seattle Mariners	$2,033,688	Cincinnati Reds	$1,610,801
Boston Red Sox	$2,790,342	St. Louis Cardinals	$2,026,821	Minnesota Twins	$1,500,023
New York Mets	$2,589,062	Philadelphia Phillies	$2,025,717	Tampa Bay Rays	$1,450,793
Arizona Diamondbacks	$2,432,396	Colorado Rockies	$1,940,413	Oakland Athletics	$1,410,852
Los Angeles Dodgers	$2,349,151	Detroit Tigers	$1,922,999	Milwaukee Brewers	$1,405,790
Chicago Cubs	$2,343,446	Houston Astros	$1,902,850	San Diego Padres	$1,392,457
Atlanta Braves	$2,257,812	Baltimore Orioles	$1,898,775	Kansas City Royals	$1,338,414
Los Angeles Angels	$2,088,519	Texas Rangers	$1,836,433	Florida Marlins	$1,229,639
Chicago White Sox	$2,076,906	Toronto Blue Jays	$1,800,779	Washington Nationals	$1,119,610
San Francisco Giants	$2,038,534	Cleveland Indians	$1,632,429	Pittsburgh Pirates	$1,097,979

Figure 3.10 Average salaries per ball club in MLB

In addition to measures of central tendency, Excel also provides formulas to compute range, variance, and standard deviation:

=max(RANGE) – min(RANGE)	Computes the range as the maximum minus the minimum value.
=var(RANGE)	Computes the variance (ignores cells containing no numerical data).
=var.p(RANGE)	New function to compute the population variance.
=var.s(RANGE)	New function to compute the sample variance.
=stdev(RANGE)	Computes the standard deviation (ignores cells containing no numerical data).
=stdev.p(RANGE)	New function to compute the population standard deviation.
=stdev.s(RANGE)	New function to compute the sample standard deviation.

Example: Use the preceding formulas to compute the mean, range, variance, and standard deviation of the salaries of graduates for the University of Florida:

www.betterbusinessdecisions.org/data/u-floridagraduationsalaries.xls

All that is involved here is adding the appropriate formulas to the Excel worksheet (see Figure 3.11).

Note: The variance is displayed as dollars, even though that is not correct (it should be "square dollars," which does not make much sense). The standard deviation, on the other hand, has indeed dollars as unit.

There are a number of additional statistical functions that can be used as needed but Excel also provides a convenient tool to compute many of the most commonly used descriptive statistics such as mean, mode,

	A	B	C	D	E	F	G
1	Gender	College	Salary	Graduation Date			
2	1	7	$28,900	1.00		=MAX(C2:C1101)-MIN(C2:C1101)	$ 58,300.00
3	1	7	$28,000	1.00		=VAR(C2:C1101)	$ 48,552,771.77
4	1	1	$27,500	1.00		=STDEV(C2:C1101)	$ 6,967.98
5	1	7	$30,300	1.00			
6	1	1	$18,000	1.00		=MEAN(C2:C1101)	$ 26,064.20
7	0	7	$31,700	1.00			
8	1	3	$26.000	1.00			

Figure 3.11 Mean, range, variance, and standard deviation of salaries

median, variance, standard deviation, and more all at once and for multiple variables simultaneously.

Example: The following Excel spreadsheet contains some data about life expectancy and literacy rates in over 200 countries of the world in 2014. Compute the mean, mode, median, variance, standard deviation, and range of the two variables:

 www.betterbusinessdecisions.org/data/life_literate.xlsx

Load the data set as usual. Then switch to the *Data* ribbon and pick the *Data Analysis* tool from our ToolPak on the far right. Select the *Descriptive Statistics* tool. Define as range the second and third columns titled "Life Expectancy" and "Literacy Rate" from B1 to C206, check the box "Label in First Row," and check the option "Summary Statistics." Then click OK.

Excel will compute a variety of descriptive statistics all at once and for all (numerical) variables in the selected range; Figure 3.12 shows the output.

We can see, for example, that for the average "Life Expectancy" we have computed the mean to be 71.68, the median to be 74.2, and the mode to be 76.4. The standard deviation is 8.77, the variance is 76.96, and the range is 40.2. Both variables have a distribution that is skewed to the left and hence the mean will be smaller than the median. Note that variance and standard deviation refer to the sample variance and standard deviation formulas.

Life Expectancy (%)		Literacy Rate (%)	
Mean	71.68487805	Mean	87.27122
Standard Error	0.612694559	Standard Error	1.183373
Median	74.2	Median	95.1
Mode	76.4	Mode	99
Standard Deviation	8.772451063	Standard Deeviation	16.94332
Sample Variance	76.95589766	Sample Variance	287.0761
Kurtosis	0.028444576	Kurtosis	2.494144
Skewness	-0.901267506	Skewness	-1.76692
Range	40.2	Range	72.3
Minimum	49.4	Minimum	27.7
Maximum	89.6	Maximum	100
Sum	14695.4	Sum	17890.6
Count	205	Count	205

Figure 3.12 *Output of Excel's descriptive statistics procedure*

Using Excel to Find Percentiles

Of course Excel can be used to find percentiles, and therefore upper and lower quartiles (which are just the 25th and 75th percentiles, respectively):

=quartile (RANGE, N)	Computes the lower quartile if $N = 1$, the median if $N = 2$, or the upper quartile if $N = 3$. Note that Excel uses a slightly different method to compute the quartiles from that described in the "Quartiles and Percentiles" section.
=percentile (RANGE, P)	Computes percentiles, where RANGE is a range of cells and P is the percentile to compute as a decimal number between 0 and 1. The data does not have to be sorted.
=percentrank (RANGE, X)	Computes the rank of a value x in a RANGE as a percentage of the data set (in other words, the percentile value of x). The data does not have to be sorted.

Note: the QUARTILE function used in Excel uses a definition that is slightly different from our (second) one earlier. Thus, you *cannot* use Excel to check your own manual answers in many cases. In fact, the calculation of the quartiles is different depending on the text or computer/calculator package being used (such as SAS, JMP, MINITAB, Excel, and TI-83 Plus); it turns out that Excel alone offers two functions to compute quartiles: QUARTILE.EXC and QUARTILE.INC (which is the same as our familiar QUARTILE function). Check the article at www.amstat.org/publications/jse/v14n3/langford.html for more details.

Example: Load the Excel spreadsheet that contains the data about life expectancy and literacy rates in 205 countries of the world in 2014. Find the upper and lower quartiles for both variables. What is the percentile value for life expectancy in Japan, the United States, and in Afghanistan?

 www.betterbusinessdecisions.org/data/life_literate.xlsx

We can use either the percentile or the quartile function to find the percentiles, or manually compute them. For the variable "Life Expectancy":

- =percentile(B2:B206, 0.25) or =quartile (B2:B206,1) gives 67.1 as Q_1
- =percentile(B2:B206, 0.75) or =quartile (B2:B206,3) gives 78.0 as Q_3
- =0.25 * N = 51.25, so we pick the number at position 52, which is 67.1
- =0.75 * N = 153.75, so we pick the number at position 154, which is 78.0

For the variable "People who Read":

- =percentile(C2:C206, 0.25) or =quartile (B2:B206,1) gives 81.4 as Q_1
- =percentile(C2:C206, 0.75) or =quartile (B2:B206,1) gives 98.9 as Q_3

To find the relative ranking (aka percentiles) for Japan, the United States, and Afghanistan we use the "percentrank(range, x)" function where we substitute the life expectancy of the respective countries for x:

- =percentrank(B2:B206, 50.5) = 0.014. Afghanistan is at the 1.4th percentile in life expectancy, that is, about 1.4 percent of countries have shorter and 98.6 percent have longer life expectancy than Afghanistan.

- =percentrank(B2:B206, 84.5) = 0.99. Japan is at the 99th percentile in life expectancy, that is, about 99 percent of countries have shorter and 1 percent has longer life expectancy than Japan.
- =percentrank(B2:B206, 79.6) = 0.828. The United States is at the 82.8th percentile in life expectancy, that is, about 82.8 percent of countries have shorter and 17.2 percent have longer life expectancy than the United States.

Drawing a Box Plot With Excel

Unfortunately Excel does not have a nice built-in facility to quickly create a box plot. You could of course use the formulas introduced earlier to compute the values needed and then draw a box plot manually. However, there is an easy-to-use Excel template that is not quite as convenient as the data analysis tools we have been using, but it is still pretty simple and useful. To use the Excel box plot template, click on the following icon to download the file:

 www.betterbusinessdecisions.org/data/boxplot.xls

When you open the file, Excel will show you a worksheet with a finished box plot already, and a column on the right in green where you can enter or paste your data (see Figure 3.13).

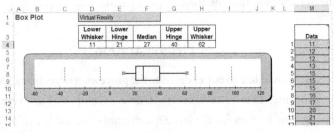

Figure 3.13 A box plot generated by an Excel template

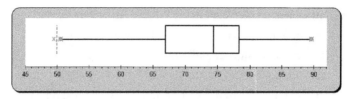

*Figure 3.14 Box plot generated by Excel template for life
expectancy data*

Simply delete the data currently in column M and replace it with your
new data to create a new plot. The box plot will update automatically.

Example: Create a box plot for the life expectancy data by country
that we considered before:

 www.betterbusinessdecisions.org/data/life.xls

When the spreadsheet opens up, mark all numerical data in column
B (the life expectancy column) but not including the column header and
copy it to the clipboard (e.g., press CTRL-c). Then open the boxplot.xls
spreadsheet and position your cursor to the first data value in column M.
Paste the copied data values (e.g., press CTRL-v) into that column and
the box plot will automatically update itself as shown in Figure 3.14.

If your picture looks slightly different, you can double-click the horizontal axis to adjust the scale (minimum and maximum) so that the picture looks like that in Figure 3.14. We can see one outlier value on the left
(check if there really are extreme values according to our definition) and
it seems that the distribution is skewed to the left. Thus, we would expect
the mean to be less than the median (verify that).

Excel Demonstration

Company S would like to better describe the processing times of tax returns
for small businesses to future clients. To do so, Company S collected the
processing time in days for the last 27 tax returns (see Table 3.10). What
would we tell a potential client about the expected processing times for
tax returns?

Table 3.10 Table of processing time

Return ID	Processing time		Return ID	Processing time
1	73		15	45
2	19		16	48
3	16		17	17
4	64		18	17
5	28		19	17
6	28		20	91
7	31		21	92
8	90		22	63
9	60		23	50
10	56		24	51
11	31		25	69
12	56		26	16
13	22		27	17
14	18			

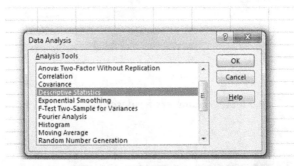

Figure 3.15 The analysis ToolPak functions available

Step 1: Enter the data in *two* columns, labeled "Return ID" and "Processing Time" into *Excel*.

Step 2: Let us describe the data by finding out the mean, median, first quartile, third quartile, range, interquartile range, and standard deviation. We can find many of these using the Analysis Tool-Pak "descriptive statistics" function, or we can use Excel formulas. In the Analysis ToolPak, click on *Descriptive Statistics* as shown in Figure 3.15.

Then, for the input range select the data, check *Labels in first row* since we included the labels, and click *Summary statistics* as shown in Figure 3.16; then click OK.

We are provided with the descriptive statistics for processing time and return ID. Note we will not need data for Return ID for our analysis. Figure 3.17 shows the output of the procedure.

From this table we can now see the average processing time, median processing time, range, and standard deviation. We can find the remaining required statistics using the formulas shown in Figure 3.18.

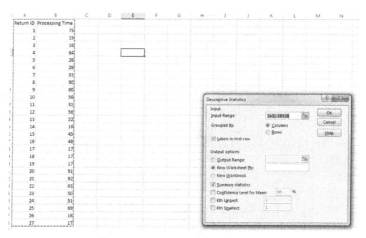

Figure 3.16 *Available parameters for descriptive statistics procedure*

Return ID		Processing Time	
Mean	14	Mean	43.88888889
Standard Error	1.527525232	Standard Error	4.865815794
Median	14	Median	45
Mode	#N/A	Mode	17
Standard Deviation	7.937253933	Standard Deviation	25.28352053
Sample Variance	63	Sample Variance	639.2564103
Kurtosis	-1.2	Kurtosis	-0.904073224
Skewness	3.68936E-17	Skewness	0.517267531
Range	26	Range	76
Minimum	1	Minimum	16
Maximum	27	Maximum	92
Sum	378	Sum	1185
Count	27	Count	27

Figure 3.17 *Output of the descriptive statistics procedure*

First Quartile	=QUARTILE(B2:B28,1)	First quartile means that 25% of the values are smaller than or equal to the first quartile number
Third Quartile	=QUARTILE(B2:B28,3)	Third quartile means that 75% of the values are smaller than or equal to the third quartile number
Range	76	The difference between the largest and smallest number
Interquartile Range	=Q5-D4	Quartile 3 - Quarter 1: which is the range for the middle 50% of the numbers, or the range between quarterile 3 and quarti
		Skewness measures the extent to which a set of data is not symetric. Positive = right skewed. Negative = left skewed
		Left skewed means that most of the values are in the upper portion of the distribution
		Right skewed means that most of the values are in the lowest portion of the distribution
		Kurtosis, measures the relative concentration of values in the center of the distribution
Skewness	=SKEW(B2:B28)	
First Quartile	18.5	First quartile means that 25% of the values are smaller than or equal to the first quartile number
Third Quartile	61.5	Third quartile means that 75% of the values are smaller than or equal to the third quartile number
Range	76	The difference between the largest and smallest number
Interquartile Range	43	Quartile 3 - Quarter 1: which is the range for the middle 50% of the numbers, or the range between quarterile 8 and quartile 1
		Skewness measures the extent to which a set of data is not symetric. Positive = right skewed. Negative = left skewed
		Left skewed means that most of the values are in the upper portion of the distribution
		Right skewed means that most of the values are in the lowest portion of the distribution
		Kurtosis, measures the relative concentration of values in the center of the distribution
Skewness	0.51726753	
	Positive = right skewed	

Figure 3.18 Computing various statistics using individual Excel commands

In conclusion, we can tell our potential client that the average processing time is around 44 days, and that based on the positively right skewed statistic, we expect most of the processing times to fall toward the lower portion of the distribution, so that there is hope that the actual processing time might be shorter.

CHAPTER 4

Probability Theory

Preview: *Probability theory is the study of likelihoods that given events will occur. Probability theory plays a role in everything from operating a local casino to the techniques used to minimize side effects and negative outcomes in a medical setting.*

No matter what the setting, probabilities can be represented by numbers between 0.0 and 1.0, where a probability of 0.0 means that there is no chance a given result will be achieved, while a probability of 1.0 means that the event will take place for certain. Probability theory often uses relative frequency to predict how often a given event will take place. That event can be anything, from the number of wins and losses for a soccer team to the number of times heads come up in a coin toss. Probability theory also examines the distribution of all results, which often is represented via a bell-shaped curve. It plays a big role in probability theory and it is an important concept for students to understand.

Learning Objectives: At the conclusion of this chapter, you should be able to:

1. Compute the expected value and variance of a probability distribution
2. Compute probabilities from binomial distributions
3. Solve business problems using binomial distributions
4. Compute probabilities from normal or continuous distributions
5. Solve business problems using normal or continuous distributions

Introduction

We will now switch gears and start involving probabilities in our discussions. Until now we talked about *descriptive statistics*, using numbers

(mean, standard deviation), graphs (pie chart, histogram), or general concepts (skewed distribution) to describe data, whether from a population
or from a sample. In subsequent chapters we want to introduce *inferential
statistics* where we draw conclusions about a population based on properties of a sample and discuss the precision and accuracy of our conclusions
in terms of probabilities. However, we will only use as much probability
as necessary; we will not study probability theory in its own right here.
This chapter will introduce the elements of probability theory that will be
useful to us in subsequent chapters. Let us start with the basics.

Definition: A *sample space* S is the set of all possible outcomes of an
experiment. An *event* is a subset of S. We will consider the *probability
of an event* as the chance, or likelihood, that this event indeed takes
place. All probabilities will be numbers between 0.0 and 1.0, inclusive,
where a probability of 0 means that an event does not happen and a
probability of 1.0 means that an event will happen for certain. We
will often use the notation $P(A)$ to denote the probability of event A
occurring. The total probability of all events must be equal to 1.0, that
is, $P(S) = 1$.

Sometimes a sample space, a set of possible events, and the probabilities assigned to each event are collectively called a *probability space*. We
could make this more mathematically rigorous: a *probability* is a function
that has as its domain a certain collection of sets that are subsets of some
sample space S and associates with each set $E \subset S$ a number between 0.0
and 1.0 so that the following properties are satisfied.

1. $P(\varnothing) = 0$ (probability of the empty set is zero) and $P(S) = 1$ (probability of all events is one).
2. $0 \leq P(E) \leq 1$ for every event E.
3. If $E = \mathrm{U}_{j=0}^{\infty} E_j$ and all E_j are mutually disjoint, then
   $P(E) = P(\mathrm{U}_{j=0}^{\infty} E_j) = \sum_{j=0}^{\infty} P(E_j)$, that is, the *probability of a union
   of disjoint sets* equals the *sum of the probabilities of each set*.

These axioms are known as the *Kolmogorov* axioms, in honor of Andrei Kolmogorov, a famous Russian mathematician who lived from 1903 to 1987. If this more rigorous definition sounds somewhat abstract, you are right. If it actually sounds too abstract for comfort, very good! In a true probability theory course we would use this above abstract definition and then continue to derive various properties of it. But for this course we will be content with saying that probabilities of events are numbers between 0 and 1 that determine the likelihood of events occurring. That should sound much simpler. In many cases these probabilities are determined by counting or as proportions.

Example: Let us say our experiment consists of tossing fair a coin once. List the sample space. What is the probability of obtaining *head*? Suppose our experiment consists of rolling a die. What is the probability of getting a 5 or a larger number? What is the probability of two dice adding to 4 when tossing them simultaneously? If we throw a dart randomly into a square with side length 1 m, what is the probability of landing in a circle of radius 10 cm in the middle of the square (bull's-eye).

The first experiment consists of throwing a single coin. There are two possible outcomes, heads or tails (coins do not land on their side). Thus, the sample space S is $\{H, T\}$. Whenever all outcomes of an experiment are equally likely, we can compute probabilities simply by counting. We have for any event E:

$$P(E) = \frac{\#\,elements\,in\,E}{\#\,elements\,in\,S},$$

where S is the sample space, as usual. In tossing a coin, for example, there are two possible outcomes, head (H) or tail (T), both equally likely (if the coin is fair). Thus, our sample space is the set $\{H, T\}$ and the probability of obtaining a head should be (# elements in $\{H\}$)/(# elements in $\{H, T\}$), or 1/2. Another way of saying this is that the chance of a head in tossing a fair coin is 1 out of 2, which in mathematics simply means "1 divided by 2." Thus: $P(\{H\}) = 0.5$.

Similarly, for a die there are six possible outcomes, all equally likely. Thus, our sample space consists of the set S = {1, 2, 3, 4, 5, 6}, and the event of obtaining a number 5 or more is composed of the event of getting a 5 or a 6. Thus, the corresponding probability should be 2 out of 6, 2/6, or 1/3. In other words: P({5 or 6}) = 2/6 = 1/3 = 0.3333.

Next, if we throw two dice simultaneously, each could show a number from 1 to 6. If we record their sum, the sample space is S = {2, 3, 4, 5, 6, 7, 8, 9, 10, 11, 12}. To compute the probabilities of these numbers occurring, we create a table where each entry inside the table denotes the sum of the die in that column and that row (see Table 4.1). Using that table to establish probabilities is again a simple exercise in counting: There are a total of 36 possible ways to throw two dice; we are interested in their sum being 4; from the table we see that there are three possible throws adding up to 4 (a 3 + 1, 2 + 2, and 1 + 3) so that our probability is 3 out of 36, or 3/36, which reduces to 1/12. Thus: P({$sum\ of\ two\ dice$ = 4}) = 3/36 = 1/12 = 0.0833.

For the final example we need to compute areas. We assume that every dart thrown will land inside the large square. Then the chance of hitting the little circle at random is the ratio of the area of that circle over the area of the square (see Figure 4.1). Recall that the area of a square with side x is x^2 and the area of a circle with radius r is πr^2. Thus, the probability of hitting a bull's-eye at random is

$$P(\{bull's\,eye\}) = \frac{area\,of\,circle}{area\,of\,square} = \frac{\pi 10^2}{100^2} = \frac{\pi}{100} = 0.0314 \ .$$

Table 4.1 Sum of two dice

	1	2	3	4	5	6
1	2	3	4	5	6	7
2	3	4	5	6	7	8
3	4	5	6	7	8	9
4	5	6	7	8	9	10
5	6	7	8	9	10	11
6	7	8	9	10	11	12

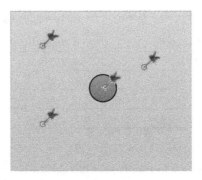

Figure 4.1 Darts thrown at a dart board

Note that the probability remains the same regardless of where the little circle is located inside the square (as long as it is completely inside the square). Also, by practicing, a dart player can significantly increase the probability of hitting a bull's-eye; the preceding number refers to darts thrown *randomly* at the board.

In more real-life experiments it may be too time-consuming or simply impossible to list all possible outcomes or to count the ones we are interested in, but we can instead use experimentation or relative frequencies to come up with approximate probabilities.

Example: Suppose we have a *weighted* coin. Find the probability of obtaining a head (*H*) in one toss of the coin.

Since the coin is weighted, the chance of getting one head is no longer 50–50. So we toss the coin 100 times and find 71 heads (and consequently 29 tails). Thus, we proclaim that

$$P(\{H\}) = 0.71 \text{ and consequently } P(\{T\}) = 1 - 0.71 = 0.29.$$

Example: Suppose that a (hypothetical) frequency distribution for the age of people in a survey is as shown in Table 4.2. What is the missing probability? What is the chance that a randomly selected person is 40 years or younger?

Table 4.2 Relative frequencies for age

Category	Probability
0–18	0.15
19–40	0.25
41–65	
66 and older	0.3

Here we simply used decimal numbers instead of percentages, that is, the entry in the first row means that 15 percent of the people in the survey were between 0 and 18 years old. One number is missing in the table but since probabilities have to add up to 1.0, the missing number is $1.0 - (0.15 + 0.25 + 0.3) = 0.3$.

The event of being 40 years or younger means that a person is either in the 0 to 18 category, with probability 0.15, or in the 19 to 40 category, with probability 0.25. Therefore, the total probability of a person being 40 years or younger is $0.15 + 0.25 = 0.40$, or equivalently 40 percent.

It is often helpful to consider probabilities in relation to frequency histograms graphically.

Example: The following data set consists of a number of variables related to the health records of 40 female patients, randomly selected. Construct a frequency histogram for the height of the 40 patients, including a chart. Then use that histogram to find:

- The probability, approximately, that a woman is 60 in. or shorter
- The probability, approximately, that a woman is 65 in. or taller
- The probability, approximately, that a woman is between 60 and 65 in. tall

For each question, shade the part of the histogram chart that you used to answer the question.

 www.betterbusinessdecisions.org/data/health_female.xls

Height	Frequency	Rel. Freq.
57 or less	1	0.025
57.1 to 58.6	1	0.025
58.7 to 60.1	3	0.075
60.1 to 61.7	6	0.15
61.8 to 63.3	8	0.2
63.4 to 64.8	11	0.275
64.9 to 66.4	3	0.075
66.5 and mo	7	0.175
Total	40	1

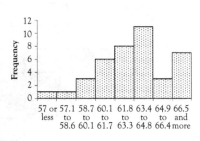

Figure 4.2 Relative frequency distribution of height

We construct a frequency histogram using the appropriate Analysis ToolPak procedure as described in Chapter 2. We have manually specified the bin boundaries and modified the histogram table slightly to clarify the bin boundaries. We also computed the relative frequency for each row, defined as the number in that row divided by the total number of observations. The results are shown in Figure 4.2.

Using this chart it is now easy to answer the questions. Note that our bin boundaries do not exactly correspond to the boundaries posed in the questions, but we can use the closest bin boundary available to get the *approximately* right answer.

- $P(women\ 60\ in.\ or\ less) = (1 + 1 + 3)/40 = (0.025 + 0.025 + 0.075) = 0.125$
- $P(a\ women\ 65\ in.\ or\ more) = (3 + 7)/40 = (0.075 + 0.175) = 0.25$
- $P(women\ between\ 60\ and\ 65\ in.) = (6 + 8 + 11)/40 = (0.15 + 0.2 + 0.275) = 0.625$

To illustrate these probabilities, we have shaded the respective portions in Figure 4.3.

To be sure, our probabilities are approximate only because the bin boundaries do not *exactly* match the questions. In addition, we have not really computed, for example, that the probability of a *general* woman to be between 60 and 65 in. tall is 62.5 percent. Instead, we computed that the probability of a *randomly selected woman from our sample of 40 women* is between 60 and 65 in. tall is 62.5 percent. But if in turn the entire sample

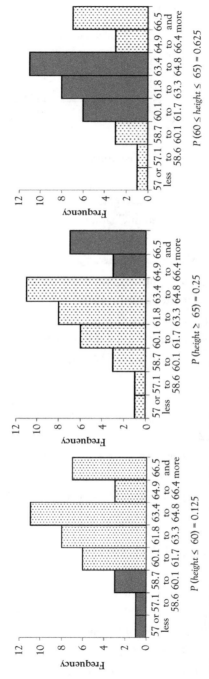

Figure 4.3 Relevant categories of the probability distribution

was truly randomly selected, then it is a fair guess to propose that *the probability of any woman to be between 60 and 65 in. tall is 62.5 percent,* or, phrased differently, that *62.5 percent of all women are between 60 and 65 in. tall.* Of course we have generalized from the *women in our sample* to the set of *all women*, which might seem reasonable but the big question is whether such an inference really works and how well it works. We will tackle that in the next chapter; first we need more background information.

The Normal Distribution

If you compute a lot of frequency histograms and their associated charts you will notice that most of them differ in detail but have somewhat similar shapes: the chart is usually "small" on the left and right sides with a "bump" in the middle. With a little bit of imagination you might say that such distributions look somewhat similar to a "church bell" (see Figure 4.4).

Figure 4.5 shows several histogram charts with the imagined "church bell" shape super imposed (all of the data comes from the health_female.xls and health_male.xls data files).

These bell-shaped distributions differ from each other by the location of their hump and the width of the bell's opening, and they have a special name.

Definition: A distribution that looks bell-shaped is called a *normal distribution.* The position of the hump is denoted by *m* and stands for the mean of the distribution, and its width is denoted by *s* and corresponds to the standard deviation. Thus, a particular normal distribution with mean *m* and standard deviation *s* is denoted by *N(m, s)*.

The special normal distribution *N(0, 1)*, that is, bell-shaped with mean 0 and standard deviation 1, is called the *standard normal distribution.*

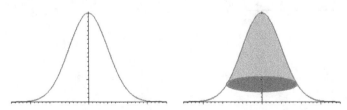

Figure 4.4 The bell curve

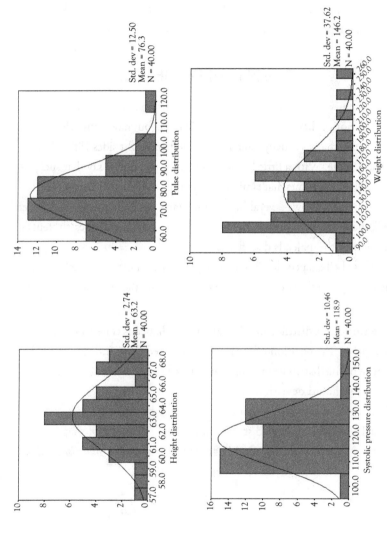

Figure 4.5 Sample frequency histograms with superimposed normal curve

Figure 4.6 shows three normal distributions. Remember that they simply represent relative frequency charts, with the height of each bar corresponding to the probability of a randomly selected number falling in that bin.

Side note: The bell-shaped normal distribution is frequently called the *Gaussian* normal distribution, named after the famous German mathematician Carl Friedrich Gauss (1777–1855). It can be modeled mathematically by the exponential function $N_{n,s}(x) = \dfrac{1}{s\sqrt{2\pi}} e^{-\frac{(x-\mu)^2}{2s^2}}$, where *m* stands for the mean and *s* for the standard deviation of the distribution. Figure 4.7 shows four normal distributions with different parameters. For each, the mean *n* shows where the top of the hill is, which is also the axis of symmetry, and indicates the most likely occurrence. The standard deviation *s* specifies the width of the hill.

Computing Normal Probabilities with Excel

Instead of creating a frequency histogram with (more or less) arbitrary bin boundaries, we can compute the mean and the standard deviation of the data and use the normal distribution with that particular mean and standard deviation to compute the probabilities we are interested in.

Example: Consider the Excel data set health_female.xls, showing a number of variables related to the health records of 40 female patients, randomly selected.

 www.betterbusinessdecisions.org/data/health_female.xls

Compute the mean and standard distribution for the height variable of that data set and then use the corresponding normal distribution to visualize:

- The probability, approximately, that a woman is 60 in. or shorter
- The probability, approximately, that a woman is 65 in. or taller
- The probability, approximately, that a woman is between 60 and 65 in. tall

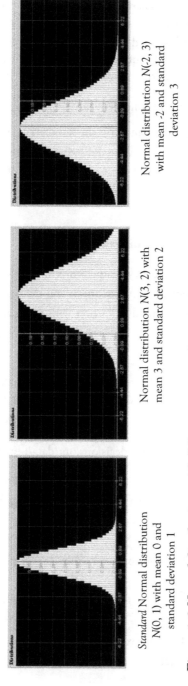

Standard Normal distribution $N(0, 1)$ with mean 0 and standard deviation 1

Normal distribution $N(3, 2)$ with mean 3 and standard deviation 2

Normal distribution $N(-2, 3)$ with mean -2 and standard deviation 3

Figure 4.6 Normal distributions with different means and standard deviations

You can see a picture of Carl Friedrich Gauss on a German 10 DM bill (approximately $6). In the center of the bill you can see a small graph of the normal distribution. Note that this currency was replaced by the EURO in 2002

N(0,1)
N(0,2)
N(−1, 0.8)
N(0.5, 1.2)

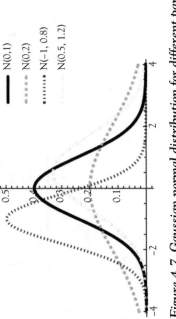

Figure 4.7 Gaussian normal distribution for different parameters

As explained in Chapter 3, we can use Excel to quickly compute the mean and standard deviation to be as follows: mean $\mu = 63.2$ and standard deviation $\sigma = 2.74$. The normal distribution with these parameters is $N_{63.2,\,2.74}(x) = 0.1456\,e^{-0.0666(x-63.2)^2}$ (see Figure 4.8).

We can now use that graph to visualize the various probabilities by shading the appropriate area under that curve (see Figure 4.9).

If you happen to have had calculus prior to this course, you might remember that the area under a curve is computed via integration (do not worry, if you have not had calculus or you do not care about it, just skip to the next paragraph). Therefore, the probabilities are:

$$P(height \le 60) = \int_{-\infty}^{60} 0.1456\,e^{-0.0666(x-63.2)^2}\,dx = 0.1214,$$

$$P(height \ge 65) = \int_{65}^{\infty} 0.1456\,e^{-0.0666(x-63.2)^2}\,dx = 0.2556,$$

$$P(60 \le height \le 65) = \int_{60}^{65} 0.1456\,e^{-0.0666(x-63.2)^2}\,dx = 0.6230.$$

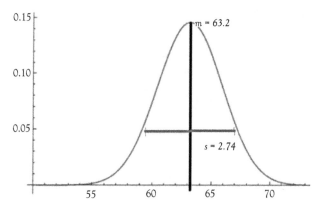

Figure 4.8 Graph of the normal distribution N(63.2, 2.74)

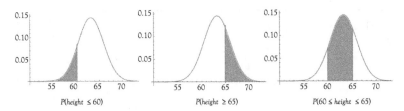

Figure 4.9 Shading the relevant portion of the normal distribution N(63.2, 2.74)

To evaluate these integrals is actually pretty difficult, even if you remember your calculus well; we have used an advanced computer program called Mathematica to get the answers. The good news is that Excel can easily compute these areas under a normal distribution as well, but there is a catch.

> **Definition**: To compute probabilities under a normal distribution Excel provides the formula *NORMDIST(X, m, s, true)*, where *m* and *s* are the mean and standard deviation, respectively, and the last parameter should always be set to "true." The value of that formula *always* represents the probability (aka area under the curve) on the *left* side under the normal distribution *up to* the value of *X*: *NORMDIST(X, m, s, true)* = $P(x \leq X)$, where *x* is *N(m, s)*.

If you are using this formula in Excel, do not forget to start it with an equal sign, as you would do for any Excel formula. For example:

Note that the last value happens to be exactly the area we need to answer the first of our three questions. Therefore: $P(x \leq 60)$ = *NORMDIST(60, 63.2, 2.74, true)* = 0.1214. The original method, using the actual frequency histogram, yields 0.125. Both computed values are close to each other, but using the normal distribution and Excel is *way* faster *and* allows for arbitrary boundary points to be used.

Excel formula	Mathematical notation	Computed area	Value
= NORMDIST(0, 0, 1, true)	$P(x \leq 0)$ x standard normal $N(0, 1)$	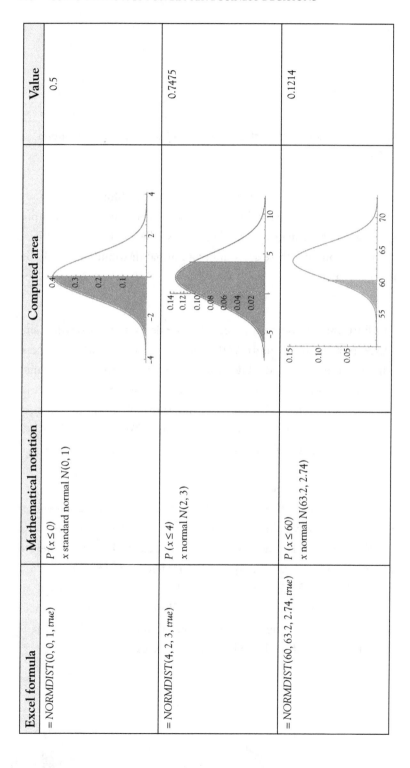	0.5
= NORMDIST(4, 2, 3, true)	$P(x \leq 4)$ x normal $N(2, 3)$		0.7475
= NORMDIST(60, 63.2, 2.74, true)	$P(x \leq 60)$ x normal $N(63.2, 2.74)$		0.1214

Other probabilities can be computed in a similar way, using the additional fact that the probability of everything must be 1. For example, suppose we want to use an $N(63, 2)$ normal distribution to compute the probability $P(height \geq 65)$. We cannot simply use the Excel formula $NORMDIST(65, 63, 2, true)$ because that formula computes, as always, $P(x \leq 65)$, not what we want (in fact, it is kind of the opposite). However, we know that the probability of everything is 1 so that:

$$P(height \leq 65) + P(height \geq 65) = 1.$$

To compute a probability like $P(60 \leq height \leq 65)$, we can apply a similar trick, shown in Figure 4.10.

Now, in fact, we can use Excel to rapidly compute probabilities without ever constructing a frequency histogram at all. In fact, we do not even need to have access to the complete data set. All we need is to know the mean and the standard deviation of the data so that we can pick the right normal distribution.

Example: Consider the Excel data set health_male.xls, showing a number of variables related to the health records of 40 male patients, randomly selected. Without constructing a frequency histogram for the height of the 40 patients, find the following probabilities.

- What is the probability, approximately, that a man is 60 in. or shorter?
- What is the probability, approximately, that a man is 65 in. or taller?
- What is the probability, approximately, that a man is between 60 and 65 in. tall?

Instead of constructing a complete frequency histogram, we quickly use Excel to compute the mean and the standard deviation of our data. Then we use the $NORMDIST$ function, just as earlier, but of course using the mean and standard deviation for *this* data set. Here we go:

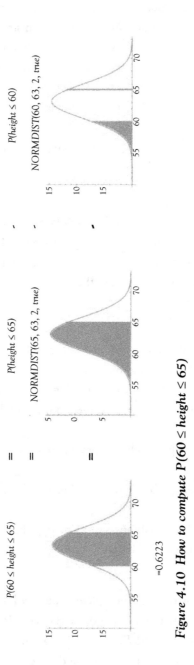

Figure 4.10 How to compute P(60 ≤ height ≤ 65)

mean height:	68.3	
st. dev.	3.02	
P(height <=60) =	0.002995	=NORMDIST(60,68,3,3.02, TRUE)
P(height >=60) =	0.862741	=1-NORMDIST(65,68.3,3.02, TRUE)
P(60 <= height <=65) =	0.134265	=NORMDIST(65,68.3,3.02, TRUE) - NORMDIST (60,68.3,3.02, TRUE)

Note that the probability of a man being less than 60 in. tall is now about 0.003, or 0.3 percent, much lower than the probability for a woman. That makes sense, since men are, on average, taller than woman (68.3 in. versus 63.2 in.), so the probability of a man being less than 60 in. tall should indeed be lower than the comparable probability for women. The other figures equally make sense. Note also that all three probabilities add up to 1 (approximately). Again, that makes sense—explain.

Important: The computed probabilities will be (approximately) correct *under the assumption* that the height of men is indeed normally distributed.

Now it should be clear how to use various normal distributions together with Excel to quickly compute probabilities. To practice, here are a few exercises for you to do. The answers are listed, but not how to get them. Remember, sometimes you need to use 1 − *NORMDIST* or subtract two *NORMDIST* values from each other—draw a picture of the normal curve, shade the desired area, and determine how that area relates to the Excel function *NORMDIST*.

Example: Find the indicated probabilities, assuming that the variable *x* has a distribution with the given mean and standard deviation.

1. *x* has mean 2.0 and standard deviation 1.0. Find $P(x <= 3.0)$ [= 0.8413].

2. x has mean 1.0 and standard deviation 2.0. Find $P(x >= 1.5)$ [= 0.4013].

3. x has mean −10 and standard deviation 5.0. Find $P(-12 <= x <= -7)$ [= 0.3812].

4. x is a standard normal variable. Find $P(x <= -0.5)$ [= 0.3085].

5. x is a standard normal variable. Find $P(x >= -0.5)$ [= 0.6915].

6. x is a standard normal variable. Find $P(x >= 0.6)$ [= 0.2742].

7. x is a standard normal variable. Find $P(-0.3 <= x <= 0.4)$ [= 0.2733].

The Inverse Normal Problem

While we now can easily compute probabilities $P(x < a)$ for given values of a, we sometimes want to do just the opposite: given a probability p, find a cut-off value a such that $P(x < a) = p$. Excel has just the function for us, as usual.

Definition: If x is $N(\mu, \sigma)$, that is, normal with mean μ and standard deviation σ, then the Excel function **NORMINV**(p, μ, σ) gives the value of a such that $P(x < a) = p$. Thus, the Excel functions *NORMDIST* and *NORMINV* are inverses of each other.

Of course, once we can find values of a such that $P(x < a) = p$, we can also find cut-off values if the prescribed probability has a different form. Perhaps an example will clarify this:

Example: If x is standard normal, find a such that $P(x < a) = 0.4$. What if x was $N(4, 1.5)$? Can you use the *NORMINV* function to find b such that $P(x > b) = 0.05$ if x is $N(5, 1)$?

For the first question, we know right away that a must be less than 0 because the distribution is normal with mean 0 and standard deviation 1. Thus, if a probability of the form $P(x < a)$ wants to be less than 50 percent, a must be negative. In fact, $a = NORMINV(0.4, 0, 1) = -0.2533$.

Indeed, we can check that $NORMDIST(-0.2533, 0, 1, true) = 0.4$, which is of course the inverse of the problem.

If the variable x was $N(4, 1.5)$ instead of the standard normal and we again wanted to find a such that $P(x < a) = 0.4$, then it is easy to see that a has to be less than the mean of 4. In fact, $a = NORMINV(0.4, 4, 1.5) = 3.6200$. We could verify this again using $NORMDIST$ but we will leave that to you.

Finally, with a little imagination and the picture of the normal distribution in our mind we can figure out that to find b such that $P(x > b) = 0.05$ is equivalent to $P(x < b) = 0.95$ so that $b = NORMINV(0.95, 5, 1) = 6.6448$. Indeed, to double-check: $P(x > 6.6448) = 1 - P(x < 6.6448) = 1 - NORMDIST(6.6448, 5, 1, true) = 0.05$.

Normal Distribution and Its Standard Deviation

While the mean of a normal distribution is easy to see (it is the line of symmetry through the top of the mountain), it seems harder to visualize the standard deviation. It is relatively simple to decide which of the two normal distributions has the smaller variance, but as it turns out even if you have only one normal distribution you can "see" the standard deviation.

Definition: If x is normally distributed with mean m and standard deviation s, then the *three-sigma rule of thumb* states (compare Figure 4.11):

- The interval $(m - s, m + s)$ contains ≈68 percent of the data.
- The interval $(m - 2s, m + 2s)$ contains ≈95 percent of the data.
- The interval $(m - 3s, m + 3s)$ contains ≈99 percent of the data.

This rule can be used to verify whether a given distribution of data is normal or not: check how much of the data is within one, two, and three standard deviations of the mean and compare it with the three-sigma rule of thumb: if there is an approximate match, the distribution is likely normal.

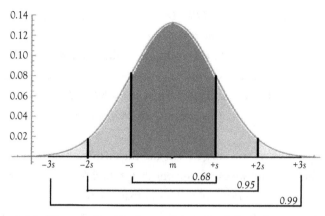

Figure 4.11 Normal distribution and standard deviation

Example: Bags of chips have an average weight of 425 g, with a standard deviation of 2.5 g. Assuming the weight is normal, how many bags in a box of 500 bags weigh between 420 and 430g?

We want to find:

$$P(420 \leq x \leq 430) = NORMDIST(430, 425, 2.5, true)$$
$$-NORMDIST(420, 425, 2.5, true),$$

which works out to 0.9545. This matches with our observation that the interval $(m - 2s, m + 2s)$ contains approximately 95 percent. Thus, we expect $0.95 \cdot 500 = 475$ bags will have the desired weight.

Incidentally, the preceding rule explains why we can approximate the standard deviation s as $range/4$, as we saw in Chapter 3: the interval $m - 2s$ to $m + 2s$ contains approximately 95 percent of the data, or in other words, the strip from $m - 2s$ to $m + 2s$ has a width of $4s$ and contains 95 percent of the data, approximately. Thus, $4s \approx range$ or $s \approx range/4$.

Converting to z-Scores

It turns out that you can easily convert one normal distribution into another. This is particularly handy when converting an arbitrary normal distribution to the standard normal $N(0,1)$.

Transformation Formula for Normal Distributions: If x is normal with mean m and standard deviation s, then $z = \dfrac{x - m}{s}$ has the *standard* normal distribution, that is, the mean of z is 0 and its standard deviation is 1. The number $\dfrac{x - m}{s}$ is frequently called the *z-score* of x.

This formula allows us to compute probabilities of normally distributed variables in (at least) two ways.

Example: Suppose x is normally distributed as $N(5, 2)$, that is, normal with mean 5 and standard deviation 2. Then compute $P(2 < x < 6)$ using (a) the original parameters and (b) using z-scores.

For part (a) we compute as usual:

$$P(2 < x < 6) = NORMDIST(6, 5, 2, true) - NORMDIST(2, 5, 2, true)$$
$$= 0.6915 - 0.0668 = 0.6247$$

By the transformation formula the variable $z = \dfrac{x - 5}{2}$ is $N(0, 1)$. But if $x = 2$ then the z-score is $z = \dfrac{2 - 5}{2} = -1.5$ and the z-score of $x = 6$ is $z = \dfrac{6 - 5}{2} = 0.5$. Thus:

$$P(2 < x < 6) = P(-1.5 < z < 0.5)$$
$$= NORMIDST(0.5, 0, 1, true) - NORMDIST(-1.5, 0, 1, true)$$
$$= 0.6915 - 0.0668 = 0.6247$$

Thus, as long as you know how to compute probabilities of the standard normal distribution you can actually compute probabilities of *any* normal distribution. Therefore, Excel includes a special function to compute probabilities of the standard normal.

Definition: The Excel function $=NORMSDIST(Z)$ computes the probability $P(z < Z)$ if z has a standard normal distribution. In other words, $NORMSDIST(Z) = NORMDIST(Z, 0, 1, true)$.

The *NORMSDIST* has the advantage that it is somewhat simpler to use but offers no other benefits. Thus, we will stick with *NORMDIST(Z,* 0, 1, *true*) as a reminder that the standard normal distribution has mean 0 and standard deviation 1.

Discrete and Continuous Random Variables

Previously we have used the term "variable" without properly defining it; we relied on common sense. Since we are currently adding a solid foundation to our discussion anyway, we might as well do the same for our most basic terminology.

Definition: A *random variable* is a variable whose values are numerical outcomes of an experiment. A *discrete* random variable can take only distinct values; a *continuous* one can take *any* value within a range.

Let us say we are tossing a single coin once. A random variable needs to assign numbers to the events in the sample space. Thus, we define a random variable x by saying, for example, that $x(\{H\}) = 0$ and $x(\{T\}) = 1$. If we toss a coin twice, a random variable could count the number of H's, so that $x(\{T,T\}) = 0$, $x(\{T,H\}) = x(\{H,T\}) = 1$, and $x(\{H,H\}) = 2$. These two variables are discrete. As an example for a continuous variable, consider an experiment that measures the height of people. A random variable x could simply be the height of a person in inches. For discrete random variables it is convenient to define them via a table of values including their probabilities, while continuous random variables are often represented as the graph of a function called the *probability density function*.

Mean and Standard Deviation for Discrete Random Variables

Of course we can compute the mean or standard deviation of discrete random variables. It is similar to computing those parameters for frequency tables but we need to take into account that the distinct values of our random variable can occur with different probabilities.

Definition: The *mean* μ (or *expected value* $E(x)$) of a discrete random variable x with values $x_1, x_2, ..., x_n$ is:

$$\mu = x_1 P(x = x_1) + x_2 P(x = x_2) + \cdots + x_n P(x = x_n)$$

$$= \sum x_i P(x = x_i).$$

The *variance* σ^2 of a discrete random variable x is:

$$\sigma^2 = (x_1 - \mu)^2 P(x = x_1) + (x_2 - \mu)^2 P(x = x_2) + \cdots + (x_n - \mu)^2 P(x = x_n) =$$

$$= \sum (x_i - \mu)^2 P(x = x_i) = \sum x_i^2 P(x = x_i) - \mu^2.$$

The standard deviation is, as usual, the square root of the variance:

$$\sigma = \sqrt{\sigma^2}$$

This looks pretty intimidating but once you work through an example everything should clear up and you should have no problems. Note that interpreting the mean of a random variable as the *expected value* is particularly interesting.

Example: Suppose you want to open a new pizzeria. You do some research and you find that 30 percent of comparable pizzerias operate at a loss of $35,000, 40 percent break even, 20 percent make a profit of $25,000, and 10 percent make a profit of $95,000. How much money can you expect to make if you go through with your plans? What is the standard deviation?

First, we will convert the information into our new lingo: we define the random variable x to measure how much profit a pizzeria makes. Thus, x has four distinct values with the probabilities as shown in column 2 of Table 4.3.

Table 4.3 Finding the expected profit opening a pizzeria

x (Profit) ($)	$P(x = x_i)$	$x_i P(x = x_1)$	$x_i^2 P(x = x_1)$
−35,000	0.3	−10,500	367,500,000
0	0.4	0	0
25,000	0.2	5,000	125,000,000
95,000	0.1	9,500	902,500,000
		4,000	1,395,000,000

To find the mean, or the expected value, we multiply $x_i P(x = x_1)$ and add column 3 to the table. Since we also need to find the standard deviation, we add one more column containing $x_i^2 P(x = x_1)$. Then we find the total of column 3, which will be the expected value of x. Thus, the expected value of x is $4,000, which means that statistically speaking you can expect a profit of $4,000 if you open the pizzeria.

To compute the variance (and hence the standard deviation), we add up the fourth column and use the preceding formula to compute the variance: $\sigma^2 = 1,395,000,000 − 16,000,000 = 1,379,000,000$ so that the standard deviation becomes $37,134.89.

Mean and Standard Deviation for Continuous Random Variables

Defining mean and standard deviation for continuous random variables requires integration of functions—that is, areas under curves—and is generally beyond the scope of this text. Still, for completeness, we list the definitions here as well.

Definition: The mean μ, or *expected value E(x)*, of a continuous random variable x with density function p(x) is:

$$\mu = E(x) = \int_{-\infty}^{\infty} x \, p(x) dx.$$

The variance σ^2 of the continuous random variable x is:

$$\sigma^2 = \int_{-\infty}^{\infty} (x - \mu)^2 \, p(x) dx.$$

The standard deviation is, as usual, the square root of the variance: $\sigma = \sqrt{\sigma^2}$.

Even though we do not know how to integrate, here is a relatively simple example.

Example: Suppose we constructed a dial with a spinner, similar to a wheel of fortune, and spin it randomly (see Figure 4.12). Define the random variable x to be the angle at which the spinner comes to a rest. Compute the mean and variance of x.

The random variable x can take any value between 0 and 360: it is therefore a continuous variable. Since you are spinning randomly, every angle is equally likely, so x is called a *uniformly* distributed random variable. The probability density function for x must be constant, since every value between 0 and 360 is equally likely: $p(x) = c$ for $0 \leq x \leq 360$ (see Figure 4.13).

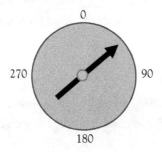

Figure 4.12 A continuous "wheel of fortune"

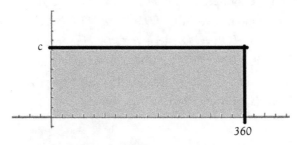

Figure 4.13 Uniform distribution

We know that the total probability has to be 1, as always, so that the area of the rectangle with width 360 and height c must be 1. Therefore, $360\, c = 1$, so that

$c = \dfrac{1}{360} = 0.0028$. Now we can find the mean and variance:

$$\mu = \int_{-\infty}^{\infty} x\, p(x)dx = \int_{0}^{360} \frac{x}{360}\, dx = 180\,,$$

$$\sigma^2 = \int_{-\infty}^{\infty} (x - \mu)^2\, p(x)dx = \int_{0}^{360} (x - 180)^2 \frac{1}{360}\, dx = 10{,}800\,.$$

Other Distributions

There are many different distributions. In fact, any function $p(x)$ that is non-negative for all x and with the total area under the curve being 1 can generate a probability distribution. We already introduced the normal distributions and worked extensively with them, and in the previous section we introduced a uniform distribution for $0 \le x \le 360$. Now we will introduce two additional ones.

Definition: Two other frequently used continuous distributions are the *Student t*-distribution and the *F* distribution. Both have complicated density functions but in terms of Excel they are defined via:

- **Student *t*-distribution:** *TDIST*(x, df, tails), where df stands for degree of freedom and *tails* is 1 (to compute one tail) or 2 (to compute two tails). *TDIST*(x, df, 1) = P(X > x) and *TDIST*(x, df, 2) = P(X > x) + P(X < −x) for positive x.
- *F* **distribution:** *FDIST*(x, df1, df2), where df1 and df2 stand for degrees of freedom 1 and 2, respectively. *FDIST*(x, df1, df2) = P(X > x).

You can see their graphs in Figures 4.14 and 4.15.

The *t*-distribution looks similar to the standard normal distribution but its peak is not quite as high whereas its tails are wider. If the degree of freedom is high, the *t*-distribution is nearly identical to the standard normal distribution. The *F* distribution, on the other hand, looks completely different (see Figure 4.14). In particular, it has no axis of symmetry. We will need these distributions in later chapters, at which point we will also explain the significance of the degree of freedoms. Right now we just want to familiarize ourselves with new ways to compute probabilities.

Note that the Excel definitions of both *TDIST* and *FDIST* give the probabilities at the *tail* end of the distribution whereas *NORMDIST* gives the probability *to the left* of *x*. See Figure 4.15.

Example: Suppose *x* is distributed according to a *t*-distribution with six degrees of freedom. Use Excel to find $P(x \geq 1.5)$ and $P(|x| \leq 1)$. Also verify that for large degrees of freedom the *t*-distribution and the standard normal distribution are approximately the same. Finally, compare the one-tailed probabilities $P(x \geq 1.5)$ if *x* is distributed according to the *F* distribution with $df1 = 10$ and $df2 = 2$ with the standard normal one.

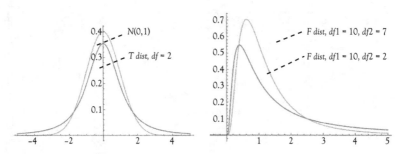

Figure 4.14 *t-distribution versus standard normal (left) and two F distributions (right)*

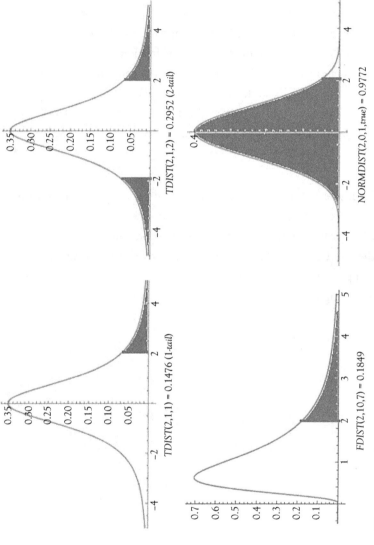

Figure 4.15 One- and two-tailed t-distribution versus standard normal and F distribution

Assuming x is distributed according to a t-distribution with $df = 6$, we have $P(x \geq 1.5) = TDIST(1.5,6,1) = 0.092$. On the other hand, $P(|x| \leq 1)$ $= 1 - TDIST(1,6,2) = 0.8220$.

To verify that a t-distribution with high degrees of freedom is about equal to the standard normal distribution, we compare $TDIST(1,1000,1)$ $= 0.15878$ with $1 - NORMDIST(1,0,1,true) = 0.15865$ and repeat those calculations for different values of x. You will find that the probabilities agree very well indeed.

If x is distributed according to the F distribution with $df1 = 10$ and $df2$ $= 2$ then $P(x \geq 1.5) = FDIST(1.5,10,2) = 0.4651$. On the other hand, if x is $N(0, 1)$ then $P(x \geq 1.5) = 1 - NORMDIST(1.5,0,1,true) = 0.06680$.

The Inverse Probability Problem

We have seen that before that we can also solve the *inverse probability* problem: instead of finding the probability $P(x < a)$ for a given value of a, we compute that value of a that results in a given probability $p = P(x < a)$. If x is normal, then we can use the Excel function *NORMINV*. Similarly, Excel offers the functions **TINV** and **FINV** that are similar to *NORMINV*, but with slight differences in the interpretation of their inputs.

- If x is distributed according to a t-distribution with degrees of freedom df, then the Excel function **TINV**(p, df) returns that value a such that $P(x < -a) + P(x > a) = P(|x| > a) = p$.
- If x is distributed according to an F distribution with degrees of freedom $df1$ and $df2$, then the Excel function **FINV**(p, $df1$, $df2$) returns that value a such that $P(x > a) = p$.

The functions *TINV* and *TDIST* are inverse of each other, as are *FINV* and *FDIST*.

The Central Limit Theorem

In the "Introduction" section we saw that we can use frequency distributions to compute probabilities of various events. Then we determined that we could use various *normal* distributions as a shortcut to compute those probabilities, which was very convenient. Using that technique we were able to compute all kinds of probabilities just based on the fact that we knew the mean and sample standard deviation of the distribution. We had to assume, however, that the (unknown) distribution of the variable in question was normal with the computed mean and standard deviation as parameters.

As it turns out, there is some mathematical justification for that; it says, in effect, that most distributions—in some sense—are "normal." That theorem, called the *Central Limit Theorem*, is one of the corner stones of statistics. It has many practical and theoretical implications, some of which we will explore in subsequent chapters.

In this course we will simply state the theorem without any proof. In more advanced courses we would provide a justification or mathematical proof, but for our current purposes it will be enough to understand the theorem and to apply it in subsequent chapters.

If we want to talk colloquially, we have actually already seen the Central Limit Theorem. We noted previously that "most histograms are (more or less) bell-shaped," which is in fact one way to state the Central Limit Theorem. To state this theorem precisely, we need to specify, among other things, exactly which normal distribution we are talking about.

Central Limit Theorem for Means: Suppose x is a variable for a population whose distribution has a mean m and standard deviation s but whose shape is unknown. Suppose further we repeatedly select random samples of size N from that population and compute the sample mean each time. Finally, we plot the distribution (histogram) of all these sample means. Then the distribution of all sample means is approximately normal (bell-shaped) with mean m (the original mean) and standard deviation $\dfrac{s}{\sqrt{N}}$.

This theorem is perhaps somewhat hard to understand, so here is a more colloquial restatement.

Central Limit Theorem, colloquial version: No matter what shape the distribution of a population has, the distribution of *means* computed for samples of size N is approximately bell-shaped (normal). The approximation gets better as N gets larger. Moreover, if we know the mean and standard deviation of the original distribution, the mean for the sample means will be the same as the original one, while the new standard deviation will be the original one divided by the square root of N.

The importance of this theorem is that it allows us to start with an *arbitrary* and possibly unknown distribution, yet use the *normal* distribution with appropriate mean and standard deviation to perform various computations, at least approximately.

Example: Roll a single die once and record the number on the upper face. What is the distribution for this experiment? Now roll two dice and record the average of the numbers on the up faces. What is the distribution for this experiment? Finally, roll three dice, record the average, and determine the distribution. Relate your results to the Central Limit Theorem.

If we roll a single die, the numbers 1 to 6 are all equally likely to come up. Thus, the probability for each outcome is 1/6 so that the distribution looks like Figure 4.16.

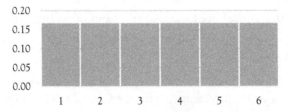

Figure 4.16 Uniform distribution for tossing one die

Table 4.4 *Average for tossing two dice*

	1	2	3	4	5	6
1	2/2	3/2	4/2	5/2	6/2	7/2
2	3/2	4/2	5/2	6/2	7/2	8/2
3	4/2	5/2	6/2	7/2	8/2	9/2
4	5/2	6/2	7/2	8/2	9/2	10/2
5	6/2	7/2	8/2	9/2	10/2	11/2
6	7/2	8/2	9/2	10/2	11/2	12/2

Note that the mean $m = 3.5$ and the standard deviation $s = 1.7078$.

If we throw two dice and record their average, we get the outcomes 2/2, 3/2, 4/2, 5/2, 6/2, 7/2, 8/2, 9/2, 10/2, 11/2, and 12/2. We can list these outcomes in Table 4.4, similar to what we did before.

As before, we can determine the probabilities by counting to create the distribution in Figure 4.17.

Now we throw three dice and record the average. There are $6 \times 6 \times 6 = 216$ total possibilities, with probabilities like $P(average = 3/3) = P(\{1,1,1\}) = 1/216$, $P(average = 4/3) = P(\{1,1,2\}, \{1,2,1\}, \{2,1,1\}) = 3/216$, and so on. We could show the outcomes in a three-dimensional table, but instead we simply show the resulting distribution in Figure 4.18. While we are at it, we also show the result of recording the average of four dice.

We can see that as the sample size N increases, the distribution looks more and more bell-shaped (normal), exactly as the Central Limit Theorem predicts.

The Central Limit Theorem Applet

If you want to see the Central Limit Theorem in action, check out the Central Limit Applet (see Figure 4.19; it requires the latest version of the Java plug-in, which you can download for free).

Try the following:

- Click on the preceding link for the Central Limit Theorem applet.
- Click on the "Start CLT Applet" button (the applet might take a few seconds to initialize).

Outcome	Probability
2/2	1/36
3/2	2/36
4/2	3/36
5/2	4/36
6/2	5/36
7/2	6/36
8/2	5/36
9/2	4/36
10/2	3/36
11/2	2/36
12/2	1/36

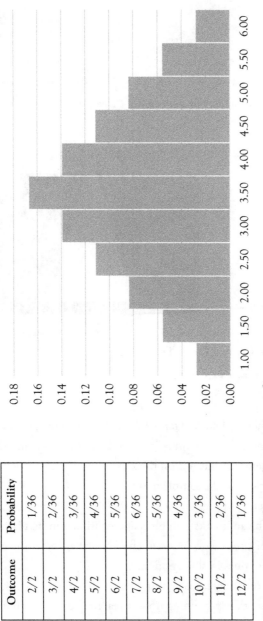

Figure 4.17 Distribution for tossing two dice

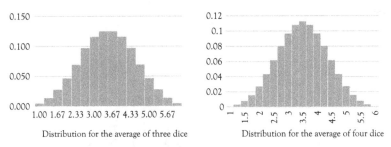

Distribution for the average of three dice   Distribution for the average of four dice

Figure 4.18 Distribution for tossing three and four dice

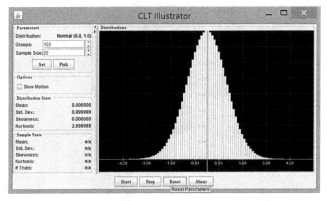

Figure 4.19 Central Limit Theorem Applet

Source: http://www.mathcs.org/java/programs/CLT/clt.html

- o When you click "Start," the program will pick a random sample from a population, compute the mean, and mark where that mean is on the x-axis to start a frequency distribution for the sample mean.
- o Then the program picks another random sample, computes its mean, marks it in blue, and continues in that fashion—check the "Slow Motion" checkbox to see what the program does in slow motion.
- After the program is running for a while, notice that the blue bars are slowly building up to a real frequency distribution (the yellow bars underneath show the distribution of the underlying population from which the random samples are selected).

Now try the following:

- Let the program run (at regular speed) for a while. What shape is the distribution of the random samples (blue bars), at least approximately?
- Experiment with different distributions (click on [Pick] to choose another distribution). What shape does the distribution of the sample means (blue chart) have when you pick other distributions for the population? Is that true regardless of the underlying population distribution (yellow chart)?
- What is the mean for the distribution of the sample means (blue chart) in relation to the mean of the distribution of the original distribution (yellow chart)? The figures for the sample means are shown in the category "Sample Stats," but make sure to run the program for a while before looking at the numbers. Note that these numbers represent the "sample mean" for the distribution of all sample means, and the "sample standard deviation" for the distribution of all sample means (yes, it sounds odd, but that is what it is).
- Is there a relation between the standard deviation of the sample means (blue chart) and that of the original population (yellow chart)? Experiment with sample sizes 16, 25, 36, 49, and 64 to find the relation, but make sure to press the Reset button before using new parameters or sample sizes, and let the program run for a while before estimating the sample stats.

If you have done everything correctly, you have just discovered the Central Limit Theorem! Relax: if you have any trouble with that applet, or if you are not exactly sure what it shows and how it works, do not worry. In this class we are interested in the consequences of the Central Limit Theorem, coming up in the next chapter, and not in that theorem in and of itself.

Proportions and the Binomial Distribution

Of the continuous distributions the normal ones are the most important, but they require a *numerical* variable. Is there anything we can do for *categorical* variables? It turns out that if our data is such that it falls into exactly two categories, it can be modeled by a *binomial distribution*.

Definition: Suppose a random experiment has exactly two outcomes. We (arbitrarily) call one of them *success* (*S*) and the other one *failure* (*F*). Suppose further that the *probability of success* is p (and hence the probability of failure is $q = 1 - p$). Assume finally that this experiment is repeated independently N times and the random variable x counts the *number of successes*. Then x is a *binomial random variable* and has the *binomial distribution $B(p, N)$*.

Note: A random experiment with exactly two outcomes where the probability of success does not change is sometimes called a *Bernoulli Trial*, named after the well-known Swiss mathematician Jacob Bernoulli (1654–1705). As so often, the preceding definition sounds really complicated but once you see examples it will become much clearer.

Example: Find the parameters for the following binomial distributions.

- Flip a coin 33 times and count the number of heads.
- It turns out that individuals with a certain gene have a 0.70 probability of contracting a certain disease. We conduct a study of 100 individuals with that gene to count the number of individuals who will contract the disease.
- Consider a population of 25,000 voters in a given state. The proportion of voters who favor candidate A is equal to 0.40.

We can describe each of these situations using our terminology for a binomial distribution. In the first case of flipping a single coin, we (arbitrarily) consider heads to be a success (this would be our Bernoulli trial). Then the probability of success is $p = \dfrac{1}{2}$. Since we repeat this experiment 33 times, the random variable x counting the number of successes is $B(1/2, 33)$.

In the second case we consider it a success to contract the disease (which may sound odd). Then $p = 0.7$ and since we repeat this 100 times, we have a $B(0.7, 100)$ distribution. We could just as well consider it a success *not* to contract the disease (avoiding a disease does sound more successful). In that case $p = 1 - 0.7 = 0.3$ and this variable, call it y, counting the number of successes, is $B(0.3, 100)$.

For the last case we consider a vote for candidate A a success so that $p = 0.4$. Since we have 25,000 voters, our distribution is $B(0.4, 25,000)$.

It turns out that there is a (relatively) simple formula for a binomial distribution but it requires the formula $c_{n,k} = \binom{n}{k} = \dfrac{n!}{k!(n-k)!}$, where $n! = n \cdot (n-1) \cdot (n-2) \cdot \ldots \cdot 3 \cdot 2 \cdot 1$ and $0! = 1$. We pronounce $n!$ as "n *factorial*" and $c_{n,k}$ or $\binom{n}{k}$ as "n *choose* k" or "*choose* k *out of* n." For example $4! = 4 \cdot 3 \cdot 2 \cdot 1 = 24$ and

$$C_{8,3} = \binom{8}{3} = \frac{8}{3!(8-3)!} = \frac{8}{3!5!} = \frac{8 \cdot 7 \cdot 6 \cdot 5 \cdot 4 \cdot 3 \cdot 2 \cdot 1}{3 \cdot 2 \cdot 1 \cdot 5 \cdot 4 \cdot 3 \cdot 2 \cdot 1} = \frac{6\ 8\ 7}{3\ 2\ 1} = 2 \cdot 4 \cdot 7 = 56.$$

Note that "n choose k" *always* comes out an integer even though at first glance that seems unlikely.

Definition: Suppose a random variable x is $B(p, N)$. Then x is a discrete binomial random variable and its distribution is

$$P(x = k) = C_{N,k} \cdot p^k (1-p)^{N-k}.$$

The mean of x is $\mu = np$ and the variance is $\sigma^2 = np(1-p)$.

This is pretty nifty. It gives us the probability of getting k successes in N total tries, each of which has probability of success p.

Example: Create the probability distribution for counting heads in flipping a coin six times.

Some of the probabilities are easy to determine. For example, the probability of obtaining six heads should clearly be $(0.5)^6$. Also, the probability of obtaining no heads is equal to the probability of getting six tails, which again is $(0.5)^6$. For the probabilities in between we need to apply the preceding formula; see Table 4.5 and Figure 4.20 for the results.

Table 4.5 Binomial distribution B(1/2, 6)

k	P(X = k)
0	$C_{6,0} \cdot (0.5)^0 (0.5)^6 = \dfrac{6!}{0!6!}(0.5)^6 = (0.5)^6 = 0.015625$
1	$C_{6,1} \cdot (0.5)^1 (0.5)^5 = \dfrac{6!}{1!5!}(0.5)^6 = 6 \cdot 0.5^6 = 0.09375$
2	$C_{6,2} \cdot (0.5)^2 (0.5)^4 = \dfrac{6!}{2!4!}(0.5)^6 = \dfrac{6 \cdot 5}{2 \cdot 1}(0.5)^6 = 0.234375$
3	$C_{6,3} \cdot (0.5)^3 (0.5)^3 = \dfrac{6!}{3!3!}(0.5)^6 = \dfrac{6 \cdot 5 \cdot 4}{3 \cdot 2 \cdot 1}(0.5)^6 = 0.3125$
4	$C_{6,4} \cdot (0.5)^4 (0.5)^2 = \dfrac{6!}{4!2!}\left(0.5\dfrac{1}{2}\right)^6 = \dfrac{6 \cdot 5}{2 \cdot 1}\left(\dfrac{1}{2}\right)^6 = 0.234375$
5	$C_{6,5} \cdot (0.5)^5 (0.5)^1 = \dfrac{6!}{5!1!}\left(\dfrac{1}{2}\right)^6 = 6\left(\dfrac{1}{2}\right)^6 = 0.09375$
6	$C_{6,6} \cdot \left(\dfrac{1}{2}\right)^6 \left(\dfrac{1}{2}\right)^0 = \dfrac{6!}{6!0!}\left(\dfrac{1}{2}\right)^6 = \left(\dfrac{1}{2}\right)^6 = 0.015625$

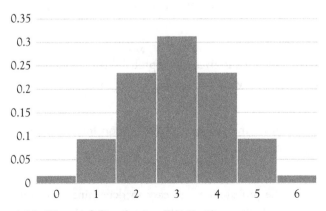

Figure 4.20 Binomial distribution B(1/2, 6)

Using Excel to Compute the Binomial Distribution

Excel, of course, includes functions to easily compute $P(x = k)$ if x is $B(p, N)$.

FACT(n)	computes $n!$
COMBIN(n, k)	computes "n choose k," that is, the number of ways to select k objects from n objects
BINOMDIST(x, N, p, false)	computes probability of obtaining k successes in N trials if the probability of success is p

Example: Use Excel to create the distribution chart for $B(0.2, 40)$, that is, the distribution of selecting k successes out of 40 trials with probability of success $p = 0.2$. Describe the distribution. Find $Q1$ and $Q3$ as well as the mean and the median.

Using Excel's *BINOM.DIST* (or *BINOMDIST* in Excel 2007) function it is easy to create the probability distribution for $B(0.2, 40)$; see Figure 4.21. We can then create the cumulative probability chart to determine $Q1 = 7$, $Q3 = 11$, and the median = 9, as explained in Chapter 3. The mean of $B(0.2, 40)$ is 8. The distribution in Figure 4.21 looks approximately normal but shifted slightly to the right.

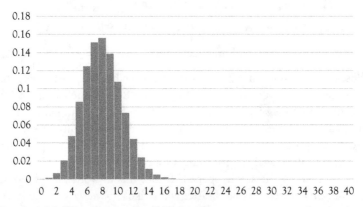

Figure 4.21 Distribution for B(0.2, 40)

Let us conclude this chapter with an interesting application that might give you pause for thought.

 **Example:** The National Aeronautics and Space Administration (NASA) flew a total of 135 space shuttle missions from 1982 to 2011. In 1986 the shuttle *Challenger*, the 25th shuttle launch, broke apart 73 sec into its flight, leading to the deaths of all seven crew members. A subsequent investigation, led by famous physicist Richard Feynman, found out that a simple O-ring failure caused by cold weather resulted in this disaster. Assuming that space shuttle launches are independent and that the probability of each successful launch is approximately 99.2 percent, find the probability of 25 successful shuttle launches in a row. Determine how many successful launches it takes before the probability of N successful launches in a row drops to 50 percent. Should you then launch the $N+1$ shuttle? What is the probability of 135 successful launches in a row?

Let x be a variable that counts the number of successful shuttle launches. Because of our assumptions, x has a binomial distribution with $B(0.992, N)$. Thus, the probability of 25 successful launches (and no failures) is $P(x = 25) = 0.992^{25} = 0.8181$ or about 82 percent. The probability of 135 successes in a row is similarly $0.992^{135} = 0.3381$ or only 33 percent.

To find N such that the probability of N successful launches drops below 50 percent we need to solve $P(x = N) = 0.992^{N} = 0.5$. We can take the natural logarithm on both sides to find that $N = \dfrac{\ln(0.5)}{\ln(0.992)} = 86.3$. Thus, the probability of 87 successful launches has dropped to less than 50 percent. However, the probability of the 88th launch is again 99.2 percent, regardless of what happened before. Such is the nature of the binomial distribution: no matter how close the probability of success p is to 1, the probability of N successes in a row eventually drops to zero! Still, each trial has again a probability of success p, regardless of how many successes in a row already happened. To put this in words: in a binomial distribution it is *certain* that disaster will strike *eventually*, but you *cannot* predict when.

Excel Demonstration

Recall that to solve a probability problem using a binomial distribution, you would need the number of successes you are looking for, the number of trials, and the probability of success. In the following text is a quick tip sheet on the scripts to use in Excel for specific situations. Note that TRUE/FALSE represents whether or not we are looking for the cumulative probability. In other words, if we are looking for the probability of 5, and if we were to say TRUE in our script, that means we would get the probability of everything up to and including 5 (the cumulative amount). If we say FALSE (meaning we are saying NO to the cumulative) that means we only want 5, not the cumulative value.

Rules for Finding Binomial Probabilities in Excel

- If the question asks you to find the probability of exactly one number, use *BINOMDIST(successes,trials,probability,FALSE)*.
- If the question asks you to find the probability of up to and including a number (less than or equal to a number), use *BINOMDIST(successes,trials,probability,TRUE)*.
- If the question asks you to find the probability of less than a number, use *BINOMDIST(successes,trials,probability,TRUE) – BINOMDIST(successes,trials,probability,FALSE)*.
- If the question asks you to find the probability of at least one number (greater than or equal to a number), use *(1 – BINOMDIST(successes,trials,probability,TRUE)) + BINOMDIST(successes,trials,probability,FALSE)*.
- If the question asks you to find the probability of greater than a number, use *1 – BINOMDIST(successes,trials,-probability,TRUE)*.

Example: Company P, the paper products manufacturer, has a customer service and return department. A customer service representative's records show that the probability that a newly sold product needing to be returned in the first 90 days is 0.05. If a sample of three new products is selected:

a. What is the probability that none needs to be returned?

b. What is the probability that at least one needs to be returned?

c. What is the probability that more than one needs to be returned?

The key parameters to this problem are: sample size (trials) $N = 3$, probability of "success" $p = 5$ percent, and number of "successes" (a) exactly 0, (b) 1 or more, or (c) more than one. To solve in Excel, we would use the following formulas:

a. *BINOMDIST(0,3,0.05,FALSE)* to get the result of: 0.857375 or around 86 percent

b. 1 – *BINOMDIST(0,3,0.05,FALSE)* to get the result of: 0.142625 or around 14 percent

c. 1 – *BINOMDIST(1,3,0.05,TRUE)* to get the result of: 0.142625 or around 14 percent

Example: Company S, the accounting firm, knows that to resolve client inquires on the same day is highly important for keeping client satisfaction. This means the client relations department works quickly to resolve inquiries on the same day. Past data from the customer relationship management database indicates that the likelihood is 0.70 that client inquiries that come in on a Monday (the busiest day of the week) will be resolved on the same day. For the first five inquiries submitted on a given Monday:

a. What is the probability that all 5 will be resolved on the same day?

b. What is the probability that at least 3 will be resolved on the same day?

c. What is the probability that fewer than 2 will be resolved on the same day?

The key parameters for this problem are: sample size (trials) $N = 5$, probability of success $p = 70$ percent, and number of successes (a) exactly 5, (b) 3 or more, or (c) fewer than two. To solve this in Excel, we would use the following formulas:

a. $=BINOMDIST(5,5,0.7,FALSE)$ to get the result of: 0.16807 or around 17 percent

b. $=1 - BINOMDIST(3,5,0.7,TRUE) + BINOMDIST(3,5,0.7,FALSE)$ to get the result of 0.83692 or around 84 percent

c. $=BINOMDIST(2,5,0.7,TRUE) - BINOMDIST(2,5,0.7,FALSE)$ to get the result of 0.03078 or about 3 percent

Solving Probability Problems Using Normal Distribution Techniques

Company P determined that its truck drivers making deliveries are spending a lot of time on the road, and the trucks are becoming worn out quickly. Company P determined that the annual distance traveled per truck is normally distributed, with a mean of 72,000 miles and a standard deviation of 17,000 miles.

a. What proportion of trucks can be expected to travel between 38,000 and 62,000 miles in the year?

b. What percentage of the trucks travel less than 35,000 miles in the year?

c. What percentage of the trucks travel more than 57,000 miles in the year?

d. How many miles will be traveled by more than 72 percent of the trucks?

In Excel 2013, go to Formulas, and click Insert Function (which is the *fx* entry in the input line). Type in *NORMDIST* and select GO. Double-click on the *NORMDIST* option (see Figure 4.22).

To solve question A of finding the probability of traveling between 38,000 and 62,000, find the probability of 62,000 and then subtract from the probability of 3800,000:

- To find the probability of 62,000, input 62,000 for X, 72,000 for MEAN, 17,000 for Standard Deviation, and TRUE for Cumulative. The probability for 62,000 is 0.27 (see Figure 4.23).
- Now change X to 38,000 and the probability is 0.02.
- Subtract 0.27 and 0.02 to get 0.25 or 25 percent as the answer to A.

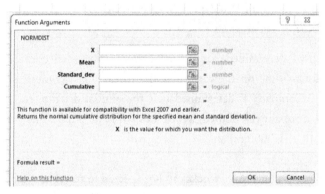

Figure 4.22 Dialog for NORMDIST function

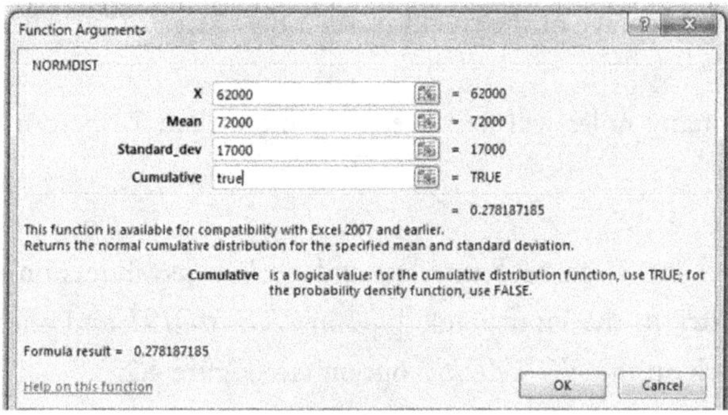

Figure 4.23 The standard normal probability for x = 62,000

To solve question B, leave the same dialog box up and leave the mean, standard deviation, and cumulative value as they were. Replace X with 35,000 to get 0.01 or 1 percent for B.

To solve question C, find the probability of less than or equal to 57,000 first by replacing X with 57,000 and leaving cumulative as True. This gives you 0.18 or 18 percent as the probability of getting less than or equal to 57,000. To find the probability of getting more than 55,000, subtract 0.18 from 1 to get 0.82 or 82 percent, which is the solution.

To solve question D, we must use the inverse function of *NORMDIST* since we want to compute a cut-off value for *x* to get a specified probability. Go to Insert Function and type in *NORMINV* (see Figure 4.24).

You are asked to find how many miles will be traveled by more than 72 percent of the trucks, so you are looking for the instances that fall *above* 72 percent, which is the top 27 percent. If it had asked us for less than 72 percent of the trucks then we would have been concerned with those trucks in the 0 to 72 percent range, not the 73 to 100 percent range. Input the following numbers into the dialog box shown in Figure 4.24.

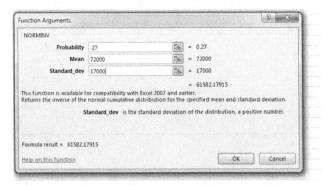

Figure 4.24 Dialog for NORMINV function

As you can see, the answer to D is 61,582 miles.

CHAPTER 5

Estimation

Preview: *Estimation is an important concept to understand no matter what field you work in. Estimating outcomes may seem like a simple matter, but it is actually a complicated process. In order to create an accurate estimation, it is important to not only gather the right information but also to make the proper inferences from that data. The sample size plays a role here as well and can have a profound impact on the accuracy of the estimate: a large sample size yields better estimates than a small one. We will provide our estimates in the form of confidence intervals, which in turn come with a margin of error. If you have ever reviewed polling data for a presidential election, you know that all of those polls report a margin of error, which varies from poll to poll. Margin of error is defined as the amount allowed for miscalculation. If a poll reports that candidate A has the support of 52 percent of the population while candidate B enjoys the support of 48 percent of the people and the margin of error is 3 percent, candidate A could have the support of between 49 percent and 55 percent of the people surveyed, while support for candidate B could be between 45 percent and 51 percent. These deviations may be small, but they can mean the difference between one candidate and the other prevailing on election day. We will provide estimates for the population mean, the difference of population means, and for proportions.*

Learning Objectives: At the conclusion of this chapter, you should be able to:

1. Construct and interpret confidence interval estimates for the mean and the proportion
2. Determine the sample size necessary to develop a confidence interval estimate for the mean or proportion
3. Use confidence interval estimates in solving business problems

Introduction

Up to now we discussed *descriptive* statistics (Chapters 1 to 3) and we developed some basic understanding of probability theory (Chapter 4). Beginning with this chapter we will talk about *inferential* statistics, which will be based on the theory we developed in Chapter 4. The principal idea is that we want to estimate parameters of a population based on information gathered from a random sample.

Confidence Intervals for Means

Let us start by estimating the mean of a population, given that we know the mean of a particular sample. In other words, if a sample of size, say, 100 is selected at random from some population, it is easy to compute the mean of that sample. It is equally easy to then use that sample mean as an estimate for the unknown population mean. But just because it is easy to do does not necessarily mean it is right.

For example, suppose we randomly select 100 people from the population of all people in the United States, measure their height, and compute the average height of our sample to be, say, 164.432 cm. If we now wanted to know the average height of *everyone* in our population (i.e., everyone in the United States), it seems reasonable to estimate that the average height of everyone is 164.432 cm as well. However, if we think about it, it is of course highly unlikely that the average for the entire population comes out *exactly* the same as the average for our random sample of just 100 people. It is much more likely that our sample mean of 164.432 cm is only *approximately* equal to the (unknown) population mean. It is the purpose of this section to clarify, using probability theory, what exactly we mean by "approximately equal."

Example: Consider the following data set for approximately 400 cars, assumed to be collected at random. We would like to make predictions about *all* automobiles, based on that random sample. In particular, the data set lists miles per gallon, engine size, and weight of 400 cars, but we would like to know the average miles per gallon, engine size, and weight of all cars, based on this sample.

 www.betterbusinessdecisions.org/data/cars.xls

It is of course simple to compute the mean of the various variables of the sample, starting with gas mileage. We find that the sample mean gas mileage is $\bar{x}$ = 23.5 miles per gallon (mpg), the sample standard deviation s = 7.82 mpg, and the sample size n = 398. We need to know how well this sample mean $\bar{x}$ predicts the actual and unknown population mean μ. Our best guess is clearly that the average mpg for all cars is 23.5 mpg—it is after all pretty much the only number we have—but how good is that estimate?

In fact, we know *more* than just the sample mean: we *also* know that all sample means are distributed normally, according to the Central Limit Theorem, and that the distribution of all sample means (of which ours is just one) is normal with the same mean as the population mean and a standard deviation of $7.82/\sqrt{398}$ = 0.3920.

Let us say we want to estimate a (unknown) population mean so that we are, say, 95 percent certain that the estimate is correct (or 90 percent, or 99 percent, or any other predetermined notion of certainty we might want to have). In other words, we need to compute a lower limit a and an upper limit b in such a way as to be 95 percent sure that our (unknown) population mean is between a and b (see Figure 5.1). That interval (a, b) is known as a *95 percent confidence interval* for the unknown mean. Using standard probability notation we can rephrase this: we want to find a and b so that $P(a < \mu < b) = 0.95$ (see Figure 5.1).

Using symmetry and focusing on the part of the distribution that we can compute with Excel, this is equivalent to finding a value of a such that $P(x < a) = 0.025$, since $P(x < a) + P(a < x < b) + P(x > b) = 1$ and $P(x < a) = P(x > b)$ (see Figure 5.2).

But that is an *inverse* normal problem as described in Chapter 4 and the Excel function *NORMINV* will come to the rescue: a = *NORMINV* (0.025, 23.5, 0.3290) = 22.8552.

Similarly, to find b such that $P(x > b) = 0.025$ implies that b = *NORMINV*(0.975, 23.5, 0.3290) = 24.1448. Thus, we conclude that the unknown population mean is between 22.8551 and 24.1448 with 95

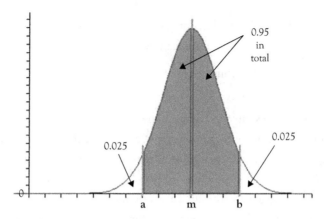

Figure 5.1 P(a < μ < b) = 0.95 *and related probabilities*

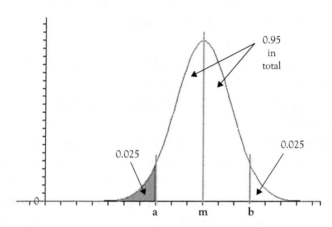

Figure 5.2 P(x < a) = 0.025 *and related probabilities*

percent certainty. Alternatively, we say that the 95 percent confidence interval for the average gas mileage of all cars is (22.8551, 24.1448).

Example: Again using our data on cars, as earlier, find the 95 percent confidence interval for the engine size of all cars.

We compute the sample mean to be 193 in.³ with a standard deviation of 104.55 in.³ and the sample size $n = 398$. To find a 95 percent confidence interval, we need to find a such that $P(x < a) = 0.025$ and b

such that $P(x > b) = 0.025$, assuming that x is $N(193,104.55/\sqrt{398})$. Thus, since $104.55/\sqrt{398} = 5.2406$:

- $a = NORMINV(0.025,193,5.2406) = 182.7286$
- $b = NORMINV(0.975,193,5.2406) = 203.2714$

Therefore, our 95 percent confidence interval is (182.73, 203.27) or, in other words, we are 95 percent certain that the unknown population mean—in this case the size of the engines of all cars—is between 182.73 and 203.2, with the mean 193 right in the middle.

Note that the preceding discussion is based on the Central Limit Theorem. It lets us use a normal distribution for the sample means even if the underlying distribution of the original data is unknown. However, that approximation works best for *large* sample sizes n, so for small n we need to employ a slightly different procedure. Thus, we will summarize our procedure for finding a confidence interval for a population mean μ, depending on the sample size n.

Large Sample Size

Here we will summarize the procedure to find a confidence interval for a *large* sample size n. In fact, we will consider n to be large if $n > 30$.

Confidence Interval for Mean, $n > 30$ (with Excel): Suppose we have selected a random sample with size $n > 30$ and with *sample* mean m and *sample* standard deviation s. Then the $p\%$ confidence interval for the unknown population mean μ is the interval (a, b), where

- $a = NORMINV((1 - p)/2, m, s/\sqrt{N})$
- $b = NORMINV((1 + p)/2, m, s/\sqrt{n})$

Note: the sample mean m will always be half way between a and b, that is, $(a + b)/2 = m$. You could use this relationship to quickly check your calculations.

Example: We want to know the average weight of cheese that comes in 8 oz packages. We select a random sample of 100 packages, weigh them, and find that the sample mean is 7.8 oz with a standard deviation of 0.8 oz. Estimate the average weight of all 8 oz packages, using a 95 percent confidence interval.

We have $N = 100 > 30$, so our preceding procedure for a large sample size is valid. Thus, we find:

- $a = NORMINV\left(\dfrac{1-0.95}{2}, 7.8, \dfrac{0.8}{\sqrt{100}}\right)$

  $= NORMINV(0.025, 7.8, 0.08) = 7.6432$

- $b = NORMINV\left(\dfrac{1+0.95}{2}, 7.8, \dfrac{0.8}{\sqrt{100}}\right)$

  $= NORMINV(0.975, 7.8, 0.08) = 7.9568$

Note that $\dfrac{a+b}{2} = \dfrac{7.6432 + 7.9568}{2} = \dfrac{15.6}{2} = 7.8 = m$ so that our calculations check out.

We have found that the average weight of all 8 oz packages of cheese is between 7.6432 oz and 7.9568 oz and we are 95 percent certain of this estimate.

Incidentally, this would mean that it is likely that these 8 oz packages of cheese are mislabeled! They should of course contain 8 oz of cheese on average, but we found that the (unknown) average is less than 7.9568 with 95 percent certainty. In other words, there is a small chance that the average weight of all cheeses is indeed 8 oz, but that chance is less than 5 percent. Thus, we are relatively certain that the cheese manufacturer is indeed mislabeling their cheese. This kind of argument, in fact, will be formalized in the next chapter on hypothesis testing. For now we will be content with obtaining estimates together with their certainty.

By the way, do you think a 99 percent confidence interval would be wider or narrower than the 95 percent interval (7.6432, 7.9568)? You will find the answer later in this section but you should try to think about it already.

The preceding summary works well but it relies on Excel. We can, however, use the z-score introduced in "The Normal Distribution" section to compute *some* confidence intervals without resorting to Excel at all.

According to our preceding summary, a *standard* normal distribution has a 95 percent confidence interval (a, b) where $a = NORMINV(0.025, 0, 1) = -1.96$ and $b = NORMINV(0.975, 0, 1) = 1.96$. Thus, if we start with a normal distribution with mean m and standard deviation s, then $(x - m)/s$ is *standard* normal and has a 95 percent confidence interval $(-1.96, 1.96)$. In other words, the confidence interval goes from $(x - m)/s = -1.96$ to $(x - m)/s = 1.96$, or equivalently, solving for x, from $x = m - 1.96\,s$ to $x = m + 1.96\,s$. Thus, the 95 percent confidence interval for x is $(m - 1.96\,s, m + 1.96\,s)$.

Now we can finish up this discussion by resorting to the Central Limit Theorem: if x has a distribution with mean m and standard deviation s then the sample means are normal with mean m and standard deviation $s/\sqrt{N}$. But then the sample means have a 95 percent confidence interval from $m - 1.96\,s/\sqrt{N}$ to $m + 1.96\,s/\sqrt{N}$. Putting everything together, we can summarize an alternative method of computing confidence intervals, at least for the ones most commonly used.

Confidence Interval for Mean, $N > 30$ (Alternate Version): Suppose we have selected a random sample with size $N > 30$ and with sample mean m and sample standard deviation s. Then:

- A 90 percent confidence interval goes from $m - 1.645 \cdot \dfrac{s}{\sqrt{N}}$ to $m + 1.645 \cdot \dfrac{s}{\sqrt{N}}$.

- A 95 percent confidence interval goes from $m - 1.96 \cdot \dfrac{s}{\sqrt{N}}$ to $m + 1.96 \cdot \dfrac{s}{\sqrt{N}}$.

- A 99 percent confidence interval goes from $m - 2.58 \cdot \dfrac{s}{\sqrt{N}}$

  to $m + 2.58 \cdot \dfrac{s}{\sqrt{N}}$.

Each of the intervals is centered at the mean m. The term $s/\sqrt{N}$ is known as the *standard error*.

Note: As you could have (hopefully) guessed from our preceding discussion, the 90 percent and 99 percent intervals use the constants $NORMINV(0.05, 0, 1) = -1.645$ and $NORMINV(0.005, 0, 1) = -2.58$, respectively. The improvement of this alternate version is based on the fact that you do *not* need Excel to compute any of these constants, a simple, plain calculator would do just fine here (unless you want to find an interval different from 90 percent, 95 percent, or 99 percent).

Example: In an earlier example we analyzed the gasoline efficiency of cars. Recall that we looked at a sample of size $N = 398$ with $m = 23.5$ and $s = 7.82$. Find a 90 percent, 95 percent, and 99 percent confidence interval for the average mpg of all cars.

Using our alternate version the problem is pretty easy:

- 90 percent confidence: from $23.5 - 1.645 \cdot \dfrac{7.82}{\sqrt{398}} = 22.85$ to $23.5 + 1.645 \cdot \dfrac{7.82}{\sqrt{398}} = 24.14$, or in interval notation (22.85, 24.14)

- 95 percent confidence: from $23.5 - 1.96 \cdot \dfrac{7.82}{\sqrt{398}} = 22.73$ to $23.5 + 1.96 \cdot \dfrac{7.82}{\sqrt{398}} = 24.27$, or (22.73, 24.27)

- 99 percent confidence: from $23.5 - 2.58 \cdot \dfrac{7.82}{\sqrt{398}} = 22.49$ to $23.5 + 2.58 \cdot \dfrac{7.82}{\sqrt{398}} = 24.51$, or (22.49, 24.51)

Thus, we are 90 percent certain that the average mpg for all cars is between 22.85 and 24.14; we are 95 percent certain that it is between 22.73 and 24.27, and we are 99 percent certain it is between 22.49 and 24.51.

Usually you only need to compute one of these intervals, depending on your preferred level of certainty. There is a price to pay, though: the more certain you want to be, the bigger your interval will turn out. Eventually, a 100 percent confidence interval would be $(-\infty, +\infty)$: you are clearly 100 percent certain that the unknown population mean is in that interval (after all, any number is) but that answer, while correct, does not help at all.

Small Sample Size

As we mentioned, the derivation of the formulas for confidence intervals uses the Central Limit Theorem, which works better for larger values of N (the sample size). For $N > 30$ we declare the sample size big enough but for smaller N we need to be more careful. In this case the method is based on the Student's t-distribution, but is otherwise similar to before. Since all t-distributions have a mean of zero, we cannot generalize our first procedure to find confidence intervals. However, the alternate method works fine.

Confidence Interval for Mean, $N \le 30$ (Alternate Version): Suppose we have selected a random sample with size $N \le 30$ and with sample mean m and sample standard deviation s. Compute the number $t_p =$ $TINV(1 - p, N - 1)$, where $TINV$ is inverse of the t-distribution with degrees of freedom $df = N - 1$ and p is the confidence interval to compute. Then:

- The $p\%$ confidence interval goes from $m - t_b \cdot \dfrac{s}{\sqrt{N}}$ to $m + t_b \cdot \dfrac{s}{\sqrt{N}}$.

This is similar to the alternate method for large N, but the multiplier t_p depends not only on which percentage interval we want to find but also on the sample size N. It turns out, however, that the multiplier t_p is always greater than the corresponding multiplier z_p for large N (e.g., $z_p = 1.96$ for a 95 percent confidence interval) so that a confidence interval using the small sample size procedure is always *bigger* than the one using the large sample size procedure.

Example: Suppose you want to measure the efficacy of a new blood pressure drug. Since trials involving human beings are expensive, you test the new drug on only 10 randomly selected patients. You find that the average decrease of blood pressure in the group tested was 15 mmHg with a standard deviation of 2 mmHg. Since we are dealing with medication given to humans, we want to be very sure about my results, so we want to know a 99 percent confidence interval.

The sample size is $N = 10$, which is considered small, so that the "small size" procedure applies. We need to find $t_{0.99}$ using $N - 1 = 9$ as degrees of freedom: $t_{0.99} = TINV(0.01,9) = 3.2498$. Thus, our 99 percent confidence interval goes from $m - t_p \dfrac{s}{\sqrt{N}} = 15 - 3.2498 \cdot \dfrac{2.1}{\sqrt{10}} = 12.84$ to $m + t_p \dfrac{s}{\sqrt{N}} = 15 + 3.2498 \cdot \dfrac{2.1}{\sqrt{10}} = 17.16$, or in interval notation (12.84, 17.16).

Using Excel to Compute Confidence Intervals

We have used Excel to find various confidence intervals using the mean m and standard deviation s of a data set. This works fine even if we do not have access to the entire data, as long as we know N, m, and s. If we do know the complete data set, Excel offers yet another method to compute confidence intervals and a host of other parameters all at once and for several variables simultaneously.

Example: Consider the following data set for approximately 400 cars that we analyzed before. Find 95 percent confidence intervals for the average miles per gallon, engine size, and weight of cars using this data.

 www.betterbusinessdecisions.org/data/cars.xls

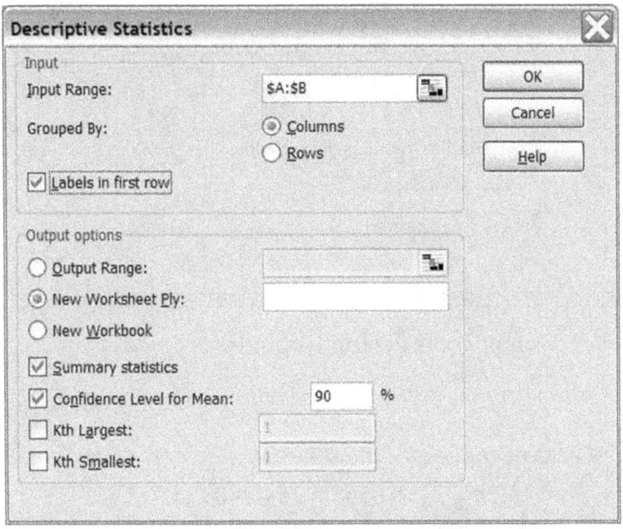

Figure 5.3 Descriptive statistics procedure options

We will use the "Descriptive Statistics" tool of Excel's Analysis Tool-Pak. Load the data set specified, then choose "Data Analysis ..." from the "Data" ribbon, and select "Descriptive Statistics" from the choice of available procedures (see Figure 5.3).

Select as input range the first few columns, including "Miles per Gallon," "Engine Size," "Horse Powers," and "Weight in Pounds" and make sure to check the "Labels in First Row" box, the "Summary Statistics" box, and the "Confidence Level for Mean," as shown in Figure 5.3. We also need to specify the level of confidence for the "Confidence Level for Mean"—enter 90 percent and then click "Okay."

You should see a number of parameters for our data set, including the familiar mean, median, variance, and standard deviation as well as our new descriptors *standard error* and *confidence level (90 percent)*—see Figure 5.4. To find the actual confidence intervals in the form we are used to, we need to add/subtract the *Confidence Level* to/from the *Mean*. In our case we have:

- 90 percent confidence interval of *average miles per gallon*:
  - from 23.4957 − 0.6468 = 22.8489 to 23.4957 + 0.6468 = 24.1425

Miles Per Gallon		Engine Size (cube in)		Weight in pounds	
Mean	23.49571788	Mean	192.8576826	Mean	2960.97985
Standard Error	0.3923287	Standard Error	5.250663581	Standard Error	42.6904038
Median	23	Median	146	Median	2800
Mode	13	Mode	97	Mode	2130
Std. Deviation	7.816778561	Std. Deviation	104.6187307	Std. Deviation	850.600269
Variance	61.10202707	Variance	10945.07881	Variance	723520.818
Kurtosis	-0.503100544	Kurtosis	-0.731931558	Kurtosis	-0.7222187
Skewness	0.463130954	Skewness	0.713505114	Skewness	0.490132
Range	37.6	Range	451	Range	4408
Minimum	9	Minimum	4	Minimum	732
Maximum	46.6	Maximum	455	Maximum	5140
Sum	9327.8	Sum	76564.5	Sum	1175509
Count	397	Count	397	Count	397
Confidence Level (90%)	0.646810388	Confidence Level (90%)	8.656824709	Confidence Level (90%)	70.3841213

Figure 5.4 Output of the descriptive statistics procedure

- 90 percent confidence interval of *average engine size*:
  - from 192.8577 − 8.6568 = 184.2008 to 192.8577 +
    8.6568 = 201.5145073
- 90 percent confidence interval of *average weight (in pounds)*
  - from 2960.9799 − 70.3841 = 2890.5957 to 2960.9798 +
    70.3842 = 3031.3640

Comparing Confidence Intervals

To finish up our discussion of estimating the mean we want to investigate the relation between the various intervals we could compute.

Example: Suppose we compute, for the same sample data, both a 90 percent and a 99 percent confidence interval. Which one is larger?

To answer this question, let us first look at an example: we compute both a 90 percent and a 99 percent confidence interval for the "Horse Power" in the preceding data set about cars, using Excel. The procedure of computing the numbers is similar to the one earlier; here are the answers:

- The sample mean for the "Horse Power" is 104.27.
- The 90 percent confidence level results in 3.19, so that the 90 percent confidence interval goes from 104.27 − 3.19 to 104.27 + 3.19, or from 101.08 to 107.46.
- The 99 percent confidence level results in 5.01, so that the 99 percent confidence interval goes from 104.27 − 5.01 to 104.27 + 5.01, or from 99.26 to 109.28.

Since the 99 percent interval (99.26, 109.28) includes the 90 percent interval (101.08, 107.46), we conjecture that in general a 99 percent confidence interval is always larger than a 90 percent confidence interval (see Figure 5.5).

That makes sense: If we want to be more certain that we have captured the true (unknown) population mean correctly, we need to make our interval larger; the larger the interval, the better our chance of capturing the unknown population mean. Hence, a 99 percent confidence interval must be wider than a 90 percent confidence interval.

Another way to argue is that every 99 percent interval is automatically also a 90 percent interval, because if we are 99 percent certain to include the mean, we are in particular 90 percent certain to include it. The other way around is not true. Thus, the 99 percent interval must contain the 90 percent interval and must therefore be wider.

Last, we want to compare the two methods for computing confidence intervals: the one based on a normal distribution (for $N > 30$) and the other one based on the t-distribution (for $N \leq 30$). First, we will consider an example.

Example: A crime scene investigator finds an unknown liquid at a crime scene. To help identify it, she decides to determine its boiling point. Heating up the entire liquid would destroy the evidence, so instead she takes nine small samples and determines their boiling points. It turns out that the sample mean is 86.5°C with a sample standard deviation of 0.6°C. Find a 95 percent confidence interval for the boiling point of the substance, using the small and the large sample size method (even though only one of the methods is appropriate, technically speaking).

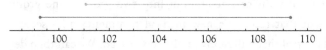

Figure 5.5 90 percent (top) versus 99 percent (bottom) confidence interval

| 86.0 | 86.2 | 86.4 | 86.6 | 86.8 | 87.0 |

Figure 5.6 Small sample size (bottom) versus large sample size (top) confidence interval

Small sample method: We need to find the multiplier $t_{0.95}$ = $TINV(0.05,8) = 2.3060$ and the standard error $\dfrac{s}{\sqrt{N}} = \dfrac{0.6}{\sqrt{9}} = 0.2$. Then the 95 percent confidence interval goes from $86.5 - 2.306 \cdot 0.2 = 86.0388$ to $86.5 + 2.306 \cdot 0.2 = 86.9612$ (see Figure 5.6).

Large sample method: The multiplier for a 95 percent confidence interval is always 1.96 while the standard error is the same as before. Thus, the interval goes from $86.5 - 1.96 \cdot 0.2 = 86.108$ to $86.5 - 1.96 \cdot 0.2 = 86.892$ (see Figure 5.6).

Our conjecture is, therefore, that the small sample size method yields a wider interval than the large sample size method. This is indeed true because the t-distribution has "thicker" tails than the standard normal distribution; hence the cut-off value x_0 where $P(|x| > x_0) = 0.05$ will be larger for the t-distribution than for the standard normal one.

Therefore using the t-distribution will yield a more conservative, that is, wider, confidence interval for any sample size; we could do away with the large sample size procedure entirely and not be wrong. However, doing so might make our interval unnecessarily wide and our estimate for the population mean would not be as sharp as it could be.

Confidence Intervals for Difference of Means

Now we will discuss confidence intervals for the difference of two means. This procedure applies if we have two samples whose means we want to compare. There are many situations where this is useful; perhaps the most important one relates to medical trials, where people are frequently divided at random into two groups: one group called treatment that receives a new medical treatment and a second group called control that will receive a placebo instead. We can then determine the efficacy of the treatment by comparing the means of treatment and control.

We distinguish between two cases, that of equal variance and of unequal variances of the two populations.

Equal Variances

Suppose we have two populations with (unknown) means μ_1 and μ_2 and standard deviations σ_1 and σ_2, respectively. Moreover, assume that the two variances are equal, approximately. If we select independent samples of sizes n_1 and n_2, respectively, from these populations, then the distribution of the difference of the sample means $\bar{x}_2 - \bar{x}_1$ has *joint mean*

$$\mu = \mu_2 - \mu_1 \text{ and } \textit{pooled standard deviation } S_p = \sqrt{\frac{(n_1 - 1)s_1^2 + (n_2 - 1)s_2^2}{n_1 + n_2 - 2}}$$

as well as *joint standard error* $SE = S_p \sqrt{\dfrac{1}{n_1} + \dfrac{1}{n_2}}$. The confidence interval

for $\mu_2 - \mu_1$ goes from $(\bar{x}_2 - \bar{x}_1) - t_p \cdot SE$ to $(\bar{x}_2 - \bar{x}_1) + t_p \cdot SE$, where SE is the joint standard error, and the multiplier $t_p = TINV(1 - p, df)$, $TINV$ is the inverse of the t-distribution with degrees of freedom $df = n_1 + n_2 - 2$ and p is the confidence interval to compute.

These formulas apply if the variances are approximately equal. How can you tell? As a guideline, compute the ratio of the sample variances $s_1^2 \big/ s_2^2$. If that ratio is between 0.5 and 2.0, we will assume that the population variances are approximately the same and the formulas listed earlier apply. In fact, there are quite a number of formulas here, but as the next example shows, if you compute them one at a time, things are not as bad as they look.

Example: We want to determine if there is a difference in the spending habits between men and women at soccer games. A randomly selected sample of 45 men spent an average of $21 with a standard deviation of $4. A randomly selected sample of 57 women, on the other hand, spent an average of $19 with a standard deviation of $3. Find a 95 percent confidence interval for the difference of means and interpret the answer.

First we check the ratio of the sample variances to test the assumption of equal variances:

$$s_1^2 \Big/ s_2^2 = \frac{4^2}{3^2} = \frac{16}{9} = 1.778 \, .$$

The ratio is less than 2, so that according to our guidelines our formulas apply. Next, we compute the pooled standard deviation S_p:

$$S_p = \sqrt{\frac{(n_1 - 1)s_1^2 + (n_2 - 1)s_2^2}{n_1 + n_2 - 2}} = \sqrt{\frac{(45 - 1)4^2 + (57 - 1)3^2}{45 + 57 - 2}}$$

$$= \sqrt{\frac{(44 \cdot 16 + 56 \cdot 9)}{100}} = \sqrt{\frac{1208}{100}} = 3.476 \, .$$

Note that S_p is between the two original variances. Next, we go for the joint standard error SE:

$$SE = S_p \sqrt{\frac{1}{n_1} + \frac{1}{n_2}} = 3.476 \sqrt{\frac{1}{45} + \frac{1}{57}} = 3.476 \cdot 0.1994 = 0.6931 \, .$$

Finally we need to find the multiplier $t_p = TINV(1 - p, df)$, where $df = n_1 + n_2 - 2 = 100$:

$$t_p = TINV(0.05, 100) = 1.9840 \, .$$

But now we have all ingredients in place to compute the given confidence interval. It goes from $(19 - 21) - 1.984 \cdot 0.6931 = -3.3751$ to $(19 - 21) + 1.984 \cdot 0.6931 = -0.62489$.

Thus, our 95 percent confidence interval for the difference of means is $(-3.3751, -0.62489)$. In particular, we can say with 95 percent certainty that the difference of population means $\mu_2 - \mu_1$ is negative, which implies that $\mu_2 < \mu_1$. In other words, we are 95 percent sure that women spend less money, on average, than men at soccer games. This seems obvious, considering the sample means for men and women, but just because one sample mean is less than another does not imply that the first *population* mean is necessarily less than the other *population* mean. The point of the preceding example is that in this case we *can* infer from the sample about the population, and we can even specify the degree of certainty.

Note that $t_p = 1.9840$ is close to 1.96, the multiplier we used for large sample size confidence interval for a single mean. This makes sense, since for large sample sizes the *t*-distribution is close to the normal distribution. However, for simplicity we will stick to using the *t*-distribution for difference of means regardless of the sample sizes.

Unequal Variances

The procedure in the case of unequal variances is similar except that the formula to compute the degrees of freedom for the *t*-distribution is different (and much more complicated).

If the variances for the two populations are different, the confidence interval for $\mu_2 - \mu_1$ as before goes from $(\bar{x}_2 - \bar{x}_1) - t_p \cdot SE$ to

$$(\bar{x}_2 - \bar{x}_1) + t_p \cdot SE \quad \text{where} \quad SE = \sqrt{\frac{s_1^2}{n_1} + \frac{s_2^2}{n_2}} \quad \text{and} \quad t_p = TINV(1 - p, df),$$

where *TINV* is the inverse of the *t*-distribution with degrees of freedom

$$df = \frac{\left(\frac{s_1^2}{n_1} + \frac{s_2^2}{n_2}\right)^2}{\frac{\left(\frac{s_1^2}{n_1}\right)^2}{n_1 - 1} + \frac{\left(\frac{s_2^2}{n_2}\right)^2}{n_2 - 1}} \quad \text{(use the nearest integer) and } p \text{ is the confidence interval to}$$

compute.

This procedure is similar to the one before but the degree of freedom for the *t*-distribution is a lot more complicated.

Example: A female student did poorly in a class and suspects the teacher is biased against women. She complains to the department chair who investigates the situation. The chair selects a random sample of 21 women and 9 men who have previously taken a class with the teacher. It turns out that the average grade for the men is 3.4 with standard deviation 0.9 and for the women it is 2.9 with a standard deviation of 1.5. What can you conclude?

First, we need to decide on a confidence interval. We choose a 90 percent confidence interval (which means that we are somewhat favorably disposed toward the student). Next, we check the ratio of the two standard deviations to determine which of our procedures applies:

$$\frac{s_1^2}{s_2^2} = \frac{0.9^2}{1.5^2} = \frac{0.81}{2.25} = 0.36.$$

Since that ratio is not between 0.5 and 2, we need to assume unequal variances. We compute the standard error SE:

$$SE = \sqrt{\frac{s_1^2}{n_1} + \frac{s_2^2}{n_2}} = \sqrt{\frac{0.9^2}{9} + \frac{1.5^2}{21}} = \sqrt{0.09 + 0.1071} = 0.4440.$$

The multiplier $t_{0.90} = TINV(0.1, df)$, but the degree of freedom is hard to compute:

$$df = \frac{\left(\frac{s_1^2}{n_1} + \frac{s_2^2}{n_2}\right)^2}{\frac{\left(\frac{s_1^2}{n_1}\right)^2}{n_1 - 1} + \frac{\left(\frac{s_2^2}{n_2}\right)^2}{n_2 - 1}} = \frac{\left(\frac{0.9^2}{9} + \frac{1.5^2}{21}\right)^2}{\frac{\left(\frac{0.9^2}{9}\right)^2}{9 - 1} + \frac{\left(\frac{1.5^2}{21}\right)^2}{21 - 1}} = \frac{0.1971^2}{\frac{0.0081}{8} + \frac{0.0115^2}{20}} = \frac{0.0387}{0.00159} = 24.4$$

The next closest integer to that value is 24, so we know that $df = 24$. Thus

$$t_{0.1} = TINV(0.1, 124) = 1.7109.$$

Now we have all the ingredients so that the 90 percent confidence interval goes from

$$(3.4 - 2.9) - 0.4440 \cdot 1.7109 = -0.2596 \text{ to}$$
$$(3.4 - 2.9) + 0.4440 \cdot 1.6572 = 1.2596.$$

This means, in particular, that our 90 percent confidence interval includes 0, and if the difference of means was indeed 0, there would be no difference in the scores of men and women. Thus, it is perfectly possible, based on our calculations, that on average the instructor in question shows no bias toward men or women. Therefore, the department chair will dismiss the accusation. Note that this does not mean that there *truly* is no bias; it is just that based on the available data we cannot conclude that there is.

The question of whether there is or is not a difference in the average score is actually better suited for a "test of hypothesis," which we will tackle in the next chapter. But first we want to apply the concept of estimation to proportion.

Note that another difference of means situation applies in the case of *paired differences*. This situation arises if we take two measurements from each member of a population. For example, we might be interested in figuring out whether consumption of wine or beer has a different impact on a person's concentration. We could divide our participants at random into two groups, give wine to one and beer to the other, and measure the level of concentration for each group. This would be a difference of means situation, just as we covered already. Alternatively, I could give everyone in my population wine, measure their level of concentration, then (after waiting an appropriate time) give everyone beer, and again measure their concentration. This is advantageous, for example, if the total available sample size is small. We will not develop this situation here but refer the reader, for example, to www.real-statistics.com/students-t-distribution/paired-sample-t-test/ for a nice discussion of this situation.

Estimating Proportions

As we mentioned in the previous chapter, many variables are categorical not numerical, so that the idea of estimating the mean does not even apply (since there *is no* mean). In special cases, however, we can resort to the idea of proportions and we could try to estimate them. This section will explain how that works.

Example: The General Social Science survey from 2008 includes data provided by a random sample of adults in the United States. You will find, among many other variables, answers to the question: Did humans develop from animals? Based on that sample data, provide an estimate of how many people in the entire United States think that way.

 www.betterbusinessdecisions.org/data/gss2008-short-2.xls

Looking at the file we find the data for that question in column AH. The data is categorical, so the first thing we need to do is count all the "true" and all "false" values. As we learned in Chapter 2, Excel's Pivot tool will do that for us. Here are the steps, in case you forgot:

1. Click on the "Insert" ribbon and select the "Pivot" menu choice.
2. Make sure the entire table is selected; then click "OK."
3. Drag the field "SCI: HUMANS DEVELOPED FROM ANIMALS" onto the *Row Fields*; then drag the same field also onto the *Value Fields*.

This should finish the pivot table (see Figure 5.7) and show that 651 out of 1,316 answered "false" while 665 out of 1,316 answered "true."

Incidentally, the total number of people participating in this survey was 2,023 but only 1,316 answered this particular question. Thus, as far as analyzing this question is concerned, the sample size is $n = 1,316$. To phrase this as a proportion problem, we need to define success (and failure): We call it a *success* if someone believes that humans developed from animals, since then the probability of success p is exactly what we want to know. What we do know is the ratio of success for our sample, which is $\hat{p} = \dfrac{665}{1316} = 0.5052$. To finish the problem, we need to know the standard error SE and the multiplier m, as is usual for all confidence intervals.

Definition: Suppose x is a binomial random variable with probability of success p. If we take a random sample of size n, we can compute the sample proportion of success $\hat{p}$ as $\hat{p} = \dfrac{x}{n}$, where x counts the number of successes. Then the standard error SE of the sample is $SE = \sqrt{\dfrac{\hat{p} \cdot (1 - \hat{p})}{n}}$ and we can compute a confidence interval for p from $\hat{p} - Z_p \cdot SE$ to $\hat{p} + Z_p \cdot SE$ where $z_p = 1.645$ for a 90 percent confidence interval, $z_p = 1.96$ for a 95 percent confidence interval, and $z_p = 2.54$ for a 99 percent confidence interval. This procedure is valid as long as there are at least 10 successes and 10 failures.

```
Count of SCI: HUMANS DEVELOPED FROM ANIMALS
SCI: HUMANS DEVELOPED FROM ANIMALS          ▼ Total
FALSE                                           651
TRUE                                            665
(blank)
Grand Total                                    1316
```

Figure 5.7 Counts for the question: did humans develop from animals?

Now we can complete our example. Note that there were over 600 successes and failures so that the assumptions of our procedure are satisfied. We know that $\hat{p} = \dfrac{665}{1316} = 0.5052$ so that the standard error is

$SE = \sqrt{\dfrac{\hat{p}\,(1 - \hat{p})}{n}} = \sqrt{\dfrac{0.5052 \cdot 0.4948}{131}} = 0.0138$. Finally, suppose we want to compute a 95 percent confidence interval. It goes from $\hat{p} - 1.96\ SE = 0.5052 - 1.96 \cdot 0.0138 = 0.47815$ to $\hat{p} + 1.96\ SE = 0.5052 + 1.96 \cdot 0.0138 = 0.53225$.

Summary

Instead of providing a *point estimate* for an unknown population parameter we provide an interval instead, called *confidence interval*. The interval is based on a *random sample of size n*. Three particular confidence intervals are most common: a 90 percent, a 95 percent, or a 99 percent confidence interval (other intervals are possible). Each interval has the form:

$$\text{from } P - m \cdot SE \text{ to } P + m \cdot SE, \text{ or } P \pm m \cdot SE,$$

where P is a point estimator for the parameter being estimated, SE is the standard error, and m is a multiplier based on the standard normal or the t-distribution. The quantity $m \cdot SE$ is known as the *margin of error*.

- **Population mean μ, large sample:** point estimator $P = \bar{x}$,

  standard error $SE = \dfrac{s}{\sqrt{n}}$, multiplier $m = 1.645, 1.96$, or 2.54

- **Population mean μ, small sample:** point estimator $P = \bar{x}$, standard error $SE = \dfrac{s}{\sqrt{n}}$, multiplier $m = TINV(0.05, df)$, $TINV(0.025, df)$, or $TINV(0.005, df)$ with $df = n - 1$
- **Difference of means $\mu_2 - \mu_1$, equal variances**

(if $0.5 < \dfrac{s_1^2}{s_2^2} < 2$): point estimator $P = \bar{x}_2 - \bar{x}_1$, pooled

standard deviation $S_p = \sqrt{\dfrac{(n_1 - 1)s_1^2 + (n_2 - 1)s_2^2}{n_1 + n_2 - 2}}$, standard

error $SE = S_p\sqrt{\dfrac{1}{n_1} + \dfrac{1}{n_2}}$, multiplier $m = TINV(0.05, df)$,

$TINV(0.025, df)$, or $TINV(0.005, df)$ with $df = n_1 + n_2 - 2$
- **Difference of means $\mu_2 - \mu_1$, unequal variances** (if

$\dfrac{s_1^2}{s_2^2} \leq 0.5$ or $2 \leq \dfrac{s_1^2}{s_2^2}$): point estimator $P = \bar{x}_2 - \bar{x}_1$, stan-

dard error $SE = \sqrt{\dfrac{s_1^2}{n_1} + \dfrac{s_2^2}{n_2}}$, multiplier $m = TINV(0.05,$

$df)$, $TINV(0.025, df)$, or $TINV(0.005, df)$ with

$$df = \dfrac{\left(\dfrac{s_1^2}{n_1} + \dfrac{s_2^2}{n_2}\right)^2}{\dfrac{\left(\dfrac{s_1^2}{n_1}\right)^2}{n_1 - 1} + \dfrac{\left(\dfrac{s_2^2}{n_2}\right)^2}{n_2 - 1}} \quad \text{(use the closest integer)}$$

- **Probability of success:** point estimator $\hat{p} = \dfrac{x}{n}$, standard error

$SE = \sqrt{\dfrac{\hat{p}(1 - \hat{p})}{n}}$, multiplier $m = 1.645, 1.96,$ or 2.54

The preceding multipliers refer, in that order, to a 90 percent, 95 percent, and 99 percent interval. The certainty of the estimate is denoted by its confidence level.

Excel Demonstration

Company P wants to estimate the mean sales volume for all employees within the company. The sales director selects a sample of employees and calculates the average sales. The director now wants to be able to construct a confidence interval for the average of sales for the entire population of sales representatives in the company. The director decides that a 95 percent confidence level is sufficient and pulls the average sales from a sample of 14 representatives:

Rep 1: 24,000	Rep 2: 22,000	Rep 3: 23,000
Rep 4: 21,000	Rep 5: 22,000	Rep 6: 22,000
Rep 7: 18,000	Rep 8: 19,000	Rep 9: 21,000
Rep 10: 21,000	Rep 11: 18,000	Rep 12: 19,000
Rep 13: 21,000	Rep 14: 17,000	

Step 1: Insert the data into Excel with the labels in column A and the numbers in column B.

Step 2: Run the descriptive statistics: Go to "Data | Data Analysis | Descriptive Statistics." For the "Input Range," select Cells B1 through B14. Check the "Summary Statistics" and the "Confidence

Figure 5.8 Parameters for the descriptive statistics procedure

Level for Mean" boxes and type in 95 percent into the "Confidence Level" field. Compare your input with Figure 5.8; then click OK.

After you click OK, the descriptive statistics are provided, which are as follows:

Column1	
Mean	20,571.42857
Standard Error	551.8628365
Median	21,000
Mode	21,000
Standard Deviation	2,064.881659
Sample Variance	4,263,736.264
Kurtosis	−0.82560218
Skewness	−0.240896459
Range	7,000
Minimum	17,000
Maximum	24,000
Sum	288,000
Count	14
Confidence Level (95.0%)	1,192.227175

Step 3: Construct the upper and lower limits of the confidence interval. Recall that the "confidence level" is the product of the appropriate multiplier and the standard error.

- **Lower Limit**: Mean (20,571.42) − Confidence Level (1,192.22) = 19,379.20
- **Upper Limit**: Mean (20,571.42) + Confidence Level (1,192.22) = 21,763.64

You could write the 95 percent confidence interval as: $19,379.20 $\leq \mu \leq$ $21,763.64. In other words, you can be 95 percent confident that the average sales per representative is somewhere between $19,379.20 and $21,763.64.

CHAPTER 6

Hypothesis Testing

Preview: *It is one thing to develop a hypothesis but quite another to actually prove it beyond a reasonable doubt. Your intuition may lead you to believe that men and women who are obese are more likely to die early than those who are of normal weight. While that conclusion may seem logical, you cannot simply assume that it is true. In order to prove or disprove the hypothesis, you must first develop a series of experiments to determine the truth or falsehood of your assumption. You might look at the distributions of weight across a given population and compare that information to mortality statistics. In the case of early mortality and excess weight, the purpose of the study is to find out whether obese individuals do in fact have shorter life spans than their thinner counterparts. When developing a statistical test, we introduce a null hypothesis, which refers to the status quo, and a competing alternative hypothesis. We then gather data that in turn will support either the null or the alternative hypothesis. If we find sufficient evidence to support the alternative, we reject the null hypothesis. In the case outlined earlier, the null hypothesis would mean there is no difference in longevity between obese individuals and nonobese ones, whereas the alternative one is that nonobese people would live longer. We will develop statistical tests for a mean, a difference of means test, and a test for a proportion.*

Learning Objectives: At the conclusion of this chapter, you should be able to:

1. Describe the basic principles of hypothesis testing
2. Use hypothesis testing to test for a mean, a difference of means, and a proportion
3. Evaluate the assumptions of each hypothesis-testing procedure
4. Avoid the pitfalls involved in hypothesis testing
5. Describe the ethical issues involved in hypothesis testing

Introduction

In the previous chapter we investigated how to provide estimates for population parameters based on sample data, complete with error estimation. Now we want to handle "Yes or No" questions such as "Is the average weight of a bag of chips really 450 gr?" or "Is new medication X better than medication Y?"; of course we want to include an error estimate with our answer. The technical term for what we will describe in this chapter is "hypothesis testing."

Innocent Until Proven Guilty: Hypothesis Testing as a Trial by Jury

Consider the following case: A company is labeling their product to weigh, on average, 10 oz. However, the last time we bought that product it only weighed 8.5 oz, so either we were unlucky to get one of the rare but possible cases where the weight differs a lot from the listed mean or the manufacturer is cheating and puts less product in the package than they are claiming on the label. We suspect that the company is indeed cheating and want to determine whether our suspicion is true or not.

If the company was correct in saying that their packages weigh 10 oz on average, it does not mean that each and every package weighs exactly 10 oz. However, it is likely that most packages weigh *close* to 10 oz and only a few weigh a lot less or more. Conversely, if I found a package that weighs a lot more or a lot less than 10 oz, then it seems likely that the company's claim may be wrong. In fact, the chances that the original claim is incorrect are higher the more the weights of our sample differ from 10 oz.

As another example, we suppose a new medical drug claims to work better in lowering a person's cholesterol level than currently existing drugs. From past experiments we know that the existing drugs lower cholesterol levels by 10 percent, on average. We want to determine whether the new drug is really more effective than the existing ones.

To check the assumption that the new drug works better than old drugs, we could test it on a sample of, say, 100 patients. If we find that the drug for these 100 patients lowers the cholesterol level by more than

10 percent it seems likely that it indeed works better than the other drugs. In fact, the higher the difference to 10 percent, the more likely it seems that the drug is really better. The question is: What exactly do we mean when we say that the difference should be higher than 10 percent. Is 11 percent already good enough? Or should we require a difference of 20 percent before conceding that the new drug is better than the old ones.

In general, we are interested in testing a particular hypothesis and we want to decide whether it is true or not. Moreover, we want to associate a probability with our decision so that we know how certain (or uncertain) we are about our decision.

We will approach this problem like a trial. Recall that in a standard trial in front of a judge or jury there are two mutually exclusive hypotheses: The defendant is either guilty or not guilty.

During the trial evidence is collected and weighed either in favor of the defendant being guilty or in favor of the defendant being not guilty. At the end of the trial the judge (or jury) decides between the two alternatives and either convicts the defendant (if he/she was assumed to be proven guilty beyond a reasonable doubt) or lets them go (if there was sufficient doubt in the defendant's guilt). Note that if the judge (or jury) decides a defendant is not guilty, it does not necessarily mean he/she is innocent. It simply means there was not enough evidence for a conviction. Now we will formalize this procedure.

Definition: A statistical test involves four elements.

- **Null Hypothesis** (written as H_0): The "tried and true situation," "the status quo," or "innocent until proven guilty."
- **Alternative Hypothesis** (written as H_a): This is what you *suspect* is *really* true, the new situation, "guilty beyond a reasonable doubt"—in general, it is the opposite of the null hypothesis.
- **Test Statistics**: Collect evidence—in our case we usually select a random sample and compute some number based on that sample data.

- **Rejection Region**: Do we reject the null hypothesis (and therefore accept the alternative, which was the opposite of null hypothesis) or do we declare our test inconclusive? Moreover, if we do decide to reject the null hypothesis, what is the probability that our decision is correct?

Please note that our final conclusion is *always one of two options*: We either *reject* the null hypothesis or we declare the test *inconclusive*. We never conclude anything else, such as accepting the null hypothesis.

- Rejecting the null hypothesis when in fact it is true is called *type-1 error*. It should, of course, be small so that we can be confident in our decision to reject the null hypothesis.
- Accepting the null hypothesis when in fact it is false is called a *type-2 error*. This type of error is not covered by our procedure since we will never accept the null hypothesis; we instead declare our test inconclusive if necessary.

Most importantly, your conclusion should always be stated in terms that are easy to understand for anyone, even if they had no statistical training, and it is preferable using the terms of the original hypothesis

Example: A new antihypertensive drug is tested. It is supposed to lower blood pressure more than other drugs. Other drugs have been found to lower the pressure by 10 mmHg on average, but we suspect (or hope) that our new drug will work better. To collect evidence, we select a random sample of size $n = 62$ (say), administer the new drug, and find a sample mean of 11.3 and a sample standard deviation of 5.1. Is the new drug better than the old drugs, that is, does the new drug lower blood pressure more than other drugs?

Since the sample mean is 11.3, which is more than other drugs, it looks like this sample mean supports the claim (because the mean from our sample is indeed bigger than 10). But the question is whether that difference is so big that it could not have happened by chance if the null hypothesis was true. In other words, we want to know if the difference is *statistically significant.* To find out, we set up the four components of a statistical test.

- The null hypothesis H_0 is the "tried and true" assumption that all drugs are about the same and the new drug has about the same effect as all other drugs. Thus, the null hypothesis is that the average decrease in blood pressure (the population mean) is 10 mmHg, just as for all other drugs. Thus H_0: $\mu = 10$.
- The alternative hypothesis H_a is what we hope to be true, that is, the new drug results in a higher decrease than the traditional dugs. Thus, the alternative hypothesis is that the average decrease in blood pressure (the population mean) is different from 10 mmHg. Hence H_a: $\mu \neq 10$.
- For our test statistics we collect evidence in the form of a random sample. We found that for this random sample the sample mean is 11.3 mmHg, the sample standard deviation is 5.1 mmHg, and the sample size N is 62. These figures convert into a standard z-score of $z = 2.007$ (as we will soon see).
- Rejection region: Finally we use the test statistics $z = 2.007$ to compute the probability p that this could happen due to chance if the null hypothesis was true. This p is the probability of committing an error in deciding to reject the null hypothesis when in fact it was true (the type-1 error). If that error is small, we do indeed decide to reject the null hypothesis; otherwise we will declare the test to be inconclusive. It turns out that $p = 0.044$ or 4.4 percent (see the following text for the computation).

So, if we decide to reject the null hypothesis, this decision is invalid with a probability of about 4 percent. That is an acceptable risk for us, so we indeed decide to *reject the null hypothesis* and thus accept the alternative. This means, in terms of our original problem, that there is sufficient evidence to conclude that the new drug is better than the existing drugs in lowering blood pressure. In fact, our alternative hypothesis is that the new drug is different from the old drugs, but since the sample mean is indeed bigger, the difference must be that the new drug works better.

Testing Hypothesis for Mean

In this section we will answer the question: Is the population mean μ equal to a particular number or not? We will follow the outline of a statistical test as described in the previous section, but adjust the four elements of the test to our situation of testing for a population mean. It turns out that such a test is slightly different depending on the sample size n.

Large Sample Size (n > 30)

Our first test is a test for a sample mean when the sample size is relatively large:

- Null hypothesis: H_0: $\mu = \mu_0$ where μ_0 is a fixed number
- Alternative hypothesis: H_a: $\mu \neq \mu_0$

- Test statistics: $z_0 = \dfrac{\bar{x} - \mu_0}{\left(s/\sqrt{n}\right)}$

- Rejection region: $p = 2P(z > |Z_0|) = 2(1 - NORMDIST$ $(ABS(z_0), 0, 1, true))$. If p is small, reject the null hypothesis; otherwise the test is inconclusive.

In other words, we compute the z-score to help us decide between null and alternative hypotheses. This makes sense, since we know that sample means are normal by the Central Limit Theorem if the sample size is large. Thus, assuming the null hypothesis is true, the distribution of sample means itself has mean μ_0 with standard deviation $s/\sqrt{n}$. Therefore, the difference between the actually measured sample mean $\bar{x}$ and the assumed population mean μ_0 being large would be unlikely, so that if that difference *was indeed large* the null hypothesis could not be true and we are inclined to reject it. Converting to z-scores enables us to compute the actual probability p that the sample mean could be as far away from μ_0 as has been measured, assuming the null hypothesis was true.

In most cases you pick a predetermined number a, called the *level of significance*, *before* you start any calculations, that specifies the maximum error you are willing to accept. Then you conduct the test as described and reject the null hypothesis if $p < a$; if not, the test was inconclusive. Typically, $a = 0.1$, $a = 0.05$, or $a = 0.01$ (compare this to a 90 percent, 95 percent, or 99 percent confidence interval, respectively).

Let us review the previous example, now that we have introduced the appropriate formulas.

Example: A new antihypertensive drug is tested. It is supposed to lower blood pressure more than other drugs. Other drugs have been found to lower the pressure by 10 mmHg on average, so we suspect (or hope) that our drug will lower blood pressure by more than 10 mmHg. To collect evidence, a random sample of size $n = 62$ was selected (say), which was found to have a sample mean of 11.3 and a sample standard deviation of 5.1. Conduct a test at the $a = 0.05$ level of significance.

The two competing hypotheses are:

$$H_0 : \mu = 10.0$$

$$H_a : \mu \neq 10.0.$$

The test statistics is:

$$z_0 = \frac{x - \mu_0}{\left(s / \sqrt{n}\right)} = \frac{11.3 - 10.0}{5.1 / \sqrt{62}} = \frac{1.3}{0.6477} = 2.007.$$

The rejection region is:

$$p = 2P(z > |z_0|) = 2(1 - NORMDIST(ABS(2.007), 0, 1, true)) = 2 * 0.022 = 0.044.$$

Since $0.044 = p < a = 0.05$, we reject the null hypothesis and accept the alternative. Thus, the new drug is more effective than the old one with an error of 4.4 percent.

Comments

- The null hypothesis for this test is that the population mean is equal to a particular number. That number is usually thought of as the "default value," the "status quo," or the "best guess" value. It is usually mentioned explicitly somewhere in the problem.
- The alternative hypothesis could actually be split into two cases: a so-called two-tailed test where $\mu \neq \mu_0$ or a one-tailed test where either $\mu > \mu_0$ or $\mu < \mu_0$. However, for simplicity we will restrict ourselves to the more conservative two-tailed case here while discussing one-tailed tests in a later section.
- Please note that even if we reject a null hypothesis and hence accept the alternative it is still possible that the null hypothesis is true. However, the probability with which that can happen is p, which is small if we choose this answer (smaller than our predetermined comfort level a). This error of rejecting the null hypothesis even though it is true is called a *type-1 error*.
- In our statistical language there are two outcomes for a test: reject H_0 or inconclusive test. For real problems, however, you should always phrase your conclusion in terms that are relevant for the particular problem and easy to understand even if you knew nothing about statistics.

After all this talk it is high time for another example.

Example: Bottles of ketchup are filled automatically by a machine that must be adjusted periodically to increase or decrease the average content per bottle. Each bottle is supposed to contain 18 oz. It is important to detect an average content significantly above or below 18 oz so that the machine can be adjusted; too much ketchup per bottle would be unprofitable, while too little would be a poor business practice and open the company up to law suits about invalid labeling. We select a random sample of 32 bottles filled by the machine and compute their average weight to be 18.24 with a standard deviation of 0.7334. Should we adjust the machine? Use a comfort level of 5 percent.

We can see right away that the average weight of our sample, being 18.24 oz, is indeed different from what it is supposed to be (18 oz), but the question is whether the difference is statistically significant (or "large enough" so that it would be unlikely if the null hypothesis was true). Our statistical test for the mean will provide the answer. The two competing hypotheses are:

$$H_0: \mu = 18.0$$

$$H_a: \mu \neq 18.0.$$

The test statistics is:

$$z_0 = \frac{\bar{x} - \mu_0}{\left(s/\sqrt{n}\right)} = \frac{18.24 - 18.0}{0.7334/\sqrt{32}} = \frac{0.24}{0.1296} = 1.852.$$

The rejection region is defined via:

$$p = 2P(z > |z_0|) = 2\left(1 - NORMDIST(1.852, 0, 1, true)\right) = 0.064.$$

This time we have $0.064 = p > \alpha = 0.05$ so that our test is *inconclusive*. For our example, this means that we do not know conclusively if the machine works correctly or not. In particular, we would not adjust the machine at this time.

Example: In a nutrition study, 48 calves were fed "factor X" exclusively for six weeks. The weight gain was recorded for each calf, yielding a sample mean of 22.4 lb and a standard deviation of 11.5 lb. Other nutritional supplements are known to cause an average weight gain of about 20 lb in six weeks. Can we conclude from this evidence that, in general, a six-week diet of "factor X" will yield an average weight gain of 20 lb or more at the 1 percent level of significance? In other words, is "factor X" feed significantly better than standard supplements?

Null hypothesis: $H_0: \mu = 20$, that is, there is no improvement, everything is as it has always been.

Alternative hypothesis: H_a: $\mu \neq 20$ (we actually want to know whether "factor X" results in *higher* average weight gains, so that our alternative hypothesis really should be H_a: $\mu > 20$ but that would be a one-tailed test, which we will not conduct.

Test statistics: Sample mean is 22.4, standard deviation is 11.5, and sample size is 48. That makes the z-score $z_0 = \dfrac{22.4 - 20.0}{11.5 / \sqrt{48}} = 1.446$.

We finally use Excel to compute $p = 2 * (1 - NORMSDIST(1.446)) = 0.148$ or 14.8 percent. This probability is relatively large: If we reject the null hypothesis, the probability that we make a mistake is 14.8 percent. This is larger than our comfort level of 1 percent, so our conclusion is: The test is inconclusive, which means there is not enough evidence to decide whether "factor X" feed is better (or worse) than the regular feed.

Example: A group of secondary education student teachers were given 2.5 days of training in interpersonal communication group work. The effect of such a training session on the dogmatic nature of the student teachers was measured as the difference of scores on the "Rokeach dogmatism test" given before and after the training session. The difference "post minus pre score" was recorded as follows:

$$-16, -5, 4, 19, -40, -16, -29, 15, -2, 0, 5, -23, -3,$$
$$16, -8, 9, -14, -33, -64, -33.$$

Can we conclude from this evidence that the training session makes student teachers less dogmatic (at the 5 percent level of significance)?

We can easily compute (using Excel) that the sample mean is -10.9 and the standard deviation is 21.33. The sample size is $N = 20$, which is a problem, since N should be at least 30 to use the procedure introduced earlier. So, we need to define the procedure to test for a sample mean if the sample size is small before we can continue.

Small Sample Size (n ≤ 30)

In this section we will adjust our statistical test for the population mean to apply to small sample situations. Fortunately (sic!), this will be easy—in fact, once you understand one statistical test, additional tests are easy since they all follow a similar framework.

The only difference in performing a "small sample" statistical test for the mean as opposed to our "large sample" test is that we do not use the normal distribution as prescribed by the Central Limit theorem, but instead the more conservative t-distribution introduced earlier.

Fix an error level you are comfortable with (as usual, something like 10 percent, 5 percent, or 1 percent is most common) and denote that "comfortable" error level by α (our *level of significance*). Then set up the test as follows:

- Null hypothesis: $H_0: \mu = \mu_0$, where μ_0 is a fixed number
- Alternative hypothesis: $H_a: \mu \neq \mu_0$

- Test statistics: $t_0 = \dfrac{\bar{x} - \mu_0}{\left(s/\sqrt{n}\right)}$

- Rejection region: $p = 2P(t > |t_0|) = TDIST(ABS(t_0), df, 2)$,
  where $df = n - 1$. If $p < \alpha$, reject the null hypothesis; otherwise the test is inconclusive.

Note that the null and alternative hypothesis for this test are the same as before; the calculation of the test statistics is the same as well, but the result is called t_0 instead of z_0. The final probability p, however, is computed using the t-distribution. To see how this works, let us reconsider our last example.

Example: A group of secondary education student teachers were given 2.5 days of training in interpersonal communication group work. The effect of such a training session on the dogmatic nature of the student teachers was measured as the difference of scores on the "Rokeach dogmatism test" given before and after the training session. The difference "post minus pre score" was recorded as follows:

$$-16, -5, 4, 19, -40, -16, -29, 15, -2, 0, 5, -23, -3, 16,$$
$$-8, 9, -14, -33, -64, -33.$$

Can we conclude from this evidence that the training session makes student teachers less dogmatic at the 5 percent level of significance?

We have already computed the mean $\bar{x} = -10.9$ and the standard deviation $s = 21.33$. The sample size is $N = 20$, so our test goes as follows:

- Null hypothesis: $H_0: \mu = 0$
- Alternative hypothesis: $H_a: \mu \neq 0$
- Test statistics:

$$t_0 = \frac{\bar{x} - \mu_0}{\left(s/\sqrt{n}\right)} = \frac{-10.9 - 0}{21.33/\sqrt{20}} = \frac{10.9\sqrt{10}}{21.33} = -2.285$$

- Rejection region: $p = 2P(t > 2.285) = TDIST(2.285, 20 - 1, 2)$
  $= 0.034$. Since $0.034 = p < a = 0.05$, we reject the null hypothesis and conclude that the training indeed had an impact.

To be picky, we do not want to know whether the training had an impact ($\mu \neq 0$) but we really want to know if the training made the student teachers *less* dogmatic ($\mu < 0$). Technically this amounts to a one-tailed test, which we will cover a little later in this chapter. Here is one more example.

Examples: Suppose GAP, the clothing store, wants to introduce their line of clothing for women to another country. But their clothing sizes are based on the assumption that the average size of a woman is 162 cm. To determine whether they can simply ship the clothes to the new country they select five women at random in the target country and determine their heights as follows:

149, 165, 150, 158, 153.

Should they adjust their line of clothing or they ship them without change? Make sure to decide at the 0.05 level.

By now statistical testing is second nature:

- Null hypothesis: $H_0: \mu = 162$
- Alternative hypothesis: $H_a: \mu \neq 162$

- Test statistics: $t_0 = \dfrac{\bar{x} - \mu_0}{\left(s/\sqrt{n}\right)} = \dfrac{155 - 162}{6.59/\sqrt{3}} = -2.37$

- Rejection region: $p = 2P(t > 2.37) = TDIST(2.37, 5 - 1, 2) = 0.077$. Since $0.077 = p > a = 0.05$, the test is inconclusive.

Note that our test is inconclusive, which does not mean that we accept the null hypothesis. Thus, we do not recommend *anything* to GAP. Using common sense, however, we could suggest that GAP conduct a new study but this time with a random sample of (much) larger size, something like 100 or more. Hopefully the new study will provide statistically significant evidence.

Difference of Means Test

Our next test applies to differences of means. Such tests are common when you conduct a study involving two groups. In many medical trials, for example, subjects are randomly divided into two groups: One group receives a new drug and the second receives a placebo (sugar pill). Then a researcher measures any differences between the two groups to check the efficacy of the new medication.

While our test for a single mean used the sample size to distinguish between two slightly different procedures, a test for the difference of two means uses the variances of the two underlying populations to distinguish between two different procedures. We use the ratio of sample variances s_1^2 / s_2^2 to decide which case to use:

If the ratio of sample variances s_1^2 / s_2^2 is between 0.5 and 2 we assume that the population variances are approximately equal and use the procedure for equal variances, otherwise that for unequal variances.

Equal Variances

Suppose that two independent samples with sizes n_1 and n_2, are selected from two populations that have approximately the same population variances.

Compute the *pooled standard deviation* $S_p = \sqrt{\dfrac{(n_1 - 1)s_1^2 + (n_2 - 1)s_2^2}{n_1 + n_2 - 2}}$ as

well as *joint standard error* $SE = S_p \sqrt{\dfrac{1}{n_1} + \dfrac{1}{n_2}}$. Then a two-sample test

about the difference of means goes as follows:

- Null hypothesis: H_0: $\mu_1 - \mu_2 = c$, where c is some constant
- Alternative hypothesis: H_a: $\mu_1 - \mu_2 \neq c$

- Test statistics: $t_0 = \dfrac{\bar{x}_1 - \bar{x}_2 - c}{SE}$, where SE is the joint standard error (see earlier)
- Rejection region: $p = 2P(t > |t_0|) = TDIST(ABS(t_0), df, 2)$ with $df = n_1 + n_2 - 2$. If p is small, reject the null hypothesis; otherwise the test is inconclusive.

As in previous test, "p is small" means that $p < a$ for some fixed number a, typically 0.1, 0.05, or 0.01.

Example: Two procedures to determine the amylase in human body fluids were studied. The "original" method is considered to be an acceptable standard method, while the "new" method uses a smaller volume of water, making it more convenient as well as more economical. Proponents of the new method claim that the amylase values obtained by the new method yields better results, on average, than the original method. A test using the original method was conducted on 14 subjects and the test with the new method on 15 subjects, giving the data displayed in Table 6.1. Test the claim at the 1 percent level.

Table 6.1 Data for amylase analysis example

Original	38	48	58	53	75	58	59	46	69	59	81	44	56	50	
New	46	57	73	60	86	67	65	58	85	74	96	55	71	63	74

Using Excel we find the means and standard deviations of the two variables as:

$$n_1 = 14 \, , \ \bar{x}_1 = 56.714 \text{ and } s_1 = 11.932$$

$$n_2 = 15 \, , \ \bar{x}_2 = 68.667 \text{ and } s_2 = 13.281.$$

Note that $\dfrac{s_1^2}{s_2^2} = \dfrac{11.932^2}{13.281^2} = 0.8$, which is between 0.5 and 2 so that we can indeed use the procedure for equal variances. The test for the difference of means therefore is:

- Null hypothesis: $\mu_1 - \mu_2 = 0$
- Alternative hypothesis: $\mu_1 - \mu_2 \neq 0$
  - Pooled standard deviation:

$$S_p = \sqrt{\frac{(n_1 - 1)s_1^2 + (n_2 - 1)s_2^2}{n_1 + n_2 - 2}} = \sqrt{\frac{13 \cdot 11.932^2 + 14 \cdot 13.281^2}{14 + 15 - 2}} = 12.649$$

  - Joint standard error:

$$SE = S_p \sqrt{\frac{1}{n_1} + \frac{1}{n_2}} = 12.649 \cdot 0.3716 = 4.7005$$

- Test statistic: $t_0 = \dfrac{56.714 - 68.667}{4.7005} = \dfrac{-11.952}{4.7005} = -2.5427$
- Rejection region:
  $p = 2P(t > |t_0|) = TDIST(2.5427, 27, 2) = 0.017$. Since p is (just barely) larger than 0.01, our test is inconclusive at the 1 percent level.

This means that there is not enough evidence to conclude that the two methods of checking amylase are different. In particular, neither method can be called better than the other. Now it is tempting to change the value of a to 0.05, because at that level the test *would* be conclusive. But that is *not* correct. The value of a should be chosen carefully prior to starting your experiment. Presumably whatever reason made you decide on a 1 percent value has not changed. Adjusting a after the fact amounts to fixing the data to support whatever conclusion you want to come out.

Unequal Variances

Suppose we have two independent samples with sizes n_1 and n_2, selected from populations with *unequal variances*. Compute the *joint standard error* $SE = \sqrt{\dfrac{s_1^2}{n_1} + \dfrac{s_2^2}{n_2}}$. Then a two-sample test about the difference of means goes as follows:

- Null hypothesis: H_0: $\mu_1 - \mu_2 = c$, where c is some constant
- Alternative hypothesis: H_a: $\mu_1 - \mu_2 \neq c$

- Test statistics: $t_0 = \dfrac{\bar{x}_1 - \bar{x}_2 - c}{SE}$, where SE is the standard error defined earlier
- Rejection region: $p = 2P(t > |t_0|) = TDIST(ABS(t_0), df, 2)$

  with degree of freedom $df = \dfrac{\left(\dfrac{s_1^2}{n_1} + \dfrac{s_2^2}{n_2}\right)^2}{\dfrac{\left(\dfrac{s_1^2}{n_1}\right)^2}{n_1 - 1} + \dfrac{\left(\dfrac{s_2^2}{n_2}\right)^2}{n_2 - 1}}$ (use the nearest integer). If p is small, reject the null hypothesis; otherwise the test is inconclusive

As usual, "p is small" means that $p < a$ for some fixed number a, typically 0.1, 0.05, or 0.01.

Example: The data file employeenumeric-split.xls contains the salaries for the Acme Widget Company, separated by sex. Use that data to test the hypothesis that women make at least $10,000 less on average than men at that company.

 www.betterbusinessdecisions.org/data/employeenumeric-split.xls

Since we have the raw data we could use the appropriate test procedure from the Analysis ToolPak (which you should try as practice—see the following text), but we will first use the manual procedure outlined

earlier. First, we need to find the mean and standard deviations for the two samples of our data.

	Mean (\$)	Standard deviation (\$)	N
Males	41,442	19,499.21	258
Females	26,032	7,558.02	216

Next, we need to decide if the variances are equal or not by checking the ratio of the sample variances:

$$\frac{s_1^2}{s_2^2} = \frac{19,499.21^2}{7,558.02^2} = 6.65.$$

This ratio is greater than 1, so we need to use the "unequal variance" procedure. Now we can proceed with our two-sample test as usual:

- Null hypothesis: $H_0: \mu_1 - \mu_2 \neq \$10,000$
- Alternative hypothesis: $H_a: \mu_1 - \mu_2 \neq \$10,000$
  - Joint standard error:

$$SE = \sqrt{\frac{s_1^2}{n_1} + \frac{s_2^2}{n_2}} = \sqrt{\frac{19499.21^2}{258} + \frac{7558.02^2}{216}} = 1318.4$$

  - Degree of freedom: $df = \dfrac{\left(\dfrac{s_1^2}{n_1} + \dfrac{s_2^2}{n_2}\right)^2}{\dfrac{\left(\dfrac{s_1^2}{n_1}\right)^2}{n_1 - 1} + \dfrac{\left(\dfrac{s_2^2}{n_2}\right)^2}{n_2 - 1}} = 344.26$ (closest integer) so that $df = 344$

  Test statistics: $t_0 = \dfrac{(41442 - 26032) - 10000}{1318.4} = 4.103$

- Rejection region: $p = 2P(t > 4.103) = TDIST(4.103, 344, 2) = 0.00005$. Since $p < 0.01$, we reject the null hypothesis and accept the alternative.

Thus, the difference in average salary between men and women at the Acme Widget Company is at least \$10,000 and we are very sure that this

t-test: Two-Sample assuming Equal Variances		
	Original	New
Mean	56.71429	68.66667
Variance	142.3736	176.381
Observations	14	15
Pooled Variance	160.0071	
Hypothesized Mean Difference	0	
Degrees of Freedom df	27	
t-Statistic	-2.5427	
P(T<=t) one-tail	0.008522	
t Critical one-tail	1.703288	
P(T<=t) two-tail	0.017045	
t Critical two-tail	2.051831	

t-test: Two-Sample assuming Unequal Variances		
	Male	Female
Mean	41441.78	26031.92
Variance	3.8E+08	57123688
Observations	258	216
Hypothesized Mean Difference	10000	
Degrees of Freedom df	344	
t-Statistic	4.103352	
P(T<=t) one-tail	2.54E-05	
t Critical one-tail	1.649295	
P(T<=t) two-tail	5.09E-05	
t Critical two-tail	1.966884	

Figure 6.1 Output of Analysis ToolPak two-sample t-test with equal variance (amylase example, left) and with unequal variances (salary example, right)

answer is correct (since $p = 0.00005$). Note that our test actually confirms that the difference is *not equal to* $10,000, but looking at the actual values of the means as computed by Excel we can clearly conclude that the difference must be more than $10,000 (it is certainly not less). In fact, a one-tailed test would be more appropriate here (see the "One-Tailed and Two-Tailed Tests" section), which would show indeed that men make at least $10,000 more than women.

Excel actually provides several procedures in the Analysis ToolPak to help conduct this test, including the "t-test assuming unequal variances" and the "t-test assuming equal variances." We leave the details to you, but the output Excel produces for the last two examples is shown in Figure 6.1.

Testing Hypothesis for Proportion

Finally, let us introduce one more test, namely, testing for a proportion. This will be useful because it works on non-numerical variables whereas our previous tests required numerical ones. Recall that a proportion p is the number of successes divided by the total number of tries in a Bernoulli trial that has only two outcomes called success or failure. Our goal is to decide what the (unknown) probability of success might be, or—to phrase it in terms appropriate for a test—whether the probability of success equals a specific value or not. The test has the form:

- Null hypothesis H_0: $\pi = p_0$
- Alternative hypothesis: H_a: $\pi \neq p_0$
- Test statistics: $z_0 = \dfrac{\hat{p} - p_0}{SE}$, where $SE = \sqrt{\dfrac{p_0 \cdot (1 - p_0)}{n}}$
- Rejection region: $p = 2(1 - NORMDIST(ABS(z_0),0,1,true))$; reject the null hypothesis if $p < \alpha$

Here $\hat{p} = \dfrac{x}{n}$ is the ratio of the number of successes divided by the total number of trials. This procedure is valid as long as there are at least 10 successes and 10 failures in our sample. Note that we use the standard normal distribution to compute the p-value. This is only an approximation, actually, and we could compute p exactly. However, the added accuracy is negligible, so we will not bother.

> **Example:** Providing municipal services costs money; in order to cover the rising costs, a municipality could raise taxes or cut services. The town conducts a survey, asking 200 randomly selected people if taxes should go up; it turns out that 108 vote to increase taxes and 92 vote no. If you were hired by the town as statistical consultant, how would you advise the town?

Of course at first glance it looks like the town should increase taxes, since 108 out of 200, or 54 percent, voted yes. But that is only 54 percent of the sample asked whereas we need to infer the proportion of the *entire town* from that. In fact, we need to figure out whether the population proportion is 50 percent or not, based on the sample. So, we set up our hypothesis as follows:

Null hypothesis H_0: $\pi = 0.5$
Alternative hypothesis H_a: $\pi \neq 0.5$.

If our test lets us reject the null hypothesis we would accept the alternative where $\pi \neq 0.5$. But our sample ratio of 0.54 would then imply that $\pi > 0.5$ so that we could conclude that the majority of *all* people in the town want to see taxes raised. The other outcome would be that the test is inconclusive so that we would not recommend any course of action to the town.

Once set up, the calculations are straightforward. First, let us fix our level of significance $a = 0.05$. Then:

- $\hat{p} = \dfrac{108}{200} = 0.54$ and

$$SE = \sqrt{\dfrac{p_0 \cdot (1 - p_0)}{n}} = \sqrt{\dfrac{0.5 \cdot (1 - 0.5)}{200}} = 0.0354$$

- Test statistics $z_0 = \dfrac{\hat{p} - p_0}{SE} = \dfrac{0.54 - 0.5}{0.0354} = 1.13$

- Rejection region $p = 2(1 - NORMDIST(1.13,0,1,true)) = 0.2585$

Since $0.2585 = p > a = 0.05$, our test is inconclusive. Thus, 108 out of a sample of 200 is not enough "yes" votes to convince us that the majority of the entire town is for raising taxes. Of course the town could decide to raise taxes after all, but if they claimed that based on this survey the majority of people were for raising taxes, their margin of error would be 25 percent, which should be way too high to feel comfortable about.

The preceding example is interesting because at first it seems unclear what the null hypothesis should be. Other examples are more straightforward.

Example: The General Social Science Survey from 2008 includes data provided by a random sample of adults in the United States. You will find, among many other variables, answers to the question "Did the universe begin with a huge explosion?" Based on that sample data, does the majority of people in the United States believe that this is false? Use a level of significance $a = 0.01$.

 www.betterbusinessdecisions.org/data/gss2008-short-2.xls

After loading that data file you will find the variable in column AJ. As we learned earlier, a pivot table can be used to find the ratio of true/false answers for this survey. It turns out that 606 out of 1,088 subjects responded negatively, while 482 agreed. The example clearly asked whether $\pi = 0.5$, so setting up this test should be straightforward.

We defined "success" if someone answered "no" to the question of whether the universe began with a huge explosion. Then our test works as follows:

- Null hypothesis H_0: $\pi = 0.5$
- Alternative hypothesis H_a: $\pi \neq 0.5$

   o $SE = \sqrt{\dfrac{0.5 \cdot (1 - 0.5)}{1088}} = 0.0151$

- Test statistics $Z_0 = \dfrac{\dfrac{606}{1033} - 0.5}{0.0151} = 3.7739$

- Rejection region $p = 2(1 - NORMDIST(3.7739, 0, 1, true)) = 0.00016$

Since $0.00016 = p < \alpha = 0.01$, our test is conclusive. Therefore, we reject the null hypothesis and accept the alternative. In words this means that over 50 percent of the U.S. population does *not* believe that the universe started with a huge explosion.

Note: It is generally accepted today that the universe did start with the "Big Bang" (a huge explosion) some 13.798 ± 0.037 billion years ago (according to Wikipedia). Note that the age of the universe is an estimate just like we have learned in Chapter 5 but without mentioning which confidence interval this represents.

One-Tailed and Two-Tailed Tests

All of our tests so far tested whether a parameter was equal to a fixed value or not. In many cases, however, we are interested more specifically if the parameter is bigger than a fixed value, or perhaps smaller, not just unequal.

Example: For each of the following situations, determine the null and alternative hypotheses that best reflect the question:

1. Do bottles of ketchup contain less than the indicated weight of 16 oz?
2. Does the new feed for cows result in higher weight gain than the average of 100 lb per week when using standard feeds?
3. Is the effect of a new hypertension drug different from that of the traditional drug?

1. We want to test for the mean weight of ketchup. Let x be the weight of the contents of a ketchup bottle and μ be the (unknown) population average. Then:

$$H_0: \mu = 16$$
$$H_a: \mu < 16.$$

2. We know that old feed for cows results in a weight gain of 100 lb per week on average. Let x be the weight gain for cows getting the new feed and μ be the population average. Then:

$$H_0: \mu = 100$$
$$H_a: \mu > 100.$$

3. Hypertension drugs are supposed to lower blood pressure. If μ_1 denotes the average blood pressure of patients on the new drug and μ_2 that of patients on the traditional drug, we want to test:

$$H_0: \mu_1 = \mu_2$$
$$H_a: \mu_1 \neq \mu_2.$$

Examples 1 and 2 are called one-tailed tests, whereas Example 3 is a two-tailed test. A two-tailed test at a level of significance a allocates half of that alpha to testing the statistical significance in one direction and half of the alpha to testing statistical significance in the other direction. A one-tailed test, on the other hand, concentrates the entire alpha on one of the tails of the distribution. Thus, a one-tailed test has a slightly different rejection region.

- One-tailed test for the mean (large sample size):

If $H_a: \mu > \mu_0$ then $p = P(z > z_0) = 1 - NORMDIST(z_0,0,1,true)$.
If $H_a: \mu < \mu_0$ then $p = P(z < z_0) = NORMDIST(z_0,0,1,true)$.

- One-tailed test for the mean (small sample size):

If $H_a: \mu > \mu_0$ then $p = P(t > t_0) = TDIST(t_0,df,1)$ if $t_0 > 0$.
If $H_a: \mu < \mu_0$ then $p = P(t < t_0) = TDIST(-t_0,df,1)$ if $t_0 < 0$.

- One-tailed test for the difference of two means—compute df as usual:

If $H_a: \mu_1 - \mu_2 > c$ then $p = P(t > t_0) = TDIST(t_0,df,1)$ if $t_0 > 0$.
If $H_a: \mu_1 - \mu_2 < c$ then $p = P(t < t_0) = TDIST(-t_0,df,1)$ if $t_0 < 0$.

Example: We suspect that bottles of ketchup contain less than the indicated weight of 16 oz. We collect a sample of 100 bottles and find that the sample mean is 15.5 oz with $s = 2.6$ oz. Decide at the $a = 0.05$ level.

This is a one-tailed test; here we go:

$$H_0: \mu = 16.0$$

$$H_a: \mu < 16$$

$$z_0 = \frac{15.5 - 16}{2.6/\sqrt{100}} = \frac{-0.5}{2.6} * 10 = -1.9231$$

$$p = P(z < -1.9231) = NORMDIST(-1.9231,0,1,true) = 0.0272.$$

Thus, since $p = 0.0272 < a = 0.05$, we reject the null hypothesis and thus we think that the bottles indeed contain too little content.

Note: Had we used a two-tailed test we would have found that $p = 2 * 0.0272 = 0.0544 > a = 0.05$, so that a two-tailed test would come out inconclusive. This is no coincidence: A one-tailed test is more powerful than a two-tailed test; it is possible that a two-tailed test is inconclusive but the corresponding one-tailed test results in rejecting the null hypothesis. On the other hand, if a one-tailed test is inconclusive then the corresponding two-tailed test will also be inconclusive. Thus, if we only consider two-tailed tests we might decide that a test is inconclusive when it actually might be significant (as a one-tailed test) but we will never call a test significant when in fact it is not.

Note: If we conduct a one-tailed test $H_a: \mu < \mu_0$ and the sample mean comes out *bigger* than μ_0, then the one-tailed test will always be inconclusive. That makes sense: If we suspect a population mean to be less than, say, 10, but our sample mean comes out bigger than 10, this can never support the alternative hypothesis. Thus, the test is inconclusive. Mathematically we have that if $\bar{x} > 10$ then $z_0 > 0$ so that $p = NORMDIST(z_0,0,1,true) > 0.5$ for $z_0 > 0$. A similar argument applies if we test the alternative hypothesis $H_a: \mu > \mu_0$ and the sample mean $\bar{x} < \mu_0$: this test, too, is inconclusive.

Relationship Between Confidence Intervals and Hypothesis Testing

While confidence intervals and hypothesis testing are used for different purposes, they are related. For example, to decide whether a population mean equals a certain value μ_0 you would naturally conduct a test for a mean. However, you could also compute a confidence interval as long as you interpret the answer properly:

- If a 95 percent confidence interval about the mean *includes* the number μ_0, the test whether the mean equals μ_0 would be inconclusive at the $a = 0.05$ level.
- If a 95 percent confidence interval about the mean *excludes* the number μ_0, we would reject the null hypothesis that $\mu = \mu_0$ and accept the alternative that $\mu \neq \mu_0$ at the $a = 0.05$ level.

Example: To equip soldiers with properly fitting helmets it is important to know the average head size of all soldiers. A study selected 80 soldiers at random and measured their head size. It turns out that the sample has an average head size of 56 cm with a standard deviation of 1.36 cm. Find a 95 percent confidence interval for the population mean and use it to decide if the population mean could be 56.3.

To compute a 95 percent confidence interval (for large N), we need to find $\bar{x} \pm 1.96 \dfrac{s}{\sqrt{n}} = 56 \pm 1.96 \dfrac{1.36}{\sqrt{80}} = 56 \pm 0.298$ so that the 95 percent confidence interval goes from 55.702 to 56.298. This interval does not include the hypothesized mean of 56.3 so that according to our discussion the population mean could not be 56.3 (within our alpha level of 0.05).

Let us conduct a proper test to see if we get the same answer. Our null hypothesis would be $H_0\colon \mu = 56.3$ with the alternative $H_a\colon \mu \neq 56.3$. We compute the z-score $z_0 = \dfrac{56.3 - 56}{1.36/\sqrt{80}} = 1.973$. Finally we compute the value of $p = 2 * (1 - NORMDIST(1.973, 0, 1, true)) = 0.485$. This is smaller than alpha so that we indeed reject the null hypothesis and conclude that the population mean indeed cannot be equal to 56.3.

Note that the hypothesized mean of 56.3 is *barely* outside the 95 percent confidence interval. That corresponds to the p-value being *just* smaller than 0.05. If we checked for a number well outside the 95 percent confidence interval, the corresponding p-value would be much smaller than 0.05.

Summary

Hypothesis testing lets you decide which of two mutually exclusive situations is true and provides an error estimate for your answer. Each test has four components: (1) a null hypothesis H_0, (2) an alternative hypothesis H_a, (3) test statistics, and (4) a rejection region where you compute a probability p and decide to reject H_0 (and accept H_a) if $p < a$; otherwise the test is inconclusive. The number a is called level of significance and is typically 0.1, 0.05, or 0.01. We covered the following tests.

- **Test for a mean:** (1) $H_0\colon \mu = \mu_0$ and (2) $H_a\colon \mu \neq \mu_0$; (3) test statistics $z_0 = \dfrac{\bar{x} - \mu_0}{s/\sqrt{n}}$; and (4) probability $p = 2(1 - NORMDIST(ABS(z_0), 0, 1, true))$ for large samples ($n > 30$) or $p = TDIST(ABS(t_0), N - 1, 2)$ for small samples ($n \leq 30$).

- **Test for a difference of means (equal variances):**

  (1) $H_0: \mu_1 - \mu_2 = c$ and (2) $H_a: \mu_1 - \mu_2 \neq c$; (3) test statistics

  $$t_0 = \frac{(\mu_1 - \mu_2) - c}{SE}, \text{ where } S_p = \sqrt{\frac{(n_1 - 1)s_1^2 + (n_2 - 1)s_2^2}{n_1 + n_2 - 2}} \text{ and}$$

  $$SE = S_p \sqrt{\frac{1}{n_1} + \frac{1}{n_2}}; \text{ and (4) probability } p = TDIST$$

  $(ABS(t_0), n_1 + n_2 - 2, 2)$.

- **Test for a difference of means (unequal variances):**

  (1) $H_0: \mu_1 - \mu_2 = c$ and (2) $H_a: \mu_1 - \mu_2 \neq c$; (3) test statistics

  $$t_0 = \frac{(\mu_1 - \mu_2) - c}{SE}, \text{ where } SE = \sqrt{\frac{s_1^2}{n_1} + \frac{s_2^2}{n_2}}; \text{ and (4) probabil-}$$

  ity $p = TDIST(ABS(t_0), df, 2)$, where $df = \dfrac{\left(\dfrac{s_1^2}{n_1} + \dfrac{s_2^2}{n_2}\right)^2}{\dfrac{\left(\dfrac{s_1^2}{n_1}\right)^2}{n_1 - 1} + \dfrac{\left(\dfrac{s_2^2}{n_2}\right)^2}{n_2 - 1}}$ (use

  the nearest integer).

- **Test for proportion:** (1) $H_0: p = p_0$ and (2) $H_a: p \neq p_0$; (3) test

  statistics $z_0 = \dfrac{\hat{p} - p_0}{SE}$, where $SE = \sqrt{\dfrac{p_0 \cdot (1 - p_0)}{n}}$; and

  (4) $p = 2(1 - NORMDIST(ABS(z_0), 0, 1, true))$.

While the preceding tests list are all *two-tailed* tests, they also come in a *one-tailed* variety, in which case the computation of the p-value is slightly different.

Excel Demonstration

Company P, the large manufacturer of paper products, has the business objective of developing an improved process for fulfilling orders during the 12 p.m. to 1 p.m. lunch period. The management decides to first study the fulfillment and delivery time in the current process in the plant. The fulfillment time is defined as the number of minutes that elapses from when the order enters the plant until the product is packed and ready to ship. The data collected from a random sample are presented from two assembly lines within the company. Assuming that the population variances from both lines are unequal, is there evidence of a difference in the mean fulfillment time between the two lines, using alpha = 0.05?

Step 1: Enter the fulfillment times into Excel in Column A and create a corresponding identifying label in Column B (see Figure 6.2):

Assembly Line 1: 4.22, 5.56, 3.01, 5.14, 4.78, 2.35, 3.53, 3.21, 4.49, 6.11, 0.39, 5.13, 6.47, 6.20, 3.80
Assembly Line 2: 9.77, 5.91, 8.01, 5.78, 8.72, 3.81, 8.02, 8.36, 10.48, 6.69, 5.67, 4.09, 6.18, 9.90, 5.48.

Step 2: Click on "Data," then "Data Analysis," and choose "t-Test: Two-Sample Assuming Unequal Variances."
Note: In this example we were told the variances are unequal, which is why we chose the tool we did. If you are not told, you must first check whether the variances are equal in both groups, which determines the type of t-test to perform (one that assumes equal variances or one that does not make that assumption). A conservative approach is to always assume unequal variances.

Step 3: For "Variable Range 1," enter or select the range of numbers for Assembly Line 1 in column A. For "Variance Range 2," enter or select the range of numbers for Assembly Line 2, column A.

Step 4: Since we did not use labels in the first row, we do not need to check the "Labels" box. The alpha level is set by default to 0.05, which is what we wanted to use. Compare with Figure 6.3; then Click OK.

	A	B	C
1	**Fulfillment Time**		
2	4.22	Assembly Line 1	
3	5.56	Assembly Line 1	
4		•••	
17	9.77	Assembly Line 2	
18	5.91	Assembly Line 2	
19		•••	

Figure 6.2 Fulfillment data in Excel (excerpt)

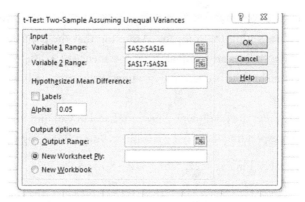

Figure 6.3 The parameters for the "t-Test: Two-Sample Assuming Unequal Variances"

The procedure should produce the following output.

t-Test: Two-Sample Assuming Unequal Variances		
	Variable 1	Variable 2
Mean	4.292666667	7.124666667
Variance	2.688206667	4.356940952
Observations	15	15
Hypothesized Mean Difference	0	
Df	27	
t Stat	−4.132318902	
P(T <= t) one-tail	0.000155796	
t Critical one-tail	1.703288446	
P(T <= t) two-tail	0.000311591	
t Critical two-tail	2.051830516	

This relates to our problem as follows.

- *Null hypothesis*: There is no difference (the two means are equal) in fulfillment time between Assembly Line 1 and Assembly Line 2.
- *Alternative hypothesis*: There is a difference (the two means are not equal) in fulfillment time between Assembly Line 1 and Assembly Line 2.

- *Results*: We have a two-tailed *p*-value of 0.0003. This is less than our alpha value, so we reject the null hypothesis and conclude that there is difference (the two means are not equal) in fulfillment time between Assembly Line 1 and Assembly Line 2.

Even though we used a two-tailed test, that is, we do not care which mean is larger, it is clear that the means are different because Assembly Line 1 has a smaller mean than line 2. Since Company P wishes to reduce fulfillment times within their manufacturing plant, the management should try to identify why there is a difference and consider implementing the work practices of Assembly Line 1 across all assembly lines as best practice.

CHAPTER 7

Association Between Categorical Variables

Preview: *When studying statistics, it can be important to understand the association, if any, between two categorical variables. To investigate this, we create a two-dimensional table where one variable defines the columns and the second the rows. Such tables are called contingency tables. We then compare the actual entries in the table with those entries that would result under the assumption that there was no association between the two variables. Then we check the combined relative difference between the actual and expected values. If this difference is small, we were correct in assuming no relation, but if the difference is large, the variables must be related. We formalize this idea into a statistical test called a chi-square test.*

For example, if there is a positive relationship between holding an MBA degree and earning more money, for example, high school graduates and college students may conclude that a graduate degree is a smart investment.

Learning Objectives: At the conclusion of this chapter, you should be able to:

1. Understand row and column percentage tables and when to use which one
2. Use the chi-square test for contingency tables
3. Understand actual versus expected theory and practice
4. Perform a chi-square test to solve a business problem

Introduction

Up to this point we have analyzed data one variable at a time. We have seen how to compute measures of central tendency, estimated parameters, and tested hypothesis but each concept applied to one variable at a time.

Now we want to investigate two (or more) variables simultaneously to discover any potential relation between them. Usually, a typical question about two variables is:

Is there some relation between one variable and another, and if so, how can one use knowledge about one variable to predict, approximately, the other?

Answers to such questions can be very useful, such as in these examples:

- If smoking causes cancer, we should stop smoking.
- If having an advanced college degree increases the chance to have a well-paying job, we should try our best to graduate college.
- If exercising increases our general state of health, we should exercise regularly.
- If a new drug really does have a positive impact on lowering blood pressure, we should take it if we have high blood pressure.

In most cases it is difficult to determine whether two variables (such as smoking and cancer) are indeed related and even harder to determine whether there is a *causal* relationship between them, that is, which is cause and which is result. (If smokers have higher cancer rates, does smoking cause cancer or does having cancer somehow induce you to smoke?) In general, correlation does not necessarily imply causation.

- The more firemen are fighting a fire, the bigger the fire is observed to be. Therefore, firemen cause an increase in the size of a fire.
- Sleeping with one's shoes on is strongly correlated with waking up with a headache. Therefore, sleeping with one's shoes on causes headaches.

Obviously, both conclusions are wrong. In the first case, the causal relationship goes the other way (a bigger fire requires more firemen), while in the second case there is an "invisible" third condition that causes both events of sleeping with one's shoes on and waking up with a headache.

Two-Dimensional Data Summary

Let us start our investigation about relationships between variables by taking a closer look at representing categorical data in tables.

Example: The residents of Green Township were asked their opinion about a new Zoning Ordinance. The answers were broken down by age of the people who were questioned. The results of the survey are summarized in Table 7.1. Convert these figures into percentages.

Table 7.1 Results of survey about zoning law

	Age 50 or under	Age over 50
For zoning law	92	87
Against zoning law	158	75

This example does not seem clear. To convert a number into percentages, we need to know the total out of which this number represents a percentage. But for the preceding table it is not clear which figure to use as total, so as a first step we expand the table by including all possible row and column totals (see Table 7.2).

Now we can convert any number into three percentage values. For example, there are 92 people aged 50 or under who voted for the zoning law. In terms of percentage, we could say:

- 92 out of a total of 179 (51.4 percent) people for the zoning law are aged 50 or under.

Table 7.2 Expanded survey results about zoning law

	Age 50 or under	Age over 50	Total
For zoning law	92	87	179
Against zoning law	158	75	233
Total	250	162	412

- 92 out of a total of 250 (36.8 percent) people aged 50 or under were for the zoning law.
- 92 out of a total of 412 (22.3 percent) people were aged 50 or younger and for the zoning law.

Thus, there are *three* possible percentage tables we could create from the preceding data (Table 7.3).

- Row percentage table using the row totals (Table 7.3b)
- Column percentage table using the column totals (Table 7.3c)
- Total percentage table using the overall total (Table 7.3d)

Row Versus Column Percentages

The total percentage table turns out to be not useful but row and column percentages are; the question is when to use which. Consider two similar but very much different questions.

- How many people, in percentage, who are for the zoning law are aged 50 or under?
- How many people, in percentage, 50 or under are for the zoning law?

These questions seem similar: We are looking at the intersection between the row "For zoning" and the column "Age 50 or under." From the first table we know that 92 people fall into that category, but that number is not in percentage. On the other hand, there are two candidates for the percentage number, 51.4 percent from the row percentages or 36.8 percent from the column percentages. Which one answers which question?

- Question 1 asks, rephrased: Out of all people who are for the zoning law, how many of them are aged 50 or under? In other words, question 1 considers all people who are for the zoning law as a total—that is a row total, so that the answer to question 1 is the row percentage 51.4 percent.

Table 7.3 (a) Raw data table (b) Row percentage table (c) Column percentage table (d) Total percentage table

(a)

	Age 50 or under	Age over 50	Total
For	92	87	179
Against	158	75	233
Total	250	162	412

(b)

	Age 50 or under (%)	Age over 50 (%)	Total (%)
For	92/179 = 51.4	87/179 = 48.6	100
Against	158/233 = 67.8	75/233 = 32.2	100
Total			

(c)

	Age 50 or under (%)	Age over 50 (%)	Total
For	92/250 = 36.8	87/162 = 53.7	
Against	158/250 = 63.2	75/162 = 46.3	
Total	100	100	

(d)

	Age 50 or under (%)	Age over 50 (%)	Total (%)
For	92/412 = 22.3	87/412 = 21.1	179/412 = 43.3
Against	158/412 = 37.5	75/421 = 18.2	233/412 = 56.7
Total	250/412 = 60.7	162/412 = 39.3	100

- Question 2 asks, rephrased: Out of all people who are 50 or under, how many of them are for the zoning law? In other words, question 2 considers all people who are 50 or under as a total—that is, a column total, so that the answer to question 2 is the column percentage 36.8 percent.

From this example we see that the key to answering questions such as these is which group is considered the "total" group for the particular question.

- If the total for that group is found in a row, use row percentages.
- If the total for that group is found in a column, use column percentages.

It seems that generating these percentage tables is a fair amount of work. Of course Excel provides an easier method for generating such tables from actual data, which we will explore soon.

Contingency Tables

In an earlier chapter we saw how to use Excel's "Pivot" function to compute counts or frequencies, using one (categorical) variable at a time. Now we want to generate tables involving two variables from a particular data set (review the "Bending the Rules: Lying or Exaggeration" section if necessary).

Example: Load the following Excel data file, which lists salary and other information about employees of a particular company. Create and interpret tables relating:

- Gender with Salary Level
- Salary Level with Years of Education
- Salary Level with Job Category

 www.betterbusinessdecisions.org/data/employeeselected.xls

With Excel, the appropriate tool to create such crosstabs tables for categorical variables is the "PivotTable …" in the "Insert" ribbon.

- Load the preceding spreadsheet into Excel.
- Click "Insert" and then "PivotTable …."
- Use the range selector tool to select the entire data set.

You will then see a table where you can drag variables from the PivotTable fields into the "Row," "Column," or "Values" areas. We will not make use of "Filters" (see Figure 7.1).

To analyze the relationship—if any—between "Gender" and "Salary Level," drag the variable "Salary Level" to the "Row" field of the table and the variable "Gender" to the "Column" field (if you accidentally drop a variable in the wrong spot, simply drag it back).

This will create a table with "Salary Levels" as rows and "Gender" as columns, but containing no data yet. Finally, drag either "Gender" or "Salary Level" into the "Data" field in the middle (in our case it does not matter which one but in Figure 7.2 we used "Salary Level") and the table will be complete—but with raw data, not percentages.

This table shows, for example, that 32 female employees out of 474 total employees earn between $10,000 and $20,000, while, for example, 45 male employees earn more than $60,000.

Similarly, we can create tables to relate "Salary Level" with "Years of Education" (see Figure 7.3). We could start again from scratch, but since we already have the Pivot table available, we can simply drag the "Salary Level" and "Gender" variables *out* of the table and drag the "Years of

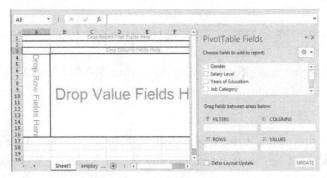

Figure 7.1 Pivot table tool

	A	B	C	D
1		Drop Report Filter Fields Here		
2				
3	Count of Salary Level	Gender		
4	Salary Level	female	male	Grand Total
5	$10K-20K	32	1	33
6	$20K-30K	144	86	230
7	$30K-40K	29	78	107
8	$40K-50K	5	28	33
9	$50K-60K	6	20	26
10	>$60K		45	45
11	Grand Total	216	258	474
12				

Figure 7.2 Results of the Pivot tool, relating income with sex (gender)

	A	B	C	D	E	F	G	H
1			Drop Report Filter Fields Here					
2								
3	Count of Salary Level	Salary Level						
4	Years of Education	$10K-20K	$20K-30K	$30K-40K	$40K-50K	$50K-60K	>$60K	Grand Total
5	8	11	32	10				53
6	12	20	134	32	3	1		190
7	14		3	3				6
8	15	2	55	45	10	3	1	116
9	16		4	16	17	14	8	59
10	17			2	1	2	6	11
11	18				1	2	6	9
12	19			1	1	3	22	27
13	20					1	1	2
14	21						1	1
15	Grand Total	33	230	107	33	26	45	474
16								

Figure 7.3 Years of education versus salary level

Education" and "Salary Level" *into* the respective row, column, and data area to create the table shown in Figure 7.3.

Similarly, we can create the table relating "Salary Level" with "Job Category"; details are left to you. To finish our discussion, we use the preceding tables to answer specific questions.

Example: Using the Excel data as before, answer the following questions in percentage.

1. How many female employees earn less than $40,000? How many males?

2. How many people earning more than $60,000 have 15 years of education or less? How many have more than 15 years of education?

At first glance it might seem that we have already created the right tables to answer these questions (see Figures 7.2 and 7.3). However, this time we want the answers in percentage, while our preceding tables contain actual numbers. And, as we have discussed in the previous section, when we want to generate percentage tables we need to decide whether we want row or column percentages.

To answer question 1, we clearly need to generate a table relating salary with gender. We will use salary as the row variable and gender as the column variable (see Figure 7.2). Question 1 uses as total all female employees, and in our table the "females" go along a column. Therefore, we need to generate column percentages.

- Double-click the "Count of Salary Level" button in your table and click on "Options" in the dialog that pops up (see Figure 7.4). Then select "% of column" in "Show values as."

You should see the final table, containing column percentages, as shown in Figure 7.5. Note that you can see that the table shows column percentages since the percentages across the columns add up to 100 percent.

Now we can answer question 1 easily: "How many female employees earn less than $40,000?" In the female column we need to add the numbers: 14.81% + 66.67% + 13.43% = 94.91%. For the male employees the answer is: 63.95 percent of males earn less than $40,000.

Actually, this seems to indicate that female employees, as a rule, earn less money than male employees. We will learn how to answer questions such as these in the next section.

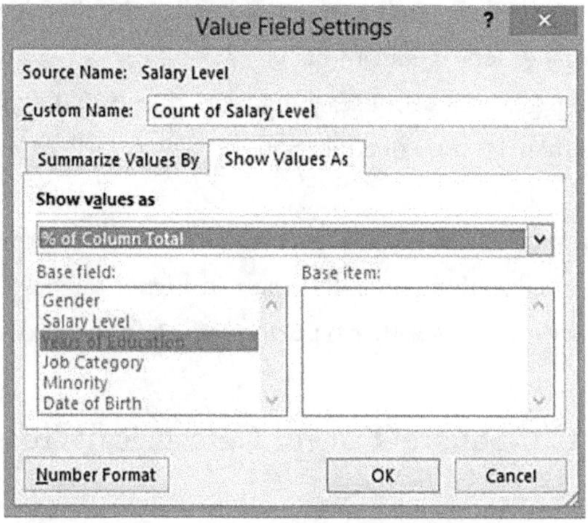

Figure 7.4 Value field settings for Pivot table

	A	B	C	D
1		Drop Report Filter Fields Here		
2				
3	Count of Salary Level	Gender		
4	Salary Level	female	male	Grand Total
5	$10K-20K	14.81%	0.39%	6.96%
6	$20K-30K	66.67%	33.33%	48.52%
7	$30K-40K	13.43%	30.23%	22.57%
8	$40K-50K	2.31%	10.85%	6.96%
9	$50K-60K	2.78%	7.75%	5.49%
10	>$60K	0.00%	17.44%	9.49%
11	Grand Total	100.00%	100.00%	100.00%

Figure 7.5 Salary level versus sex in column percentage

	A	B	C	D	E	F	G	H	I	J	K	L
1					Drop Report Filter Fields Here							
2												
3	Count of Sal	Years										
4	Salary Levi	8	12	14	15	16	17	18	19	20	21	Grand Total
5	$10K-20K	33.33%	60.61%	0.00%	6.06%	0.00%	0.00%	0.00%	0.00%	0.00%	0.00%	100.00%
6	$20K-30K	13.91%	58.26%	1.30%	23.91%	1.74%	0.87%	0.00%	0.00%	0.00%	0.00%	100.00%
7	$30K-40K	9.35%	29.91%	2.80%	42.06%	14.95%	0.00%	0.00%	0.93%	0.00%	0.00%	100.00%
8	$40K-50K	0.00%	9.09%	0.00%	30.30%	51.52%	3.03%	3.03%	3.03%	0.00%	0.00%	100.00%
9	$50K-60K	0.00%	3.85%	0.00%	11.54%	53.85%	7.69%	7.69%	11.54%	3.85%	0.00%	100.00%
10	>$60K	0.00%	0.00%	0.00%	2.22%	17.78%	13.33%	13.33%	48.89%	2.22%	2.22%	100.00%
11	Grand Total	11.18%	40.08%	1.27%	24.47%	12.45%	2.32%	1.90%	5.70%	0.42%	0.21%	100.00%

Figure 7.6 Salary level versus years of education as row percentages

It is left as an exercise to answer question 2: "How many people earning more than $60,000 have 15 years of education or less? How many have more than 15 years of education?" Figure 7.6 shows the particular table we need to figure out the answers.

By the way, is that table using row or column percentages? The correct answers are:

- 2.22 percent of people earning more than $60,000 have 15 years or less of education.
- 97.78 percent of people earning more than $60,000 have more than 15 years of education.

Again, a more interesting question would be to determine whether more years of education generally result in higher salaries (it does look that way)—we will answer that type of question in the next section.

The Chi-Square Test for Categorical Crosstabs

In the previous section we computed crosstabs tables, analyzing two categorical variables simultaneously. A natural question to ask now is:

Is there a statistically significant relationship between two (categorical) variables, or do they appear to be independent?

We should of course define the new types of variables we just introduced.

Definition: Two variables are *related* if changing the value of one will also change the value of the other. The variable that changes as a result of changing the other one is called the *dependent* variable, and the other variable is called *independent.* Note that the independent variable usually occurs first in time.

We will eventually develop a statistical test with null hypothesis and alternative hypothesis, similar to the tests we developed in Chapter 6. But the question is intuitively easy to understand, so we will give a brief discussion on how to answer it without covering all the mathematical details first.

Example: Consider the crosstabs table relating income with sex for a particular company as shown in Figure 7.2. Identify independent and dependent variables.

We do not know yet whether there is a relation between the two variables. But if there was, sex would certainly be the independent variable, while salary would be the dependent one. Thus, if there was a relation, gender would have an impact on the salary a worker makes. It is pretty clear that it cannot be the other way round: A change in salary level will certainly not change your gender. Note that gender is indeed determined prior to salary in time.

Actual Versus Expected—Theory

Let us say we are interested in figuring out whether there is a relation between sex (male/female) and smoking (yes/no), or whether the two variables are independent of each other. We conduct an experiment and ask a randomly selected group of people for their sex and whether they smoke. Then we construct the corresponding crosstabs table. Let us say the response is as shown in Table 7.4 (the actual numbers are fictitious).

Table 7.4 *Fictitious data for smoking versus sex*

	Male	Female	Totals
Smoking	30	5	35
Not smoking	10	55	65
Totals	40	60	100

Of the 35 people who smoke, 30 of them are male. Conversely, of the 65 people who do not smoke, 55 of them are female. Such an outcome—using common sense—would suggest that there is a relation between smoking and sex, because the vast majority of smokers are male, while the majority of nonsmokers are female. On the other hand, we might have obtained results as in Table 7.5 (again with fictitious numbers).

In Table 7.5 the smokers and nonsmokers are divided more evenly among men and woman, suggesting perhaps that the two variables are independent of each other (a person's sex does not seem to have an impact on their smoking habit).

Now let us see exactly how a table should look *if we assume that two variables are indeed independent.* Suppose we are again conducting our experiment and select some random sample, but for now we only look at totals for each variable separately (the actual numbers are once again fictitious). Suppose, for example:

- Number of smokers is 35 and number of nonsmokers is 65.
- Number of males is 40 and number of females is 60.
- Total number of data values (subjects) is 100.

With this information we could construct a crosstabs table as in Table 7.6.

But what kind of distribution in the various cells would we *expect* if the two variables were independent?

- We know that 35 of 100 (35 percent) smoke; there are 40 males and 60 females—if being male and female had nothing to do with smoking (the variables were independent), we would expect that 35 percent of the 40 males and 35 percent of the 60 females smoke.

Table 7.5 Different data for smoking versus sex

	Male	Female	Totals
Smoking	17	18	35
Not smoking	23	42	65
Totals	40	60	100

Table 7.6 Setting up expected values in contingency table

	Male	Female	Totals
Smoking	?	?	35
Not smoking	?	?	65
Totals	40	60	100

Table 7.7 Computing expected values

	Male	Female	Totals
Smoking	35/100 * 40 = 14	35/100 * 60 = 21	35
Not smoking	65/100 * 40 = 26	65/100 * 60 = 39	65
Totals	40	60	100

Table 7.8 How to compute expected values

	X	Y	Totals
A	r_1/total * c_1	r_1/total * c_2	r_1
B	r_2/total * c_1	r_2/total * c_2	r_2
Totals	c_1	c_2	total

- We also know that 65 of 100 (65 percent) do not smoke; there are 40 males and 60 females—if the two variables were independent, we would similarly expect that 65 percent of the 40 males and 65 percent of the 60 females do not smoke.

Under the assumption of independence we would therefore *expect* the numbers shown in Table 7.7.

Note that the cells automatically add up to the correct row and column totals. In other words, if a crosstabs table with two rows and two columns has row totals r_1 and r_2, respectively, and column totals c_1 and c_2, then if the two variables were independent we would expect the complete table to look like Table 7.8.

Now that we know what distribution to *expect* if two variables were independent and we can compare it against the *actual* distribution of numbers: if it is *not* close to the conjectured distribution, then the variables cannot be independent and thus they must be related!

With that in mind we create an effective procedure to test whether two variables are independent. First we define the table of expected values as follows.

Definition: We create a table of *expected values* as follows.

- Create a crosstabs table as usual, containing the actual or observed values (not percentage).
- Create a second crosstabs table where you leave the row and column totals as observed, but replace the count in the i-th row and j-th column by:

  (total of row i) * (total of column j)/(overall total).

Fill in all cells in this way and call the resulting crosstabs table the *expected values table*, because these numbers would be expected in this table cell if the two variables under investigation were independent.

For example, the expected value in the second row B and third column Y of Table 7.9 would be $\dfrac{20 \cdot 15}{60} = 5$.

Now, here is the clue: If the actual values are very different from the expected values, the conclusion is that the variables cannot be independent after all (because if they were independent the actual values should look similar to the expected values). We define the total difference as follows.

Definition: Let v_a be the actual value and v_e the expected value in a cell of a crosstabs table. The *total difference* between the actual and expected values is defined as the sum of $\dfrac{\left(v_a - v_e\right)^2}{v_e}$, where the sum is taken over all cells of the table. This total difference is denoted by x^2 (chi-squared):

$$x^2 = \sum \frac{\left(v_a - v_e\right)^2}{v_e}.$$

Table 7.9 How to compute an expected value

	W	X	Y	Z	*Totals*
A					10
B			$\dfrac{20 \cdot 15}{60} = 5$		20
C					30
Totals	5	10	15	30	60

The only question left to answer is: "Exactly when is this difference too large? That is: At which point can we assume that the difference between expected and actual values is so large that we have to conclude that the variables cannot be independent? Before we answer that question, let us return to our original example.

Actual Versus Expected—Example

Recall our earlier example comparing smoking versus gender. We had two hypothetical tables of actual values. For each table we compute the expected value in each cell and show it in parenthesis. Then we compute the total difference x^2 as defined earlier for both tables.

$$x^2 = \frac{(30-14)^2}{14} + \frac{(5-21)^2}{21} + \frac{(10-26)^2}{26} + \frac{(55-39)^2}{39} = 46.89$$

$$x^2 = \frac{(17-14)^2}{14} + \frac{(18-21)^2}{21} + \frac{(23-26)^2}{26} + \frac{(42-39)^2}{39} = 1.65.$$

For Table 7.10 common sense told us that the two variables were not independent and the chi-square difference turned out to be $x^2 = 46.89$. For Table 7.11 we figured that the two variables could very well be independent and the chi-square difference worked out to $x^2 = 1.65$.

Note: We compute the value of x^2 here (and in some other examples) manually, which can be quite a lot of work. In real life, we will of course use software such as Excel for that; so if you feel that computing x^2 is just too much, do not worry, we will soon show how to use Excel for this.

We developed our algorithm for the expected values using a 2 × 2 table, but that algorithm easily extends to $n \times m$ tables, that is, tables

Table 7.10 Data with large x^2

	Male	Female	Totals
Smoking	30 (14)	5 (21)	35
Not smoking	10 (26)	55 (39)	65
Totals	40	60	100

Table 7.11 Data with small x^2

	Male	Female	Totals
Smoking	17 (14)	18 (21)	35
Not smoking	23 (26)	42 (39)	65
Totals	40	60	100

with n rows and m columns. Suppose, for example, we wanted to determine whether sex (gender) and salary level in the particular company are related to each other. We create a table relating the two variables, such as Table 7.12 of actual values. Note that the table with actual values must contain counts, not percentages.

To compute the table of expected values, each entry is computed as *the product of the row and column total for that cell divided by the overall total* (see Table 7.13).

Note that the row and column totals add up correctly (except for rounding errors). If we compare expected versus actual values in Tables 7.12 and 7.13, we see that of the people making $60K or more, fewer than expected are female (0 versus 20.5) while more than expected are male (45 versus 24.5). On the other hand, in the low-income category of $10 to $20K, more than expected are female (32 versus 15.1) while fewer than expected are male (1 versus 17.9).

This seems to point toward a gender bias for salaries, that is, women make less money than men as a rule, or to phrase it differently: row and column variables do not seem independent of each other. Indeed, if we compute the total difference, we get $x^2 = 131.9$, which is quite large.

However, in a table with many rows and columns the total difference x^2 can get quite large even though each individual difference between the actual and the expected value is small, merely because we are adding up more and more terms. Thus, the big question left is: When is the

Table 7.12 2 × 6 Table of actual values

Salary level ($)	Female	Male	Total
10–20K	32	1	33
20–30K	144	86	230
30–40K	29	78	107
40–50K	5	28	33
50–60K	6	20	26
> 60K		45	45
Total	216	258	474

Table 7.13 2 × 6 table of expected values

Salary level ($)	Female	Male	Total
10–20K	33 * 216/474 = 15.1	33 * 258/474 = 17.9	33
20–30K	104.8	125.2	230
30–40K	48.8	58.2	107
40–50K	15.1	17.9	33
50–60K	11.8	14.2	26
>60K	20.5	24.5	45
Total	216	258	474

difference small enough for us to accept the independence assumption, and when is the difference so large that we can no longer assume independence and must therefore accept dependence? The answer to this question is provided by the chi-square test.

The Chi-Square Test

From Chapter 6 we know that a statistical test has four parts. We will now specify these parts to define a chi-square test of independence.

Definition: A chi-square test of independence consists of the following four parts.

- *Null hypothesis H_0:* the two variables are independent.
- *Alternative hypothesis H_a:* the two variables are dependent.

- *Test statistics*: $x^2 = \sum \dfrac{(v_a - v_e)^2}{v_e}$, where v_a is the actual and v_e the expected value in each cell of a contingency table.
- *Rejection region*: Compute the p value, which depends on the value of the test statistics x^2 and also on the number of rows and columns.

If the probability value p is small, differences between actual and expected values are judged to be significant (large) and therefore you reject the null hypothesis of independence and accept the alternative that the variables are related. If p is large, the test is inconclusive.

Typically, values of $p = 0.05$ or less are considered small enough to reject independence; the closer p is to zero the more convincing the relationship is.

Definition: One important restriction states that the chi-square test is not appropriate if any of the expected values is less than 5. You need to manually inspect all expected values to ensure none of them have a value less than 5. We call this the *rule of thumb* for a chi-square test.

How exactly is the value of p computed? We will not provide the details here but simply use the Excel function $p = chisq.test(actual\_range, expected\_range)$, where *actual_range* is the range for the actual values and *expected_range* is the range for the expected values. Note that we do not need to compute the value of x^2; the $= chisq.test$ function will take care of that.

Example: Use a chi-square test to determine if salary and gender are related.

We have created the tables of actual and expected values; they are shown in Figure 7.7.

We need to check all expected values but none is less than 5. The value of p is computed via Excel with the command =CHISQ.TEST(B2:C7,G2:H7), and turns out to be $p = 9.38713E{-}27$, which is

	A	B	C	D	E	F	G	H	I
1	Salary Level	Female	Male	Total		Salary Level	Female	Male	Total
2	$10K - $20K	32	1	33		$10K - $20K	15.1	17.9	33
3	$20K - $30K	144	86	230		$20K - $30K	104.8	125	230
4	$30K - $40K	29	78	107		$30K - $40K	48.8	58.2	107
5	$40K - $50K	5	28	33		$40K - $50K	15.1	17.9	33
6	$50K - $60K	6	20	26		$50K - $60K	11.8	14.2	26
7	> $60K	0	45	45		> $60K	20.5	24.5	45
8	Total	216	258	474		Total	216	258	474
9									
10	p-value = 9.38713E-27								

Figure 7.7 Actual and expected values in "sex versus income level"

the scientific notation for 0.00000000000000000000000000938713. Thus, p is most definitely small, so we reject the null hypothesis of independence and conclude that there *is* a relation between the two variables sex and salary. In other words, the salary level in this particular company does depend on the sex of the employees.

Example: Using the following data set, is there a relation between salary and years of schooling?

 www.betterbusinessdecisions.org/data/employeeselected.xls

After loading the data and working out the actual values via Excel's Pivot tool, we compute the expected values, which is a lot of work. The two tables are shown in Figures 7.8a and 7.8b.

Finally, we compute the chi-square test value p, again with the help of Excel: $p = 0.00$. Again the value of p is for all intent and purposes 0, so it seems that we can with a high degree of certainty conclude that there is a relation between years of education and the salary level (in other words, based on this data you make more money with more years of education, just like your parents told you).

But we failed to check if the expected values pass our "rule-of-thumb" test! In fact, quite a few of the expected values are small, certainly smaller than 5. Thus, in this case the chi-square test is *not reliable* and we should *not* believe its conclusions since the assumptions of the test were not satisfied! To remedy the problem, you could recategorize the data by using fewer groups so that hopefully the expected values in the new tables will all be above 5.

	A	B	C	D	E	F	G	H
1	Sum of Yea	Salary ▼						
2	Years of ▼	$10K-20K	$20K-30K	$30K-40K	$40K-50K	$50K-60K	>$60K	Grand Total
3	8	88	256	80				424
4	12	240	1608	384	36	12		2280
5	14		42	42				84
6	15	30	825	675	150	45	15	1740
7	16		64	256	272	224	128	944
8	17		34		17	34	102	187
9	18				18	36	108	162
10	19			19	19	57	418	513
11	20					20	20	40
12	21						21	21
13	Grand Tota	358	2829	1456	512	428	812	6395

Figure 7.8 (a) The table of actual values

16	Years of E	$10K-20K	$20K-30K	$30K-40K	$40K-50K	$50K-60K	>$60K		Grand Total
17	8	23.7	187.6	96.5	33.9	28.4	53.8		424
18	12	127.6	1008.6	519.1	182.5	152.6	289.5		2280
19	14	4.7	37.2	19.1	6.7	5.6	10.7		84
20	15	97.4	769.7	396.2	139.3	116.5	220.9		1740
21	16	52.8	417.6	214.9	75.6	63.2	119.9		944
22	17	10.5	82.7	42.6	15.0	12.5	23.7		187
23	18	9.1	71.7	36.9	13.0	10.8	20.6		162
24	19	28.7	226.9	116.8	41.1	34.3	65.1		513
25	20	2.2	17.7	9.1	3.2	2.7	5.1		40
26	21	1.2	9.3	4.8	1.7	1.4	2.7		21
27	Grand Tota	358	2829	1456	512	428	812		6395
28									
29		=CHISQ.TEST(B3:G12,B17:G26)				p=	0.00		

Figure 7.8 (b) The table of expected values

Example: Every year there are large-scale surveys, selecting a representative sample of people in the United States and asking them a broad range of questions. One such survey is the General Social Science (GSS) survey from 1996 (which contains mostly categorical data). Use the data (which is real-life data from 1996) to analyze if there is a relation between party affiliation and people's opinion on capital punishment.

 www.betterbusinessdecisions.org/data/gss96-selected.xls

After downloading and opening the data file, we construct a crosstabs table for "Party Affil" and "Capital Punishment" using the Pivot table. Then we copy the table (of actual values) to a second table and construct the expected values as described earlier (this time the table is pretty small, so computing the expected values is not that much work; see table 7.9).

Finally, we use Excel to compute the value of $p = 0.00000$ (to six digits of accuracy). Before jumping to any conclusion, we check our rule of thumb: This time the smallest expected value is 9.02, which is above 5

Actual Values				Expected Values			
Count of Cap	Capit ▾						
Party Affil ▾	Favor	Oppose	*Total*	Party Affil	Favor	Oppose	*Total*
Democrat	584	289	*873*	Democrat	671.08	201.92	*873*
Independent	740	219	*959*	Independent	737.19	221.81	*959*
Other Party	27	12	*39*	Other Party	29.98	9.02	*39*
Republican	673	89	*762*	Republican	585.75	176.25	*762*
Total	*2024*	*609*	*2633*	*Total*	*2024*	*609*	*2633*

Chi-Square Test results in		p = 0.000000	

Figure 7.9 Actual and expected values of party affiliation by "Capital Punishment"

so that it is valid to apply our chi-square test. Again p is very close to 0, implying that there is a relation between party affiliation and opinion on capital punishment.

In fact, if you compare the actual versus expected values directly for the Democrats you can see that fewer Democrats than expected favor the death penalty, while more than expected oppose it. For Republicans it is just the other way round. For independents and people with other party affiliations there seems to be little difference between actual and observed values.

So far in all our examples the variables were dependent. Of course that is not always the case.

Example: Set up the corresponding tables for actual and expected values for the data from the GSS96 survey relating people's outlook on life (variable "Life is") with their opinion on "Capital Punishment" and complete a chi-square test for independence at the alpha = 0.01 level.

After constructing the tables as required (see Figure 7.10) we see that the computed p value is $p = 0.045$, which is larger than the required alpha level of 0.01. Thus, our test is inconclusive. In particular, we cannot conclude that the variables are dependent. Note that all expected values are bigger than 5, so our chi-square test does apply.

Example: Below is the GSS Survey 2008 data file. This data set is similar to the GSS survey from 1996 but it contains a lot more variables and more recent data. Is there a relation between being born in the United States and gender?

 www.betterbusinessdecisions.org/data/gss2008-short.xls

Actual Values

Count of Life is	Capital Punishment ▾		
Life is ▾	Favor	Oppose	Grand Total
Dull	58	14	72
Exciting	653	213	866
Routine	634	155	789
Grand Total	1345	382	1727

Expected Values

Life is	Favor	Oppose	Grand Total
Dull	56.07411697	15.92588303	72
Exciting	674.447018	191.552982	866
Routine	614.4788651	174.5211349	789
Grand Total	1345	382	1727

Chi-Square test computes p = 0.045364834

Figure 7.10 Actual and expected values for "Life is …" versus opinion on "Death Penalty"

Actual Values

Count of SEX	SEX ▾		
BORN IN THIS COUN ▾	Female	Male	Grand Total
No	149	116	265
Yes	945	813	1758
Grand Total	1094	929	2023

Expected Values

Count of SEX	SEX		
BORN IN THIS COUN	Female	Male	Grand Total
No	143.31	121.69	265
Yes	950.69	807.31	1758
Grand Total	1094	929	2023

chi-square test: p = 0.452

Figure 7.11 Expected versus actual values

By now a question like this is routine. We load the data set, create a Pivot table relating the variables "born in this country" with "sex," compute the expected values, and conduct a chi-square test. The results can be found in Figure 7.11.

As it turns out, $p = 0.452$, which is way bigger than 0.05; so there is no reason to think the variables are not independent. This makes sense since it is difficult to think of a reason why being born in the United States should be related to one's gender.

Excel Demonstration

Using chi-square, we are looking to see if there is a significant difference between what we would expect results to be and what the actual results were. That is, we want to compare the expected versus observed data. We will review how to find the expected values and Microsoft Excel will help us to determine this.

Example: Company S, the accounting and tax strategy service firm, wants to determine if they are more suited to service large clients or smaller clients so that they can focus their efforts on the market segment most compatible with the organization. One variable they are interested in is client satisfaction. It has been thought that since they are a large firm, the larger clients they service are more satisfied with the services than the smaller clients, who may not be getting the individualized attention they expect.

Listed in Table 7.14 are data from a survey conducted recently where large firms and small firms responded to their client satisfaction with Company S (this is fictitious data).

We are interested in finding out if there is a significant difference in how we expected large firms to respond and what large firms actually responded with; we follow the same method for small firms. We will test this using a chi-square test with a cut-off value of $p = 0.05$. In other words, we want to know if there is a relation between the level of satisfaction and the size of the client.

Step 1: In Excel, let us first calculate the row percentage of population responses. We will take the total responses to "Not at all" (40) and divide that by the total responses (118) to determine the percentage of respondents who responded in this category; we will do that for all responses (see Figure 7.12).

We can see that 33.89 percent of all responses were "Not at all," 29.66 percent were "Somewhat," 36.44 percent were "Very" satisfied, and so on.

Table 7.14 Measures of satisfaction for large and small firms

Response	Large	Small	Total
Not at all	18	22	40
Somewhat	17	18	35
Very	26	17	43
Total	61	57	118

	A	B	C	D	E	F
1	Response	Large Firm	Small Firm	Total	Row Percent	
2	Not at all	18	22	40	0.3390	(=D2/D5)
3	Somewhat	17	18	35	0.2966	(=D3/D5)
4	Very	26	17	43	0.3644	(=D4/D5)
5	Total	61	57	118		

Figure 7.12 Satisfaction data augmented by row percentages

	A	B	C	D	E	F
1	Response	Large Firm	Small Firm	Total	Row Percent	
2	Not at all	18	22	40	0.3390	(=D2/D5)
3	Somewhat	17	18	35	0.2966	(=D3/D5)
4	Very	26	17	43	0.3644	(=D4/D5)
5	Total	61	57	118		
6						
7	EXPECTED					
8		20.68 (=B5*E2)	19.32 (=C5*E2)			
9		18.09 (=B5*E3)	16.91 (=C5*E3)			
10		22.23 (=B5*E4)	20.77 (=C5*E4)			

Figure 7.13 Actual and expected values

	A	B	C	D	E	F
1	Response	Large Firm	Small Firm	Total	Row Percent	
2	Not at all	18	22	40	0.3390	(=D2/D5)
3	Somewhat	17	18	35	0.2966	(=D3/D5)
4	Very	26	17	43	0.3644	(=D4/D5)
5	Total	61	57	118		
6						
7	EXPECTED					
8		20.68	19.32		=chisq.test(B2:C4,B8:C10)	
9		18.09	16.91			
10		22.23	20.77			

Figure 7.14 Computing the p value using chisq.test

Step 2: Since 33.89 percent of all respondents said "Not at all," we expect to see 33.89 percent of the 61 large firms to say "Not at all," as well as 33.89 percent of the 57 small firms, and so forth for the remaining groups, assuming the row and column variables are independent. Thus, we create a new table with expected values by multiplying the column totals by the row percentages in each row. We put the results below the table of actual values to create the table of expected values, as shown in Figure 7.13.

Step 3: Figure 7.13 shows what all of our "expected" results should have been if the variables were independent, and we can compare that with our actual results by computing x^2. Of course we will not do this manually but instead use Excel's CHI SQUARE TEST to compute our p-value, as shown in Figure 7.14.

We get a p-value of 0.3363505. This is much larger than our level of significance of 0.05, so we fail to reject the null hypothesis of independence and conclude that there is no significant evidence to prove that large firm and small firm actual results are different from the expected results of large firms and small firms in the population. In other words, there seems to be no relation between the level of satisfaction and the size of firms.

CHAPTER 8

Linear Regression

Preview: *Linear regression is another important concept for any researcher. Whether you are studying the relationship between sun exposure and skin cancer or the link between excess fat consumption and obesity, the concept of linear regression plays a big role. Linear regression is the approach used to explore a linear relationship between a dependent numerical variable y and one or more independent numerical variables x. The correlation between numerical values is an integral part of the linear regression approach. In some cases the correlation may be intuitive—it seems reasonable, for example, that students who had a high GPA in high school would go on to have a high GPA in college—but, as always, a thorough testing of the hypothesis will be necessary to prove or disprove it. Regardless of the subject being studied, the correlation coefficient is always a number between –1.0 and +1.0. A correlation coefficient close to +1.0 means there is a strong correlation between the two variables. In addition to computing the correlation coefficient and the equation of the least-squares regression line, we also introduce the scatter plot. A scatter plot is a type of graph in which the values of two different variables are plotted on the two axes of the chart. The pattern of points that results shows the correlation between the two variables. Once you have determined the equation of the least-squares regression line you can even use it to make predictions.*

Learning Objectives: At the conclusion of this chapter, you should be able to:

1. Use regression analysis to predict the value of a dependent variable based on an independent variable
2. Evaluate the assumptions of regression analysis
3. Determine the correlation coefficient and describe its meaning
4. Use simple regression techniques to solve business problems and make recommendations

Introduction

In Chapter 7 we saw how to create contingency tables, relating categorical variables and we computed the chi-square statistics to test if the variables are independent or not. While this type of analysis is useful for categorical data, for numerical data the resulting tables would (usually) be too big to be useful. Therefore, we need to learn different methods for dealing with numerical variables to decide whether two such variables are related. In addition, the new techniques will allow us to make predictions of future events based on events in the past.

Correlation Between Numerical Variables

We will start by determining whether there is a correlation between two numerical variables (similar to determining whether two categorical variables are related, although the procedure will be very much different).

Example: Suppose that five students were asked their high school and college GPA, with the answers shown in Table 8.1.

Table 8.1 High school and college GPA pairs

Student	HS GPA	College GPA
Bert	3.8	2.8
Jane	3.1	2.2
Justin	4.0	3.5
Susan	2.5	1.9
Wendy	3.3	2.5

We want to know if high school and college GPA are related, and if they are related, can we use the high school GPA to predict the college GPA?

Looking at this data it seems clear that the college GPA is always worse than the high school one, and the smaller the high school GPA the smaller the college GPA. This seems to indicate a relationship but it seems difficult to quantify how strong the relationship is. It also seems clear that if there was a relation, the high school GPA would be our independent variable, while the college GPA, occurring later in time, is the dependent one.

We will first discuss how to compute and interpret the so-called correlation coefficient to help decide whether two numerical variables are related or not. The formulas we need might look pretty intense but when we see the examples they should become crystal clear.

Definition: If our data is given in (x,y) pairs where x and y are numeric variables with x denoting the independent variable and y the dependent one, then compute the quantities:

$$S_{xx} = \sum x^2 - \frac{\left(\sum x\right)^2}{n},$$

$$S_{yy} = \sum y^2 - \frac{\left(\sum y\right)^2}{n},$$

$$S_{xy} = \sum xy - \frac{\left(\sum x\right)\left(\sum y\right)}{n},$$

where the "sigma" symbol indicates summation and n stands for the number of data points. With these quantities computed, the *correlation coefficient ρ (rho)* is defined as:

$$\rho = \frac{S_{xy}}{\sqrt{S_{xx}S_{yy}}}.$$

Example: Compute the correlation coefficient for the data in Table 8.1 of high school (x) and college GPA (y).

To compute the correlation coefficient for our preceding GPA example we create a table containing both variables, with additional columns for their squares as well as their product, somewhat similar to computing the variance (see Table 8.2).

Table 8.2 GPA data augmented by columns for x^2, y^2, and $x \cdot y$

Student	High school GPA (x)	College GPA (y)	x^2	y^2	$x \cdot y$
A	3.8	2.8	$3.8^2 = 14.44$	$2.8^2 = 7.84$	$3.8 * 2.8 = 10.64$
B	3.1	2.2	$3.1^2 = 9.61$	$2.2^2 = 4.84$	$3.1 * 2.2 = 6.82$
C	4.0	3.5	$4.0^2 = 16.00$	$3.5^2 = 12.25$	$4.0 * 3.5 = 14.00$
D	2.5	1.9	$2.5^2 = 6.25$	$1.9^2 = 3.61$	$2.5 * 1.9 = 4.75$
E	3.3	2.5	$3.3^2 = 10.89$	$2.5^2 = 6.25$	$3.3 * 2.5 = 8.25$
Sum	16.7	12.9	57.19	34.79	44.46

The last row contains the sum of the x's, y's, x-squared, y-squared, and $x \cdot y$, which are precisely the quantities that we need to compute S_{xx}, S_{yy}, and S_{xy}. Thus:

$$S_{xx} = \sum x^2 - \frac{\left(\sum x\right)^2}{n} = 57.19 - \frac{16.7^2}{5} = 1.412 \, ,$$

$$S_{yy} = \sum y^2 - \frac{\left(\sum y\right)^2}{n} = 34.79 - \frac{12.9^2}{5} = 1.508 \, ,$$

$$S_{xy} = \sum xy - \frac{\left(\sum x\right)\left(\sum y\right)}{n} = 44.46 - \frac{16.7 \cdot 12.9}{5} = 1.374 \, .$$

Therefore, the correlation coefficient for this data is:

$$\rho = \frac{1.374}{\sqrt{1.412 \cdot 1.508}} = 0.9416 \, .$$

Now we need to know what this number means.

Definition: The correlation coefficient ρ as defined earlier measures *how strong a linear relationship* exists between two numerical variables x and y. Specifically:

- The correlation coefficient is always a number between -1.0 and $+1.0$.

- If the correlation coefficient is close to +1.0, then there is a *strong positive linear* relationship between x and y. In other words, if x increases, y also increases.
- If the correlation coefficient is close to –1.0, then there is a *strong negative linear* relationship between x and y. In other words, if x increases, y will decrease.
- The closer to zero the correlation coefficient, the lesser the extent of the linear relationship between x and y.

Example: Determine if there is a linear relationship between high school and college GPA for the data in Table 8.1.

We have already computed the correlation coefficient to be $\rho = 0.9416$, which is very close to +1. Therefore, we can conclude that there indeed is a strong positive relationship between high school GPA and college GPA in this particular example.

Using Excel to Compute the Correlation Coefficient

While the preceding table certainly helps in computing the correlation coefficient, it is still a lot of work, especially if there are several (x, y) data points. Even using Excel to help compute Table 8.2 seems a lot of work. However, Excel has a convenient function to quickly compute the correlation coefficient without the need for a complicated table. The Excel built-in function

  =correl(x_range, y_range)

returns the correlation coefficient of the cells in *x_range* (for the x values) and the *y_range* (for the y values). All cells must contain numbers, and no cell should be empty.

Example: To use this Excel function to compute the correlation coefficient for the previous GPA example, we would enter the data and the formulas as shown in Figure 8.1.

	A	B	C	D
1	HS GPA	Coll. GPA		
2	3.8	2.8		
3	3.1	2.2		
4	4	3.5		
5	2.5	1.9		
6	3.3	2.5		
7				
8	cor. coef. =	0.941605	=CORREL(A2:A6,B2:B6)	

Figure 8.1 *Computing the correlation coefficient with Excel*

Figure 8.1 shows the correlation coefficient computed by Excel to be 0.9416, which is—of course—the same as we computed manually before.

Example: Consider the following artificial examples: Some data for x and y (which have no particular meaning right now) are listed in Table 8.3 for three different cases.

Table 8.3 *Three different cases of (x, y) points*

Case A	Case B	Case C
$x = 10, y = 20$	$x = 10, y = 200$	$x = 10, y = 100$
$x = 20, y = 40$	$x = 20, y = 160$	$x = 20, y = 20$
$x = 30, y = 60$	$x = 30, y = 120$	$x = 30, y = 200$
$x = 40, y = 80$	$x = 40, y = 80$	$x = 40, y = 50$
$x = 50, y = 100$	$x = 50, y = 40$	$x = 50, y = 100$

Guess the correlation coefficient in each case and then confirm your guess by computing it exactly (perhaps with Excel).

Just looking at Table 8.3 it seems pretty obvious that:

- In case A, there should be a strong positive relationship between x and y, so we expect the correlation coefficient to be close to +1.
- In case B, there should be a strong negative relationship between x and y, so we expect the correlation coefficient to be close to –1.

- In case C, there seems to be no apparent relationship between x and y, so the correlation coefficient should be close to zero (it is hard to say whether it is positive or negative).

Indeed, using Excel to compute each correlation coefficient confirms this:

- In case A, the coefficient equals 1.0, that is, there is a strong positive correlation—in fact, in this easy case we can see that the linear relation between x and y is $y = 2x$.
- In case B, the coefficient equals -1.0, that is, there is a strong negative correlation—the actual equation relating x with y is a little harder to see, though (but not impossible, try to guess it).
- In case C, the coefficient is 0.069, which is close to zero, so there is no correlation.

The preceding cases are artificial; real-life data is usually not so clear-cut.

Example: In a previous section we looked at an Excel data set that shows various information about employees. Here is the spreadsheet data, but this time the salary is left as an actual number instead of a category.

www.betterbusinessdecisions.org/data/employeenumeric.xls

Download this file into Excel and find out whether there is a linear relationship between the salary and the years of education of an employee.

Download the preceding spreadsheet and start Excel with that worksheet as input. Click on an empty cell in your spreadsheet and enter the formula:

=CORREL(B2:B475,C2:C475),

where the first input range B2:B475 corresponds to the salary, while the second range C2:C475 corresponds to "Years of Education." Excel will compute the correlation coefficient, which turns out to be 0.66 (see Figure 8.2).

	A	B	C	F	G	H	I
1	Gender	Current Salary	Years of Education				
2	m	$57,000	15		0.6605589		
3	m	$40,200	16		=CORREL(B2:B475,C2:C475)		
4	f	$21,450	12				
5	f	$21,900	8				
6	m	$45,000	15				
7	m	$32,100	15				
8	m	$36,000	15				
9	f	$21,900	12				

Figure 8.2 Computing the correlation coefficient between salary and education

Since the correlation coefficient is 0.66, it means that there is indeed some positive relation between years of schooling and salary earnings. But since the value is not that close to +1.0, the relationship is not super strong.

In the following sections we will introduce a more detailed analysis, which will allow us to not only determine the strength of a linear relation, but also to compute the exact equation of that relation, which we can in turn use to make predictions.

Scatter Plots

So far we have seen how to determine whether two variables are independent (chi-square test for categorical variables) or linearly related (correlation coefficient for numerical variables). In this section we will investigate the relationship, if any, graphically.

We have already defined dependent and independent variables but in our current context we say that if there is a relationship between two variables in such a way that knowledge of the first allows the computation or prediction of the second, then the first variable is called the independent variable—usually denoted by x—while the second is called the dependent variable—usually denoted by y. As before, the independent variable often refers to a time prior to that of the dependent variable.

Example: A group of 10 students was selected at random and asked for their high school GPA and their freshmen GPA in college the subsequent year. The results are shown in Table 8.4.

Table 8.4 High school versus college GPA

Student	High school GPA	Freshmen GPA
1	2.0	1.6
2	2.2	2.0
3	2.6	1.8
4	2.7	2.8
5	2.8	2.1
6	3.1	2.0
7	2.9	2.6
8	3.2	2.2
9	3.3	2.6
10	3.6	3.0

Visualize this data to see a potential relation between the two variables.

Since students go to high school prior to going to college, the high school GPA refers to a time before that of the freshmen GPA. Therefore the high school GPA is the independent variable, called x, while the freshmen GPA is the dependent variable y. That makes sense since it is conceivable that the high school GPA determines the freshmen GPA but not the other way round. With our choice of x and y, Table 8.4 translates into a series of (x, y) data points:

(2.0, 1.6), (2.2, 2.0), (2.6, 1.8), (2.8, 2.1), (3.1, 2.0), (2.9, 2.6), (3.2, 2.2), (3.3, 2.6), (3.6, 3.0).

We can now plot these points in a standard Cartesian coordinate system. Of course, we will use Excel to generate that graph for us.

- Start as usual with Microsoft Excel, with an empty spreadsheet.
- Label the first two columns "High School GPA" and "College GPA," respectively. Do not worry if you cannot see the first label in its entirety.
- Enter the data in columns, each high school GPA in the first column and the corresponding college GPA in the second.
- Use the mouse to mark all data, labels as well as numbers. Then click on the "Insert" ribbon and select "XY (Scatter)" as chart type. The resulting chart is shown in Figure 8.3.

You can customize the chart to make it look more to your liking. In our case, for example, we can double-click on the "X" axis (horizontal axis) to change the scale so that the minimum value starts at 1.8. We can also click on the "Y" axis (vertical) to change its scale so that it also starts at 1.4. After all, there are no values less than 1, so why not start the axis at that number instead of at zero? Figure 8.4 shows a possible final version of the chart (where we have also changed the background color).

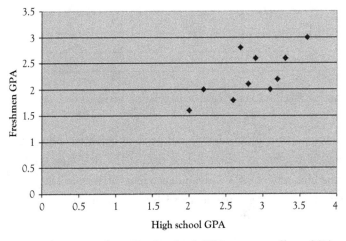

Figure 8.3 A scatter plot of high school GPA versus college GPA

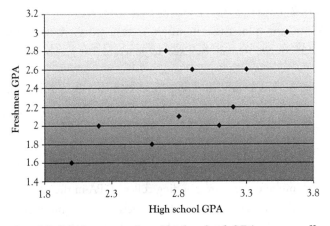

Figure 8.4 Modified scatter plot of high school GPA versus college GPA

Now that we can *see* the data it seems that there is indeed some loose relationship between high school and college GPA. The dots are not randomly distributed, and they seem to follow some pattern: low high school GPAs result in low college GPAs; higher high school scores result in better college performance; all college grades are somewhat worse than high school grades; and the dots seem to cluster around an imaginary diagonal line. If we computed the correlation coefficient it would come out to be 0.69665, confirming that there is some linear relationship between the variables but not a strong one.

In the next section we learn a precise way to determine the linear equation relating x and y and to use the projected relation to make predictions for values that are not part of the original data set.

Linear Regression

This time we again want to look at data from two variables that are possibly related, but we want to determine the exact nature of this relationship, if any, and develop some formulas that will allow us to make predictions. Let us start with the same example we have used before.

Example: A group of 10 students was selected at random and asked for their high school GPA and their freshmen GPA in college the subsequent year. The results are shown in Table 8.4. Is there a *linear* relationship between the high school GPA and the freshmen GPA? If so predict the freshmen GPA for a student with a high school GPA of, say, 3.4.

We plotted the data in a scatter plot in Figure 8.4 where we mentioned that the data seem to cluster around some imaginary diagonal line that, somehow, fits the data points in the "best possible" way. Figure 8.5 shows three candidates for such a line.

In each case we have drawn a line that somehow passes through the data points. It seems clear that:

- No straight line can pass through all data points.
- Line 1 does not fit the data points very well because too many points are to the right, or below that line.

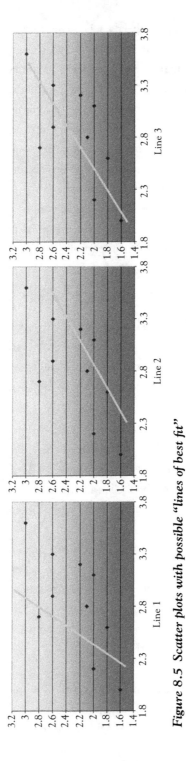

Figure 8.5 Scatter plots with possible "lines of best fit"

- Line 2 does not fit the data points very well because too many points are above the line.
- Line 3 does not fit the data points perfectly, but seems to have the best fit of these three lines.

Mathematically speaking, the line that gives the "best fit" is that line where the sum of the squares of the differences to all data points has the smallest possible value (this can be proved in multivariate calculus). Therefore, the line that fits best in that sense is called *least-squares regression line* and the process of finding it is called *least-squares linear regression*.

Least-squares Regression Line "Manually"

Our goal is to determine the equation of the "least-squares regression" line. In other words, we want to find the equation of a line that happens to be called "least-squares regression line" and that fits the data best. We know from previous algebra classes that *any* line has the equation:

$$y = mx + b,$$

where m is the slope of the line and b is the interception of the line with the y-axis. We also recall from high school that lines that go up have a positive slope (as the lines 1, 2, and 3 in Figure 8.5), while lines with negative slopes go down.

Example: Suppose we have four equations of lines as follows:
(a) $y = x - 1$ (b) $y = 2x - 1$ (c) $y = -x + 1$ (d) $y = -2x + 1$.
Match these equations to the graphs shown in Figure 8.6.
According to the equations of the lines, we know:

- $y = x - 1$ is a line with slope 1 (going up) and y-intercept -1.
- $y = 2x - 1$ is a line with slope 2 (going up more) and y-intercept -1.
- $y = -x + 1$ is a line with slope -1 (going down) and y-intercept 1.
- $y = -2x + 1$ is a line with slope -2 (going down more) and y-intercept 1.

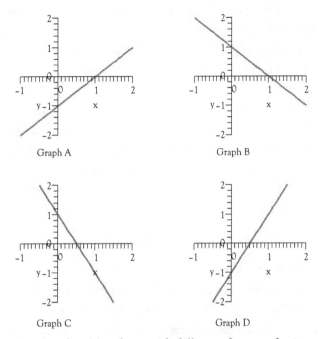

Figure 8.6 Graphs of four lines with different slopes and y-intercepts

Graphs A and D show lines going up, so both have positive slopes. Both also intersect the y-axis at –1, so both have *y*-intercept –1. But the line in graph D is steeper, so it has a bigger slope. Thus, Equation 1 matches graph A while Equation 2 matches graph D.

Similarly, both graphs B and C have negative slopes and *y*-intercept +1, but line C goes down faster and thus has a more negative slope. Therefore, Equation 3 matches graph B while Equation 4 matches graph C.

So to determine the least-squares regression line we must first and foremost find the equation of a line; this means we need to identify its slope *m* and *y*-intercept *b*. As it happens, the slope is related to the quantities S_{xx}, S_{yy}, and S_{xy} we computed in the "Linear Regression" section while the *y*-intercept is related to the averages (means) of *x* and *y*. The formulas are as follows:

- Slope $m = \dfrac{S_{xy}}{S_{xx}}$

- *y*-intercept $b = \bar{y} - \bar{x} \cdot m$

Here $\bar{x} = \dfrac{1}{n}\sum x_i$ is the mean of the x values and $\bar{y} = \dfrac{1}{n}\sum y_i$ is the mean of the y values.

In this text we will not try to determine how these formulas come about. That would be done in more advanced mathematical courses. We will be content using these equations, as in our next example.

Example: Consider the data in Table 8.4 of high school versus college GPA and compute the equation of the least-squares regression line. Also compute the correlation coefficient.

Just as we did for the correlation coefficient in the "Correlation Between Numerical Variables" section, we create the following table.

Student	x	y	x^2	y^2	$x \cdot y$
1	2.0	1.6	4.00	2.56	3.20
2	2.2	2.0	4.84	4.00	4.40
3	2.6	1.8	6.76	3.24	4.68
4	2.7	2.8	7.29	7.84	7.56
5	2.8	2.1	7.84	4.41	5.88
6	3.1	2.0	9.61	4.00	6.20
7	2.9	2.6	8.41	6.76	7.54
8	3.2	2.2	10.24	4.84	7.04
9	3.3	2.6	10.89	6.76	8.58
10	3.6	3.0	12.96	9.00	10.80
Totals	28.4	22.7	82.84	53.41	65.88

Thus, we can compute:

$$S_{xx} = \sum x^2 - \frac{\left(\sum x^2\right)^2}{n} = 82.84 - 28.4^2/10 = 2.184\,,$$

$$S_{yy} = \sum y^2 - \frac{\left(\sum y^2\right)^2}{n} = 53.41 - 22.7^2/10 = 1.881\,,$$

$$S_{xy} = \sum xy - \frac{\left(\sum x\right)\left(\sum y\right)}{n} = 65.88 - 28.4 * 22.7/10 = 1.412\,.$$

Since we already know the sums of x and of y, we can also quickly compute:

$\bar{x} = 28.4/10 = 2.84$ (mean of x),

$\bar{y} = 22.7/10 = 2.27$ (mean of y).

But now the difficult work is over and we can determine the slope and y-intercept, as well as the correlation coefficient:

Slope $m = S_{xy}/S_{xx} = 1.412/2.184 = 0.645$,

y-intercept $b = \bar{y} - m \cdot \bar{x} = 2.27 - 2.84 * 0.645 = 0.4382$,

Correlation coefficient $r = \dfrac{1.412}{\sqrt{2.184 \cdot 1.881}} = 0.6966$.

Thus, the equation of our least-squares regression line, relating high school GPA (x) and college GPA (y) is $y = 0.645 * x + 0.4382$, and the correlation coefficient of 0.6966 indicates that the relation is not very strong. We can now use our computed equation to make predictions.

Example: Using the data in Table 8.4 for high school and college GPAs, predict the college GPA for a student with a high school GPA of 3.7. Do you think your prediction is valid?

First, note that $x = 3.7$ is not one of the original high school GPA scores. But we know the general relationship between x and y (the equation of the least-squares regression line) is:

$y = 0.645 * x + 0.4382$,

which we can use for our prediction: If $x = 3.7$ then $y = 0.645 * 3.7 + 0.4382 = 2.8247$.

Thus, our prediction is that a high school GPA of 3.7 will result in a college GPA of 2.83, approximately. Moreover, because of our correlation coefficient, we are somewhat confident that our prediction is accurate.

This was a lot of work but before we use Excel to simplify the computations, let us do one more example manually.

Example: Suppose some (made-up) data for two variables x and y are as shown in the table. Use this data to predict the y value for $x = 5$ and state how confident you are in your prediction.

x	1	2	3
y	3	5	6

We create a table of x, y, x^2, and so on values, draw a scatter plot, compute S_{xx}, S_{yy}, and so forth, and finish up with the equation of the line. Figure 8.7 shows the results.

But now the difficult work is over and we can compute the slope and y-intercept, as well as the correlation coefficient, as follows:

Slope $m = Sxy/Sxx = 3/2 = 1.5$,

y-intercept $b = $ (mean of y) – (mean of x) $* m = 4.667 - 2 * 1.5 = 1.667$,

Correlation coefficient $r = 3/\text{sqrt}(2 * 4.667) = 0.982$.

Thus, the equation of our least-squares regression line relating x and y is $y = 1.5\,x + 1.667$.

Thus, if $x = 5$ we compute our prediction to be $y = 1.5 * 5 + 1.667 = 9.167$ and since the correlation coefficient is 0.982, we know that the relation is very strong. Therefore, we are pretty sure about our prediction.

Note that we are basing our prediction or forecast on only three data points. Such a small sample is generally not adequate for good predictions.

Least-Squares Regression Line "Automatically"

After all this work it should be relaxing to focus on using Excel to deliver the least-squares regression line for us, which carries out all these calculations automatically.

	x	y	x^2	y^2	xy
	1	3	1	9	3
	2	5	4	25	10
	3	6	9	36	18
Totals	6	14	14	70	31

$S_{xx} = 14 - 62/3 = 2$
$S_{yy} = 70 - 142/3 = 4.667$
$S_{xy} = 31 - 6*14/3 = 3$
mean of x = 6/3 = 2
mean of y = 14/3 = 4.667

Figure 8.7 Table of values, scatter plot, and related quantities

- Start Excel as usual and enter the data from the preceding GPA example.
- From the "Tools" menu, select the "Data Analysis ..." menu item and choose "Regression."
- In the "Regression" dialog window use the selector tools and select the X and Y range (be careful, the first range to choose is the Y range, i.e., the dependent variable, not X, i.e., the independent one). If you include labels in the X, Y ranges, make sure to check the "Labels" box (see Figure 8.8).
- To get a scatter plot including the least-squares regression line, make sure to check "Line Fit Plots" in the "Residuals" category (see Figure 8.8).

Click OK—you should see a lot of output, much of it mysterious, grouped into regions.

The Chart: This consists of a scatter plot in the X,Y coordinate system. Of course you can change the way the chart looks. At the very least you want to connect the computed points with the least-squares regression

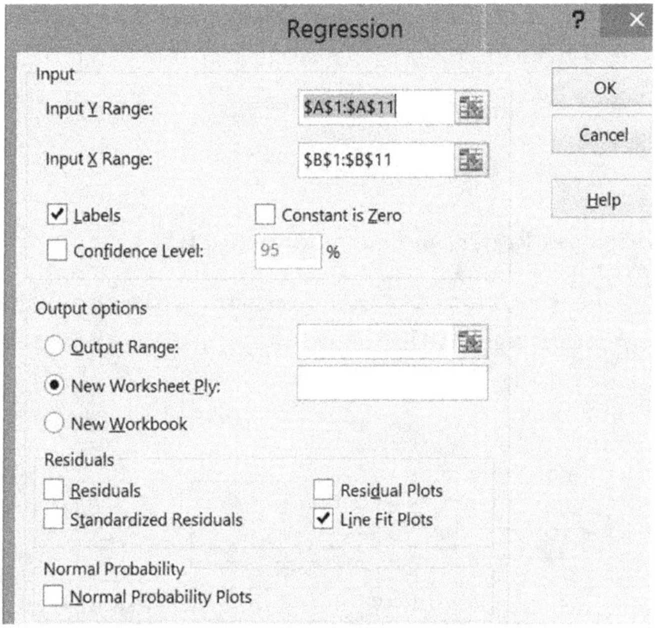

Figure 8.8 Parameters for the linear regression tool

line: double-click on the chart; then click on the data points and select "Solid line" from the options on the right. Figure 8.9 shows the result.

The Regression Statistics: This group is shown in Figure 8.10. The most important number here is "Multiple R," which has the value of 0.6966 in this case. In fact, this number is the absolute value of our previous *correlation coefficient*. If we square it, the result, called "R Square," tells us how much percentage of the variation of the dependent variable (y) is explained by the independent variable (x). In our case, 48 percent of the variation in college GPA can be explained by the high school GPA.

Note that "multiple R" is always between 0 and 1, and closer to 1 indicates a stronger relation. In our example the multiple R is reasonably close to 1, which implies that the two variables are indeed somewhat linearly (positive or negative) related (and the least-squares regression line indeed fits the data points relatively well).

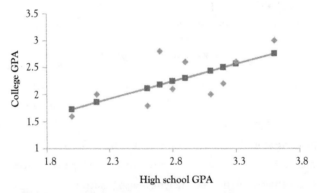

Figure 8.9 *Scatter plot of high school versus college scores, including least-squares regression line*

	A	B
2		
3	*Regression Statistics*	
4	Multiple R	0.696648942
5	R Square	0.485319748
6	Adjusted R Square	0.420984717
7	Standard Error	0.347870945
8	Observations	10
9		

Figure 8.10 *Multiple R, the absolute value of the correlation coefficient*

	A	B	C	D	E	F
10	ANOVA					
11		*df*	*SS*	*MS*	*F*	*Significance F*
12	Regression	1	0.9129	0.9129	7.5436	0.0252
13	Residual	8	0.9681	0.1210		
14	Total	9	1.8810			
15						
16		*Coefficients*	*Standard Error*	*t Stat*	*P-value*	*Lower 95%*
17	Intercept	0.433882784	0.6775	0.6404	0.5398	-1.1284
18	High School GPA	0.646520147	0.2354	2.7466	0.0252	0.1037
19						

Sheet1 / Sheet2 / Sheet3 /

Figure 8.11 The ANOVA group of our regression output

The Analysis of Variance ("ANOVA") Section: The next section produced by our regression analysis is the ANOVA section shown in Figure 8.11.

The two most important numbers in this section are the "Coefficients" for the "Intercept" and the "High School GPA." In this case "Intercept" is 0.4339 and "High School GPA" is 0.6465 (rounded). These two numbers are the slope and intercept of the least-squares regression line. In other words, the actual equation of the least-squares regression line is:

$$y = 0.6465 \cdot x + 0.4339.$$

That equation of the line can be used for predictions. For example, if we want to know the college GPA (y) for a student with a high school GPA (x) of 3.4 we substitute $x = 3.4$ in the preceding equation and we find the corresponding y value to be $y = 0.6465 * 3.4 + 0.4339 = 2.632$.

Note that from this section we see that the slope is positive, which means that the correlation coefficient is also positive.

The "Significance F" tells us whether the results are statistically significant; it should be small (less than 0.05). It gives the p-value for the testing the null hypothesis H_0: *slope* = 0 (i.e., the true regression line is really a flat line) against the alternative H_0: *slope* ≠ 0. If that p-value is small enough, we get to reject H_0 and accept the alternative (i.e., the regression equation does a better job of predicting the dependent variable rather than using a line with slope 0).

The "Residual Output" Section: This is not important for us in this context, so we ignore it.

Now we can also answer the original question: Based on our data and a least-squares regression analysis of that data, we can predict that a student with a high school GPA of 3.4 will have a college GPA of approximately 2.632. Since the correlation coefficient is 0.69, we are somewhat confident that our prediction is accurate.

Here is one more example, this time with real—and interesting—data.

Example: In the attached Excel spreadsheet you will find data about the literacy rate (percentage of people who can read) and average life expectancy of over 200 countries in the world, based on 2014 data. Load that data into Excel and perform a least-squares regression analysis to see if there is a linear relationship between literacy rate and average life expectancy. If you find that there is a relation, determine what would happen to the life expectancy of people in Afghanistan if its literacy rate could be raised to, say, 60 percent (from its current value of 29 percent).

 www.betterbusinessdecisions.org/data/life_literate.xls

Of course we will use Excel's "regression" tool we just discussed, using the literacy rate as the independent variable (x) and life expectancy as the dependent one (y). The details should be clear, so we will simply state and interpret the results: The least-squares regression line fits the data quite well as you can see from the scatter plot in Figure 8.12 as well as from the correlation coefficient of 0.67.

The coefficients of the least-squares regression line are 41.17541984 (intercept) and 0.349593582 (slope) so that the regression line has the

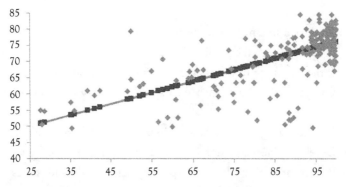

Figure 8.12 Plot of least-squares regression line

equation $y = 0.3496 \cdot x + 41.1754$. This means that if a country such as Afghanistan had a literacy rate of $y = 60$ percent, we would predict an average life expectancy of approximately $y = 0.3496 \cdot 60 + 41.1754 = 62.1514$ or approximately 62 years (as opposed to its current life expectancy of 50.5 years with a literacy rate of 28.1 percent).

Note: This does not mean that reading books causes people to live longer. After all, at the beginning of Chapter 7 we mentioned that correlation does not necessarily imply causation. But what it does mean is that if a country can raise its literacy rate, probably through a wide variety of programs and policy decisions, then a beneficial side effect seems to be that the average life expectancy goes up proportionally as well. It also means that if a country—perhaps for political reasons—does not make its life expectancy rate public, but its literacy rate is known, we can obtain a pretty good estimate of that life expectancy based exclusively on the literacy rate of the country.

Excel Demonstration

Company P, the large manufacturer of paper products, was asked by one of its retail clients to provide an analysis on the role that shelf space has on the sales of a product. The marketing manager of a large retail chain that purchases paper products from Company P has the business objective of using shelf space most efficiently. Toward that goal, she would like to use shelf space to predict the sales of a specialty paper plate product. Data collected from a random sample of 12 equal-sized stores are presented in Table 8.5.

You have been asked to answer the following questions.

1. Produce a line fit plot to demonstrate the trend in shelf space and sales along with the predicted path.
2. Is there a strong relationship between shelf space and sales?
3. Can you tell us how much shelf space accounts for the variation of sales?
4. Is there is a significant relationship between shelf space and sales?
5. Develop a linear equation for predicting sales, given shelf space.
6. Predict the weekly sales of the specialty paper product for stores with 7 ft. of shelf space for the paper product.

Step 1: Enter the data into a new Excel worksheet in two columns, including column titles.

Step 2: Click on Data, then DATA Analysis, and choose Regression.

Step 3: Fill in the *Regression* dialog box shown in Figure 8.13 and then click OK.

Table 8.5 Data on shelf space use

Shelf space (in ft.)	Sales (in thousands)
5	161
6	225
5	138
10	192
10	245
10	263
15	234
15	275
15	279
20	264
20	296
20	317

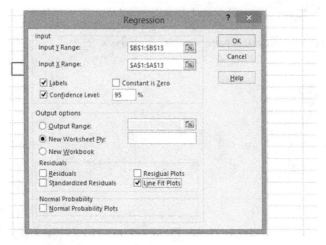

Figure 8.13 Regression dialog

- For the Y range, include the data in the Sales category (include the label).
- For the X range, include the data in the Shelf Space category (include the label).
- Check the Labels box since we have to include the label.
- Check the Confidence Level box and leave it as the default 95 percent.
- Check the Line Fit Plot box to display the least-squares regression line.

Step 4: Interpret the results shown in Figure 8.14.

Now we can answer the aforementioned questions.

1. *Produce a line fit plot to demonstrate the trend in shelf space and sales along with the predicted path.* Figure 8.15 shows the scatter plot with the least-squares regression line.

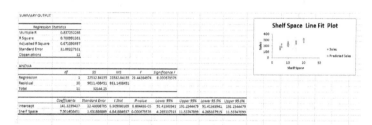

Figure 8.14 Results of the regression analysis

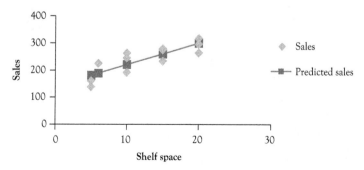

Figure 8.15 Scatter plot with regression line

2. *Is there a strong relationship between shelf space and sales?* We see from Figure 8.14 that "Multiple R" is 0.837252268. This is close to 1 so that there is a fairly strong correlation between shelf space and sales. From the plot in Figure 8.15 we see that the regression line has a positive slope, so that the correlation is fairly strong and positive.

3. *Is there a significant relationship between shelf space and sales?* From Figure 8.14 we see that the "Significance F" value is 0.000679576, which is less than our requested alpha level of 0.05, indicating that there is a significant relationship between shelf space and sales.

4. *Develop a linear equation for predicting sales, given shelf space.* We see from Figure 8.14 that the intercept coefficient is 141.3239437 and the shelf space coefficient, or slope, is 7.901408451. Thus, our least-squares regression line is $y = 141.324 + 7.901 \ x$.

5. *Predict the weekly sales of the specialty paper product for stores with 7 ft. of shelf space for the paper product.* We just found the equation of our least-squares regression line to be $y = 141.324 + 7.901 \ x$. Thus, we substitute 7 for x in the equation to get: $y = 141.324 + 7.901 \cdot 7 = 196.634$. Thus, if we gave the product 7 ft. of shelf space we can expect sales to be around $196,000.

This helps a business person to optimize the use of shelf space so that products that will result in the highest sales are given the most space on shelves.

CHAPTER 9

Analysis of Variance

Preview: *Testing for the differences between two means is a relatively straightforward exercise, but what happens when there are three or more groups? These multiple groups may have means that differ significantly from one another, which makes the comparison process much more complicated. Fortunately, there is a way to test the means no matter how many groups are involved. For example, if a researcher wanted to study the impact of listening to music on student test scores, she could randomly divide the class into three groups of students. One group would listen to popular music while they study or do homework. The second group would listen to classical music while studying and the third group would study in silence. At the conclusion of the study period, the performance of students in each group is evaluated. The analysis of variance (ANOVA) procedure is then used to determine whether there is a significant difference among a group of means, and Excel will do all calculations for you automatically.*

Learning Objectives: At the conclusion of this chapter, you should be able to:

1. Use a factor to partition an experiment into multiple groups
2. Understand the assumptions to check before using a one-way ANOVA
3. Use the one-way ANOVA to test for differences among the means of several groups
4. Understand how to obtain information about two-factor ANOVA

Introduction

We have already introduced a test for the difference of (two) means. But in many cases there are three or more groups whose means may or may not differ significantly.

Example: Many parents complain that students listen to pop music while they study. To test the impact of music on students' concentration levels, we divide 40 students randomly into three groups: Group A does not listen to any music, group B listens to pop music, and group C listens to classical music. All students study a text for 30 min and then they take a test about their understanding of the text.

There are two types of variables in this example: the performance of students on a test and the type of music students listen to. The first variable (quiz_score) is numerical, while the second (music_type) is categorical and is used to partition the first variable into three groups. This, as it turns out, is typical for an ANOVA test to compare multiple means. Note that to decide whether multiple means of various groups are different from each other, we could use multiple difference of means tests between pairs of means, but that would quickly escalate.

- For three groups we would need three comparisons: $\mu_1 \neq \mu_2$, $\mu_1 \neq \mu_3$, and $\mu_2 \neq \mu_3$.
- For four groups we would need six comparisons: $\mu_1 \neq \mu_2, \mu_1 \neq \mu_3, \mu_1 \neq \mu_4, \mu_2 \neq \mu_3, \mu_2 \neq \mu_4$, and $\mu_3 \neq \mu_4$.
- For five groups we would need 10 comparisons, and so on.

This quickly becomes a lot of work. In addition—and perhaps more important—each time we conduct a difference of means test we accept an error, typically 5 percent. These errors add up, approximately, so that checking three group means would add up to an error of 15 percent. Thus, we need a new procedure that keeps the error at a constant level even if we are comparing quite a number of means.

Definition: The ANOVA procedure is used to test for a significant difference among a group of means. The null hypothesis is: $H_0: \mu_1 = \mu_2 = \cdots = \mu_k$ and the alternative is that at least two means differ significantly: $H_a: \mu_j \neq \mu_i$.

Note that in case the ANOVA procedure is used for only *two* means it should reduce to a difference of means test. It might sound strange for a procedure that claims to test for differences of *means* to be called

ANOVA. However, it turns out that we can analyze the variances yet draw conclusions about any difference of means.

The procedure works by comparing the variance SS_B *between* group means against the variance SS_W *within* groups to determine whether the groups are all part of one larger population (no difference between means) or separate populations with different characteristics (at least two means differ significantly).

One-Factor ANOVA

Suppose we have quiz scores of students in a statistics course as follows:

2 (male), 5 (female), 1 (male), 3 (male), 6 (female), 7 (female).

We want to know if there is a difference in mean scores between males and females. Since these represent two samples only, we could use our familiar difference of means test (which incidentally results in a t-value of $t = -4.0$ and a p-value of $p = 0.016$) but we want to use a different method that will readily extend to more than two groups and their means. First, we use sex to divide the scores into two groups, as follows.

Male	Female
2	6
1	5
3	7

Definition: The variable we are interested in analyzing is called the *dependent* variable, while the variable we use to divide the dependent variable into groups is called the *independent* variable or *factor*. For ANOVA, the dependent variable should be numerical while the factor should be categorical. A *single-factor* ANOVA uses *one* factor to divide the dependent variable into groups.

For a single-factor ANOVA we will assume that all groups are approximately normal with roughly the same standard deviations. In the preceding example we are using one factor (sex) to define the groups; consequently we will perform a single-factor ANOVA. Both groups have sample variances of 1, as you can readily compute. The samples are really too small to check for normality but for this example we will simply assume everything is normal. If the variable used as factor had more values (categories), it would result in that many groups; still it would be a single-factor ANOVA.

We now compare the variance of our overall data with the variances of each group. In fact, since the variance is a function of the square difference of each point to the respective mean, we compute only the sum of the square differences to the mean instead of the full variance (see Table 9.1).

As you can see, the means for the two groups are quite different. The sums of square differences within each group are 2. Adding them together, we get $SS_W = 4$. If we ignore group membership and compute the total sum of square differences SS_T based on the overall mean 4, we get $SS_T = 28$. In other words, the variance (aka sums of squares) SS_W within the groups is much smaller than the total variability SS_T, which indicates that the means are indeed different.

More precisely, under the null hypothesis that there are no mean differences between groups in the population, we would expect only minor random fluctuation in the means of the two groups. Therefore, under the null hypothesis, it turns out that the variance SS_W *within* groups divided by the degree s of freedom *within* groups should be about the same as the variance SS_B *between* groups divided by the degrees of freedom *between* groups. We can compare those expressions via the F distribution and test whether their ratio is significantly greater than 1. Here is the formal definition of a single-factor ANOVA.

Table 9.1 Group and total variances or sum of square (SS) differences to the mean

	Male	Female
Data	2	6
	1	5
	3	7
Mean	2	6
Group SS	$(2-2)^2 + (1-2)^2 + (3-1)^2 = 2$	$(6-6)^2 + (5-6)^2 + (7-6)^2 = 2$
Total mean	4	
Total SS	$(2-4)^2 + (1-4)^2 + (3-4)^2 + (6-4)^2 + (5-4)^2 + (7-4)^2 = 28$	

Definition: Suppose we have k groups and each group contains n_j measurements, $1 \leq j \leq k$. Assume that all groups are approximately normal and that their standard deviations are approximately the same. The four components of a single-factor ANOVA are:

$$H_0: \mu_1 = \mu_1 = \cdots = \mu_k$$

$$H_a: \mu_i \neq \mu_j \text{ for some } i, j.$$

Test statistics: $f_0 = \left(\dfrac{SS_B}{df_B}\right) \Big/ \left(\dfrac{SS_W}{df_W}\right)$, where $df_B = k - 1$, $df_W = (n_1 - 1) + (n_2 - 1) + \cdots + (n_k - 1)$, sum of squares within groups $SS_W = SS_1 + SS_2 + \cdots + SS_k$, the total sum of squares SS_T, and the sum of squares between groups $SS_B = SS_T - SS_W$.

Rejection region: Reject H_0 if $p = P(f > f_0) < a$, where $P(f > f_0) = FDIST(f_0, df_B, df_W)$ using the F distribution.

Now we can finish the preceding example: $df_B = 2 - 1 = 1$, $df_W = (3 - 1) + (3 - 1) = 4$, $SS_T = 28$, $SS_W = 2 + 2 = 4$, $SS_B = SS_T - SS_W = 28 - 4 = 24$. At this point we know the variance within groups SS_W as well as the variance between groups SS_B so that $f_0 = \left(\dfrac{24}{1}\right) \Big/ \left(\dfrac{4}{4}\right) = 24$ and $p = P(f > f_0) = FDIST(24,1,4) = 0.008$.

Hence, assuming as usual that $a = 0.05$, we reject the null hypothesis and conclude that there *is* a difference between the means. Incidentally, this would have been our conclusion had we used the difference of means procedure. Now we are ready for a true ANOVA, that is, for an example with more than two groups.

Example: We want to determine if a new drug is effective in lowering blood pressure, and what dosage might work best. So we give three different levels of the drug (zero drugs, low amount, high amount) to 20 patients and measure the difference in blood pressure before and

30 min after administering the drug. The 20 people were randomly assigned to receive one of the three dosages. The results are:

Zero dosage: 4, 1, 7, 8, 2, 10
Low dosage: 11, 15, 12, 13, 18, 16, 14
High dosage: 15, 17, 12, 13, 10, 11, 10.

Is there a significant difference between the three averages? Test at the $a = 0.05$ level.

The computations for our ANOVA test are as follows:

$$\bar{x}_1 = 5.333, \bar{x}_2 = 14.14, \bar{x}_3 = 12.57, \bar{x}_{total} = 10.95$$

$$SS_1 = (4 - 5.333)^2 + (1 - 5.333)^2 + \cdots + (10 - 5.333)^2 = 63.33$$

$$SS_2 = (11 - 14.14)^2 + (15 - 14.14)^2 + \cdots + (14 - 14.14)^2 = 34.85$$

$$SS_3 = (15 - 12.57)^2 + (17 - 12.57)^2 + \cdots + (10 - 12.57)^2 = 41.71$$

so that $SS_W = SS_1 + SS_2 + SS_3 = 139.90$

$$SS_T = (4 - 10.95)^2 + (1 - 10.95)^2 + \cdots + (11 - 10.95)^2 + (10 - 10.95)^2 = 418.95$$

so that $SS_B = SS_T - SS_W = 418.95 - 139.9 = 279.065$

$$df_B = 2, df_W = 17 \text{ so that, finally:}$$

$$f_0 = \left(\frac{SS_B}{df_1}\right) \Big/ \left(\frac{SS_W}{df_2}\right) = 139.52 / 8.229 = 16.95 \text{ and therefore}$$

$$p = FDIST(16.95, 2, 17) = 0.0000085 \text{ and } p < a = 0.05.$$

Thus, we reject the null hypothesis and accept the alternative, that is, there is a significant difference between (at least two of) the means.

This is a lot of work and it is very easy to make mistakes. Fortunately, Excel has a procedure to perform these calculations automatically.

Exercise: Given the data from the previous example, use Excel to perform an ANOVA to decide whether the means differ significantly.

First, we enter the data into Excel in three columns, one column per group (see Figure 9.1).

Next, click on the "Data Analysis" on the Data ribbon, select "ANOVA: Single factor," and define as input range the data you entered, including the data labels in the first row. Make sure that "Labels in First Row" is checked and hit OK. The output of the ANOVA procedure is shown in Figure 9.2.

zero	low	high
4	11	15
1	15	17
7	12	12
8	13	13
2	18	10
10	16	11
	14	10

Figure 9.1 Data entered in columns for each group

Anova: Single Factor

SUMMARY

Groups	Count	Sum	Average	Variance
zero	6	32	5.333333	12.666667
low	7	99	14.142857	5.809524
high	7	88	12.571429	6.952381

ANOVA

Source of Variation	SS	df	MS	F	P-value	F crit
Between Groups	279.04524	2	139.522619	16.953565	0.000089	3.591531
Within Groups	139.90476	17	8.229692			
Total	418.95	19				

Figure 9.2 Output of single-factor ANOVA routine

The SUMMARY block in Figure 9.2 shows the means and variances of the three groups. In the more interesting ANOVA section we can see that $SS_B = 279.04$ and $SS_W = 139.90$. It lists the degrees of freedom next and finally shows the f_0 value of 16.95 together with the associated probability $p = 0.000089$, computed using the F distribution. Our conclusion is, just as before, to reject the null hypothesis and accept that some means differ significantly from each other.

We will show another, carefully worked out problem in the last section of this chapter; you can check that if you have any questions. You might want to work out that example manually, as we did earlier, and compare your answers.

But the idea of the ANOVA is even more powerful and applies to more complex experiments.

Two-Way ANOVA

As we mentioned, a one-factor ANOVA uses one categorical variable called factor to divide the dependent variable into groups. But complex situations often depend on more factors, which will result in two-way ANOVA or higher. As it turns out, the ANOVA procedure cannot only decide on whether means are different but detect *interaction effects* between variables, and therefore can be used to test more complex hypotheses about reality. As it turns out, in many areas of research five-way or higher interactions are not that uncommon.

However, this discussion is difficult and, while most certainly useful, is beyond the scope of this text. Thus, we will refer the reader to more advanced statistical textbooks, or better yet, appropriate online resources and we will not discuss two-way (or higher) ANOVA here. For more information, the reader can check:

- *Introduction to Probability and Statistics* by Mendenhall, Beaver, and Beaver
- *Introduction to ANOVA/MANOVA* at www.statsoft.com/ Textbook/ANOVA-MANOVA
- *Analysis of variance* at http://en.wikipedia.org/wiki/Analysis _of_variance

Excel Demonstration

Company S, the accounting firm, has an HR department that has suggested managers learn different leadership styles to help decrease employee stress levels. An experiment was conducted to determine if leadership styles (*transformational* and *transactional*) in management significantly impacted employee stress levels compared to no intervention. An employee survey was given to three groups: one group under a manager who started using a transformational motivation technique, one group under a manager who began using a transactional motivation technique, and then a control group with no new technique used. Stress levels were self-reported by the employees as shown in Table 9.2. Use alpha = 0.05.

Step 1: Start a new Excel worksheet and enter the preceding data (see Figure 9.3).

Step 2: Click on DATA, then Data Analysis, and then ANOVA: Single Factor. We are choosing Single Factor because we have only one dependent variable (stress level) that defines three categories of independent variables (transformational, transactional, control).

Step 3: In the dialog that comes up, select all of the data including the labels at once as shown in Figure 9.3. Check the box called "Labels in First Row." Notice that Alpha is automatically set to 0.05. Click OK. The output of this procedure is shown in Figure 9.4.

In a review of the p-value in the between groups row, we see a $p = 0.02$ that is less than our alpha level of 0.05, so we know there is a significant difference in stress levels between the groups.

Table 9.2 *Data for stress levels*

Transformational	Transactional	Control
0	2	6
7	5	5
3	3	8
5	0	9
2	1	5

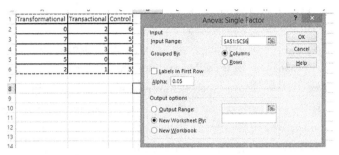

Figure 9.3 Data for stress levels of employees together with ANOVA dialog

	A	B	C	D	E	F	G	H
1	Anova: Single Factor							
2								
3	SUMMARY							
4	Groups	Count	Sum	Average	Variance			
5	Transformational	5	17	3.4	7.3			
6	Transactional	5	11	2.2	3.7			
7	Control	5	33	6.6	3.3			
8								
9								
10	ANOVA							
11	Source of Variation	SS	df	MS	F	P-value	F crit	
12	Between Groups	51.73333333	2	25.86666667	5.426573427	0.020960972	3.885293835	
13	Within Groups	57.2	12	4.766666667				
14								
15	Total	108.9333333	14					
16								
17								

Figure 9.4 Output of the single-factor ANOVA procedure

Now that we know there is a general difference between all the groups, we would like to run a post hoc test to determine if there is a significant difference between certain groups, like between transformational and control; or between control and transactional; and so on. In Excel, it is difficult to do this. However, a quick and easy way is to run a two-sample t-test between the two groups that you wish to check (only do this if you have determined that there is a significant difference between all groups).

Index

OTHER TITLES IN QUANTITATIVE APPROACHES TO DECISION MAKING COLLECTION

Donald N. Stengel, California State University, Fresno, Editor

- *Service Mining: Framework and Application* by Wei-Lun Chang
- *Regression Analysis: Unified Concepts, Practical Applications, and Computer Implementation* by Bruce L. Bowerman, Richard T. O'Connell, and Emily S. Murphree
- *Experimental Design: Unified Concepts, Practical Applications, and Computer Implementation* by Bruce L. Bowerman, Richard T. O'Connell, and Emily S. Murphree
- *An Introduction to Survey Research* by Ernest L. Cowles and Edward Nelson
- *Business Applications of Multiple Regression, Second Edition* by Ronny Richardson
- *Business Decision-Making: Streamlining the Process for More Effective Results* by Milan Frankl
- *Operations Methods: Managing Waiting Line Applications, Second Edition* by Kenneth A. Shaw

Announcing the Business Expert Press Digital Library

Concise e-books business students need for classroom and research

This book can also be purchased in an e-book collection by your library as

- a one-time purchase,
- that is owned forever,
- allows for simultaneous readers,
- has no restrictions on printing, and
- can be downloaded as PDFs from within the library community.

Our digital library collections are a great solution to beat the rising cost of textbooks. E-books can be loaded into their course management systems or onto students' e-book readers. The **Business Expert Press** digital libraries are very affordable, with no obligation to buy in future years. For more information, please visit **www.businessexpertpress.com/librarians**. To set up a trial in the United States, please email **sales@businessexpertpress.com**.

CPSIA information can be obtained
at www.ICGtesting.com
Printed in the USA
BVHW031145051122
651138BV00006B/74